Introducing .NET 6

Getting Started with Blazor, MAUI, Windows App SDK, Desktop Development, and Containers

Nico Vermeir

Apress®

Introducing .NET 6: Getting Started with Blazor, MAUI, Windows App SDK, Desktop Development, and Containers

Nico Vermeir
Merchtem, Belgium

ISBN-13 (pbk): 978-1-4842-7318-0   ISBN-13 (electronic): 978-1-4842-7319-7
https://doi.org/10.1007/978-1-4842-7319-7

Managing Director, Apress Media LLC: Welmoed Spahr
Acquisitions Editor: Joan Murray
Development Editor: Laura Berendson
Coordinating Editor: Jill Balzano

Cover image designed by Freepik (www.freepik.com)

Distributed to the book trade worldwide by Springer Science+Business Media LLC, 1 New York Plaza, Suite 4600, New York, NY 10004. Phone 1-800-SPRINGER, fax (201) 348-4505, e-mail orders-ny@springer-sbm. com, or visit www.springeronline.com. Apress Media, LLC is a California LLC and the sole member (owner) is Springer Science + Business Media Finance Inc (SSBM Finance Inc). SSBM Finance Inc is a **Delaware** corporation.

For information on translations, please e-mail booktranslations@springernature.com; for reprint, paperback, or audio rights, please e-mail bookpermissions@springernature.com.

Apress titles may be purchased in bulk for academic, corporate, or promotional use. eBook versions and licenses are also available for most titles. For more information, reference our Print and eBook Bulk Sales web page at http://www.apress.com/bulk-sales.

Any source code or other supplementary material referenced by the author in this book is available to readers on GitHub via the book's product page.

Printed on acid-free paper

Table of Contents

About the Author ix

Acknowledgments xi

Introduction xiii

Chapter 1: A Tour of .NET 6 1

  .NET 6 1

  Version Support 2

  Supported Versions 3

  A Unified Platform 4

  Roadmap 5

  Supported Operating Systems 6

  Command Line Interface 8

  Desktop Development 12

  Blazor 15

  MAUI 17

  Wrapping Up 20

Chapter 2: Runtimes and Desktop Packs 21

  .NET 6 Architecture 21

  Runtimes 22

    CoreCLR 23

    Mono 23

    WinRT 24

  Managed Execution Process 24

  Desktop Packs 25

  Wrapping Up 29

Chapter 3: Command Line Interface **31**

    Dotnet New 33

    Dotnet Restore 38

        NuGet.config 43

    Dotnet Build 46

    Dotnet Publish 52

    Dotnet Run 56

    Dotnet Test 58

    Using the CLI in GitHub Actions 60

    Other Commands 63

    Wrapping Up 64

Chapter 4: Desktop Development **65**

    WinAPI 66

    WinForms 69

        STAThread 71

        WinForms Startup 72

        The Message Loop 82

        The Form Designer 82

    WPF 91

        WPF Startup 93

        XAML Layout 95

        Visual Tree 103

        Data Binding 106

    Windows App SDK 109

        Building a Windows App SDK application 110

        Using Windows APIs with Windows App SDK 113

        Packaging 115

    Migrating to .NET 6 119

        Upgrade Assistant 122

    Wrapping Up 123

Chapter 5: Blazor **125**

Blazor WebAssembly 125

    Creating a Blazor Wasm Project 126

    Blazor Progressive Web Apps 127

    Exploring the Blazor Client Project 129

    Blazor in .NET 6 132

    Blazor Component System 134

    Creating Blazor Pages 136

    Running a Blazor App 140

Blazor Server 144

    SignalR 144

Blazor Desktop 148

Wrapping Up 152

Chapter 6: MAUI **153**

Project Structure 154

Exploring MAUI 156

    The Cross-Platform World 159

Application Lifecycle 161

MVVM 164

MVVM Toolkit 170

Wrapping Up 176

Chapter 7: ASP.NET Core **177**

Model-View-Controller 177

    Routing 185

    Views 186

    Controllers 189

Web API 200

    Controller-Based APIs 201

    Minimal APIs 215

Wrapping Up 219

Chapter 8: Microsoft Azure...**221**

Web Apps 222

    Creating an App Service 222

Static Web Apps 234

Web App for Containers 237

    Docker 238

Azure Functions 245

    Deploying Azure Functions 253

Wrapping Up 257

Chapter 9: Application Architecture **259**

Record Types...259

Monolith Architecture..263

Microservices..264

Container Orchestration 265

    Kubernetes 265

    Docker Compose 268

Dapr 270

    Installing Dapr 270

    Dapr State Management..272

Wrapping Up 273

Chapter 10: .NET Compiler Platform **275**

Roslyn 275

    Compiler API 277

    Diagnostic API..278

    Scripting API 278

    Workspace API...278

    Syntax Tree 278

    Roslyn SDK 279

Creating an Analyzer 282

Source Generators 285

Writing a Source Generator 285

Debugging Source Generators... 293

Wrapping Up 295

Chapter 11: Advanced .NET 6 297

Garbage Collector 297

The Heap 299

The Stack... 300

Garbage Collection 300

A Look at the Threadpool 301

Async in .NET 6 304

Await/Async... 304

Cancellations 308

WaitAsync 310

Conclusion 311

Index.. 313

About the Author

 **Nico Vermeir** is a Microsoft MVP in the field of Windows development. He works as an application architect at Inetum-Realdolmen Belgium and spends a lot of time keeping up with the rapidly changing world of technology. He loves talking about and using the newest and experimental technologies in the .NET stack. Nico cofounded MADN, a user group focusing on building modern applications in .NET. He regularly presents on the topic of .NET at user groups and conferences.

In his free time, you can find him enjoying rides on his motorcycle, jamming on his guitar, or having a beer with friends.

Acknowledgments

Thank you to the great people at Apress for the support during the writing of this book.

Thank you Damien Foggon for the technical review; you've helped me grow as an author and made this a better book.

A big thank you to the worldwide .NET community. Each and every one of you keeps pushing me every day to grow as a developer, as a community member, and as a person.

Introduction

Welcome to .NET 6! A very exciting new release of Microsoft's managed application runtime and SDK. .NET 6 is a release that has been long in the making; it is the next step in the one .NET dream. In this book, we will discover what .NET 6 has to offer; we will learn about exciting updates on existing frameworks like WinForms and WPF and discover new things like Minimal APIs.

We will start with a quick tour around .NET 6 in the first chapter, just to get a feel of how big this .NET release really is. In the next chapter, we will go a bit more technical and see what the different runtimes are and how a cross-platform framework like .NET still manages to run native applications on Windows, mobile, and more. In Chapter 3, we will go into the command line tooling; here we will discover that Visual Studio is not performing any magic tricks, it's just calling the CLI underneath. In Chapters 4–7, we will learn about the different application frameworks .NET hosts, from native Windows desktop to web applications with ASP.NET Core to cross-platform mobile applications. From there, we cross over into the cloud and see Azure's support for .NET 6. The final three chapters are a bit more advanced; we go into application architecture and what .NET 6 and C# 10 features help write better architectured code, and we take a look at the compiler platform, or Roslyn. And finally we end on a chapter with some more advanced topics like threading and async/await.

The book is written in a demo-based manner. Feel free to pull up your computer and follow along while reading; all the steps are explained so that we can discover the topics together.

Happy learning!

CHAPTER 1

A Tour of .NET 6

Welcome to .NET 6! An exciting new release of Microsoft's popular framework. .NET 6 is the next big step in delivering the "one .NET" vision. The vision that would unify all of .NET to have a single runtime for mobile, Web, IoT, games, and many more targets.

In this first chapter, we will look at the versioning of .NET, together with its support timeframes and release schedule. We will go over the supported operating systems, what it means to have a unified platform, and how to get started with .NET 6 using the command line interface.

.NET 6

The .NET framework has been around since the year 2000. Over the years, it has grown into a very mature, popular framework that could target many platforms. However, sharing code between those different platforms was not an easy task because of how the .NET framework was built. With .NET Core, Microsoft wanted to start from a clean slate using .NET Standard as a way to share code between the different platforms. They took the API surface of the base class library and started implementing everything anew, using modern techniques and APIs to improve performance of the framework. .NET Standard was created as an interface. It exposed parts of the BCL API; .NET Core is an implementation of that .NET Standard interface. Because .NET Standard was an abstraction, we could create .NET Standard class libraries that could be referenced from every type of platform, as long as they used the correct version of .NET Core. This quickly became confusing as .NET Core 3 was using .NET Standard 2.1, but .NET Standard 1.6 was .NET Core 1.0. The next step in unifying all of .NET was taken with .NET 5. .NET 5, which was actually .NET Core 4, was the release where .NET Core became the successor of the classic .NET Framework. The final release of the classic .NET Framework is 4.8; from that moment on, .NET Core is the main branch of the framework. To avoid confusion, later on .NET Core was renamed to simply .NET and the versioning of the

© Nico Vermeir 2022
N. Vermeir, *Introducing .NET 6*, https://doi.org/10.1007/978-1-4842-7319-7_1

classic .NET framework was taken over, hence .NET 5. .NET Standard disappeared as well; as of .NET 5, we just have .NET 5 class libraries and those are compatible with every platform that is on .NET 5. .NET 6 is one of the final steps in unifying the platform as it unifies Mono and .NET, fulfilling the "one .NET" dream.

So far we have spoken about .NET, .NET Core, and .NET Framework. This might get a bit confusing, so here is how I will talk about the different types of .NET in this book:

- .NET: This is .NET 5, .NET 6, and future releases. It is the unified release.

- .NET Core: This is the previous release that wasn't .NET Framework.

- .NET Framework: The classic .NET framework that ended on version 4.8.

Version Support

First and foremost, .NET 6 is a Long Term Support release (LTS), meaning it will receive updates for the coming 3 years (up until, and including, 2024). Non-LTS versions are supported for 1 year, usually up to 3 months after the next LTS version release.

So how do we recognize LTS versions from non-LTS versions? Simple. Every odd numbered release (.NET 5, .NET 7, etc.) will be a non-LTS release and every even numbered release (.NET 6, .NET 8, etc.) will be an LTS release (Figure 1-1). The current release cadence Microsoft has set for .NET is a new release every year around November. This release cadence was introduced with .NET 5.

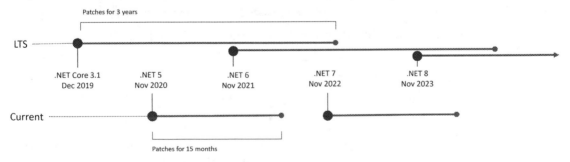

Figure 1-1. *Release timeline of .NET (Source: Microsoft)*

Why is this important? If you're starting a new software project, it's important to know that the underlying framework will not cause any security risks. No software is bug-free, so bugs and security risks will show up over the lifetime of any software; .NET is no exception. Writing your software using a version of .NET that will receive patches and updates for the coming years ensures that vulnerabilities and bugs in the framework get patched instead of potentially make your application crash, or vulnerable for attacks.

Does this mean that we can forget about the odd-numbered releases, since they are only supported for about a year? Not necessarily, it all depends on the context around the software you're developing. If you're building software that will still be in active development by the time of the next .NET LTS release, it can easily be included in the backlog to upgrade to the next version once it lands. If you're building software that will be delivered in the current non-LTS timeframe and there's no maintenance planned on the software, make sure your customer knows about the support. So, as usual it depends. Luckily, upgrading to a next release usually isn't very difficult. If you are in a consultant role, set the correct expectations to your customer.

Tip   Do not jump on the latest version of .NET just because it's the latest version, be sure to check the support status, inform your customer when applicable, and make a well-informed decision.

Supported Versions

There are multiple versions of .NET under active support at any given time. Table 1-1 gives an overview of the support status of the more recent .NET versions.

Table 1-1. *An overview of .NET versions and their support status*

Version	Original release date	Support level	End of support
.NET 6	November 2021	LTS	February 2025
.NET 5	November 2020	Non-LTS	February 2022
.NET Core 3.1	December 2019	LTS	December 2022

All details concerning support for .NET can be found in the official .NET Support Policy found at `https://dotnet.microsoft.com/platform/support/policy/dotnet-core`.

A Unified Platform

From the very start, .NET Core was meant to be cross-platform and cross-idiom. Its purpose was to bring a bunch of separate, .NET-based technologies together under one umbrella. Before .NET Core, we could do different styles of apps, but not all of those were part of .NET, for example, Mono, the open-source .NET implementation for Linux- and Unix-based systems and Xamarin, the native mobile .NET solution built on Mono.

.NET Core 3 shifted the unification of .NET into high gear by adding Windows Presentation Foundation (WPF) and Windows Forms (WinForms) support into the framework. .NET 5 expanded on this work by adding Mono; the work on Mono brought .NET into the WebAssembly world. Blazor WebAssembly was the first result of this unification. With Blazor WebAssembly, we got native .NET running in the browser, using Mono. More information on Blazor can be found in Chapter 5 of this book. .NET 6 delivers the fully realized unified vision by including Xamarin as a part of .NET instead of a separate framework.

Figure 1-2. *.NET – a unified platform (Source: Microsoft)*

Xamarin is no longer the mobile platform that happens to look like .NET. It's now a part of the framework, using .NET class libraries and .NET SDK tools to provide a great developer experience. A quick example of this is being able to use `dotnet new ios` or `dotnet new android` followed by `dotnet build` or `dotnet run`. As a result, you'll see a mobile project being created, compiled and running on either a physical device or emulator. This is the result of work that started back in .NET 5, by bringing Mono into .NET.

We'll dive deeper into Xamarin in the MAUI chapter of this book.

Roadmap

Microsoft made the decision to openly develop .NET, something they've done since .NET Core. That means that the backlog for .NET 6, and future versions, is visible to everyone. There's even a Blazor-based web application that shows an overview of what's proposed, what's in progress, and what's been completed. The website can be found at *https:// themesof.net/,* and because everything happens out in the open, the Blazor web app's source code is available at *https://github.com/terrajobst/themesof.net.*

The .NET team uses GitHub and GitHub Issues, Boards, and Milestones to keep track of their work. Although GitHub Issues is not very agile-friendly, especially when compared to tools like Azure DevOps or Jira, they have identified four categories of issues. Issues are categorized using labels. The four labels, as per their website, are as follows:

1. **Theme**: A top-level/overarching objective that will span the project leases. A theme will often have an associated document describing those objectives.

2. **Epic**: This is a higher level grouping of related user stories; it can span up to the entire release. For example, "Enterprises have a first class experience acquiring and deploying .NET 6.0."

3. **User story**: An explanation of the feature written from the perspective of the end user. Its purpose is to articulate how a software feature will provide value to the customer. Once implemented, it will contribute value toward the overall epic. For example, "As an IT Pro, I have easy access to .NET Core installer release information and scripts in my air gapped environment so I can use this to determine which updates need to be deployed."

4. **Issue**: These are all other work items. These could be bugs, features, or developer tasks. We leave it up to the engineering team/area owner how and if they want to use these.

Supported Operating Systems

Since .NET is a cross-platform framework, there are a multitude of operation systems supported. Support ranges from Windows to Linux, macOS, Android, iOS, and tvOS. Table 1-2 lists the different versions of Windows that support .NET 6.

Table 1-2. *Versions of Windows that support .NET 6*

Operating system	Version	Architecture
Windows	7 SP1, 8.1	x64, x86
Windows 10	Version 1607+	x64, x86, ARM64
Windows 11	Version 22000+	x64, x86, ARM64
Windows Server	2012+	x64, x86
Windows Server Core	2012+	x64, x86
Nano Server	Version 1809+	x64

Table 1-3 lists the supported Linux distributions with the supported versions and architecture.

Table 1-3. *Linux versions that support .NET 6*

Operating system	Version	Architecture
Alpine Linux	3.13+	x64, ARM64, ARM32
CentOS	7+	x64
Debian	10+	x64, x86, ARM64, ARM32
Fedora	33+	x64
openSUSE	15+	x64
Red Hat Enterprise Linux	7+	x64, ARM64
SUSE Enterprise Linux	12 SP2+	x64
Ubuntu	16.04, 18.04, 20.04+	x64, ARM64, ARM32

Table 1-4 lists the supported versions and architectures for macOS.

Table 1-4. *macOS versions that support .NET 6*

Operating system	Version	Architecture
macOS	10.15+	x64, ARM64

Table 1-5 lists the supported versions and architectures for Android.

Table 1-5. *Android versions that support .NET 6*

Operating system	Version	Architecture
Android	API 21+	x64, ARM, ARM64

Table 1-6 lists the supported versions and architectures for iOS and tvOS.

Table 1-6. *iOS and tvOS versions that support .NET 6*

Operating system	Version	Architecture
iOS	10.0+	x64, ARM, ARM64
tvOS	10.0+	x64, ARM, ARM64

The above tables list supported operating systems, versions, and architectures at the time of writing. The most up-to-date version of this list for .NET 6 is available at *https://github.com/dotnet/core/blob/main/release-notes/6.0/supported-os.md*.

Command Line Interface

.NET ships with a powerful Command Line Interface (CLI) tooling system since .NET Core. With the .NET command line, we can do things like creating a new project, installing tools and templates, running tests, compiling, and much more. While most of the CLI commands are rarely used manually, we can use them to script build and deploy automation. Tools like Azure DevOps or GitHub actions have full support for these commands.

The basic commands consist of:

- New

- Restore

- Build

- Publish

- Run

- Test

- Vstest

- Pack

- Migrate

- Clean

- Sln

- Help

- Store

Before we use the CLI, we have to install .NET 6 on our machine. If you have Visual Studio 2022 installed, you might already have it up and running.

We can see what version of .NET we are currently running by opening up a Powershell prompt and executing `dotnet --version`.

```
> dotnet --version
6.0.100
```

Figure 1-3. *Current installed version of .NET*

If you get another version, maybe from .NET 5, you can download the .NET 6 installer from https://dotnet.microsoft.com/download/dotnet/6.0. Make sure to download and install the SDK to get the command line tooling.

Once .NET 6 is installed, we can see what project templates we have by executing dotnet new. The tooling will list all available options if we don't specify a specific template as shown in Figure 1-4. The contents of this list depend of course on the different workloads and templates you have installed on your system.

```
> dotnet new
The list of templates was synchronized with the Optional SDK Workloads.
Template Name                      Short Name          Language       Tags
----------------------------------------------------------------------------------------------
Android Application                android              [C#]          Android
Android Activity template          android-activity     [C#]          Android
Android Java Library Binding       android-bindinglib   [C#]          Android
Android Layout template            android-layout       [C#]          Android
Android Class library              androidlib           [C#]          Android
Console Application                console               [C#],F#,VB   Common/Console
Class library                      classlib              [C#],F#,VB   Common/Library
WPF Application                    wpf                   [C#],VB      Common/WPF
WPF Class Library                  wpflib                [C#],VB      Common/WPF
WPF Custom Control Library         wpfcustomcontrollib   [C#],VB      Common/WPF
WPF User Control Library           wpfusercontrollib     [C#],VB      Common/WPF
Windows Forms App                  winforms              [C#],VB      Common/WinForms
Windows Forms Control Library      winformscontrollib    [C#],VB      Common/WinForms
Windows Forms Class Library        winformslib           [C#],VB      Common/WinForms
Worker Service                     worker                [C#],F#      Common/Worker/Web
.NET Maui Mobile Application       maui                  [C#]         Maui/Android/iOS/macOS/Catalyst
MSTest Test Project                mstest                [C#],F#,VB   Test/MSTest
NUnit 3 Test Item                  nunit-test            [C#],F#,VB   Test/NUnit
NUnit 3 Test Project               nunit                 [C#],F#,VB   Test/NUnit
xUnit Test Project                 xunit                 [C#],F#,VB   Test/xUnit
Razor Component                    razorcomponent        [C#]         Web/ASP.NET
Razor Page                         page                  [C#]         Web/ASP.NET
MVC ViewImports                    viewimports           [C#]         Web/ASP.NET
MVC ViewStart                      viewstart             [C#]         Web/ASP.NET
Blazor Server App                  blazorserver          [C#]         Web/Blazor
Blazor WebAssembly App             blazorwasm            [C#]         Web/Blazor/WebAssembly
```

Figure 1-4. *Available project templates in dotnet new*

Let's try to create, build, and run a .NET 6 WinForms application without any help from an IDE.

First we create the project by selecting the correct dotnet new template.

```
> dotnet new winforms -o "DotnetSixWinForms"
The template "Windows Forms App" was created successfully.

Processing post-creation actions...
Running 'dotnet restore' on C:\Projects\Apress\winforms\DotnetSixWinForms\DotnetSixWinForms.csproj...
  Determining projects to restore...
  Restored C:\Projects\Apress\winforms\DotnetSixWinForms\DotnetSixWinForms.csproj (in 85 ms).
Restore succeeded.
```

Figure 1-5. *Creating a WinForms project through command line*

This command created a WinForms project called DotnetSixWinForms in the current directory. Just to verify that it really is a .NET 6 project, let's have a look at the .csproj file.

Listing 1-1. WinForms project file

```
<Project Sdk="Microsoft.NET.Sdk">

  <PropertyGroup>
    <OutputType>WinExe</OutputType>
    <TargetFramework>net6.0-windows</TargetFramework>
    <Nullable>enable</Nullable>
    <UseWindowsForms>true</UseWindowsForms>
    <ImplicitUsings>enable</ImplicitUsings>
  </PropertyGroup>

</Project>
```

TargetFramework is set to net6.0-windows, so we're running on .NET 6 using the Windows compatibility pack. The compatibility packs are explained in more detail in Chapter 2. For now it means that we are running on .NET 6 but referencing some extra binaries so we can hook into the native Windows APIs, for example, to render our application or access the filesystem. Next step, let's build the project through dotnet build.

```
> dotnet build
Microsoft (R) Build Engine version 16.10.0-preview-21126-01+6819f7ab0 for .NET
Copyright (C) Microsoft Corporation. All rights reserved.

  Determining projects to restore...
  All projects are up-to-date for restore.
  You are using a preview version of .NET. See: https://aka.ms/dotnet-core-preview
  DotnetSixWinforms -> C:\Projects\Apress\DotnetSixWinforms\bin\Debug\net6.0-windows\DotnetSixWinforms.dll

Build succeeded.
    0 Warning(s)
    0 Error(s)

Time Elapsed 00:00:03.91
```

Figure 1-6. *Building the project through the command line*

I first made sure my command line was set in the directory where the .csproj or .sln file lives. If this is the case, a simple `dotnet build` suffices. The tool looks for a .csproj or .sln in its current directory and starts building it. What is happening right now is the exact same thing that happens when we build a project in Visual Studio. We call the .NET build system MSBuild and pass in parameters and a reference to a project, and it will start building. Once it is done building, you will find the familiar bin and obj folders in the project folder that you will also find after building from Visual Studio. There is no extra magic happening in Visual Studio; it triggers the same command we just executed manually.

As a final step, we execute `dotnet run` which will effectively build the project if necessary and launch it, showing a blank WinForms page as shown in Figure 1-7.

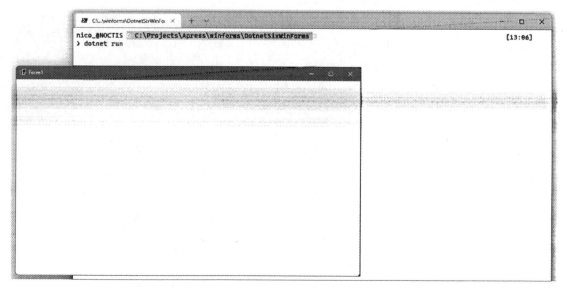

Figure 1-7. *Running a WinForms application from the command line*

We'll get deeper into the command line in Chapter 3 of this book.

Desktop Development

The desktop to this day remains a very important target for applications. Not every type of application is suited to be a web application. That's why Microsoft brought WPF and WinForms back into active development with the release of .NET Core 3. Not only that, but they are also expanding the possibilities for desktop developers.

Before they brought WPF and WinForms back, however, they were considered legacy. It was time for a new modern desktop application framework. The Universal Windows Platform saw the light of day years ago as the cross-device Windows app framework. It promised a "build once, run everywhere" experience, and they mostly delivered. But since UWP was mostly targeted at mobile experiences through Windows on tablets and phones, it kept lacking in features to make it a true successor to WPF. Today UWP has matured into a decent application framework that can deliver modern, fast applications, but it still does not have all features WPF has.

To close this gap, Microsoft has introduced the Windows App SDK. The Windows App SDK aims to bring all desktop development options closer together. The Windows App SDK brings a set of Windows APIs that are decoupled from Windows itself. The APIs are released via NuGet packages so that they can be updated out of band with the operating system.

The Windows App SDK consists of a few parts. One of the major parts is WinUI 3. WinUI 3 decouples the XAML-based UI controls of UWP from the framework and makes them available as NuGet packages. This makes it possible for Microsoft to update their control library apart from the operating system. It also makes it possible for application developers to support newer UI features on older versions of Windows, without the need of operating system upgrades.

Getting started with The Windows App SDK can be done in a few different ways, which we'll get deeper into in Chapter 4. The fastest way to get into Project Reunion is by using the WinUI templates in Visual Studio.

Blank App, Packaged (WinUI 3 in Desktop)

A project template for creating a Desktop app based on the Windows UI Library (WinUI 3) along with a MSIX package for side-loading or distribution via the Microsoft Store.

| C# | XAML | Windows | Windows App SDK | Desktop | WinUI |

Class Library (WinUI 3 in Desktop)

A project for creating a managed class library (.dll) for Desktop apps based on the Windows UI Library (WinUI 3).

| C# | XAML | Windows | Windows App SDK | Desktop | WinUI |

Blank App, Packaged with Windows Application Packaging Project (WinUI 3 in Desktop)

A project template for creating a Desktop app based on the Windows UI Library (WinUI 3). A Windows Application Packaging (WAP) project is included to create a MSIX package for side-loading or distribution via the Microsoft Store.

| C# | XAML | Windows | Windows App SDK | Desktop | WinUI |

Figure 1-8. *WinUI project templates*

The `Blank App, Packaged` template creates a new UWP project, including a package manifest for distribution through the Microsoft Store. Figure 1-9 shows the newly created solution.

Figure 1-9. *A fresh WinUI project in Visual Studio*

If you've ever built a UWP app, you might not see any difference at first sight. However, under the hood all the XAML controls this app is using are coming from a NuGet package, not from the UWP SDK like it used to. Have a look at the dependencies shown in Figure 1-13.

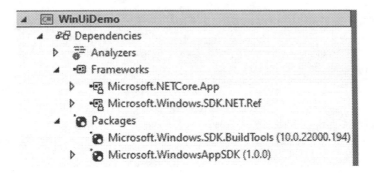

Figure 1-10. *Dependencies for a WinUI project*

Figure 1-10 shows that the Windows SDK is still referenced; we still need that for all the system calls, like creating the app's window and drawing everything on screen. The controls however all come from the *Microsoft.WindowsAppSDK* NuGet package.

An easy way to discover all the controls available in WinUI is by browsing the control gallery app available on the Windows Store *www.microsoft.com/store/productid/9P3JFPWWDZRC.*

The source code of the gallery app is available at *https://github.com/Microsoft/Xaml-Controls-Gallery/.*

Figure 1-11. *The WinUI 3 Control Gallery Sample app*

The Control Gallery Sample App is not only a demo application, but it provides XAML snippets and links to official documentation for every control in the toolkit.

Figure 1-12. *XAML snippets and links to documentation in the Control Gallery app*

Blazor

Blazor is Microsoft's answer to front-end web frameworks like Angular, Vue, and React. Its main selling point is that you can write these web apps in C# rather than JavaScript. You can still inject JavaScript and consume JavaScript libraries where you need to, but everything can basically be done through C#.

Blazor currently comes in two flavors:

- Blazor Server

- Blazor WebAssembly

Blazor Server runs all its C# logic in an ASP.NET context on a webserver and sends back the results. This is done through a SignalR connection instead of page reloads like ASP.NET MVC. This version of Blazor was released in .NET Core 3. Blazor WebAssembly was released in the .NET 5 timeframe. It runs all of its C# logic in the browser, not through some form of C# to JavaScript transpiling but through the magic of WebAssembly.

WebAssembly (abbreviated Wasm) is a binary instruction format for a stack-based virtual machine. Wasm is designed as a portable compilation target for programming languages, enabling deployment on the web for client and server applications.

Source: https://webassembly.org

Like the official description says, Wasm is a virtual execution environment in your browser. Wasm is an official W3C spec *https://www.w3.org/wasm/*.

Since Wasm is an environment that runs native code, Microsoft was able to get a version of .NET running inside of Wasm. With this, Blazor Wasm was born.

.NET 6 brings Blazor to the desktop. With Blazor Desktop, we can build hybrid applications, parts can be native UI, and parts can be web UI. It's not unlike Electron, but it differs in that applications can actually be, for example, part WPF and part web. Figure 1-13 shows a Blazor Desktop application that mixes native WPF controls with a Blazor Web Component.

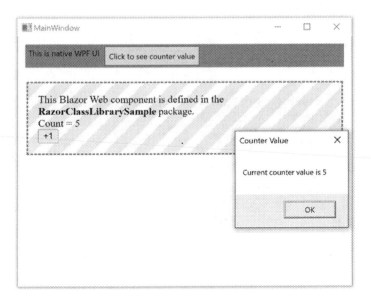

Figure 1-13. *Mixing WPF UI with Blazor Web Components (Source: Microsoft)*

As you can see in Figure 1-13, Blazor Desktop goes beyond just mixing two UI stacks. The data is shared between them. The counter increment button is web UI, while the button to see the counter value and the message box showing the value are both native Windows UI through WPF. This enables a very interesting scenario where parts of a web application can be refactored into web components to be used on both a web application and a native application.

We'll learn more about Blazor in Chapter 5 of this book.

MAUI

WPF, WinForms, and the Windows App SDK are all tightly coupled to Windows. A more cross-platform solution from Microsoft is called the .NET Multi-Platform App UI. The .NET Multi-Platform App UI, MAUI for short, is one of the biggest new parts in .NET 6. It basically is the new version of Xamarin Forms, but it's more than that. MAUI brings an entire new project system, no longer fiddling around with at least three projects in your mobile app solution. One project that contains all your mobile heads, assets, and shared code. Everything together in one .NET project.

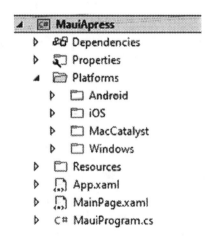

Figure 1-14. *Single project for iOS, Android, and Mac Catalyst*

MAUI no longer focuses solely on mobile either; it's now a full-fledged solution for building cross-platform, cross-idiom applications. Xamarin Forms has had support for UWP for quite some time, but it was never an important part of the framework, which resulted in a poor developer and user experience. With MAUI we can target Android, iOS, macOS, and Windows. All as first-class citizens. For Windows, this means improved UWP support, by leveraging the Windows App SDK.

As for XAML flavor, if you're building a cross-platform application with MAUI, you'll be using the same flavor of XAML you're used to from Xamarin Forms. As for macOS, Xamarin Forms has support for macOS through AppKit bindings; that support is still there.

Apple is now taking a different route for macOS development and has introduced Mac Catalyst, a framework that enables developers to build macOS desktop applications with UIKit. MAUI includes bindings for both AppKit and Mac Catalyst to suit every developer's needs. However, since Mac Catalyst is the default for Apple, MAUI also takes this as the default framework for macOS-based applications.

Getting a Xamarin Forms installation up and running has been notoriously hard so far. It's one of the most heard complaints from developers trying to get into Xamarin. You'd need to install Visual Studio with the correct mobile workload and install the correct UWP SDK versions, Android SDK version, and iOS SDK versions. Next to that, if you want to build iOS apps on Windows, you'll need a mac with the correct version of Visual Studio for Mac, Mono, and iOS SDK installed. With .NET 6 comes a tool that can check your system for MAUI compatibility and install all missing pieces for you. In pure .NET fashion, it's a command line tool that you can install through the dotnet command line.

To install:

```
dotnet tool install -g Redth.Net.Maui.Check
```

To Run:

```
maui-check
```

Running the tool will launch it in a new CLI window.

```
◉ .NET MAUI Check

▷ Synchronizing configuration... ok
▷ Scheduling appointments... ok

▷ OpenJDK 11.0 Checkup...
  - 11.0.12 (C:\Program Files\Microsoft\jdk-11.0.12.7-hotspot\bin\..)
  - 11.0.10 (C:\Program Files\Microsoft\jdk-11.0.10.9-hotspot\bin\..)

▷ Visual Studio 17.1.0-pre.1.0 Checkup...
  - 17.0.1
  - 17.1.0-pre.1.1 - C:\Program Files\Microsoft Visual Studio\2022\Preview

▷ Android SDK Checkup...
  - emulator (30.9.5)
  - build-tools;31.0.0 (31.0.0)
  - platforms;android-31 (1)
  - system-images;android-31;google_apis;x86_64 (8)
  - platform-tools (31.0.3)
  - cmdline-tools;5.0 (5.0)

▷ Android Emulator Checkup...
  - Emulator: phone_m-dpi_5_1in_pie_9_0_-_api_28 found.

▷ .NET SDK Checkup...
  - 2.2.207 - C:\Program Files\dotnet\sdk\2.2.207
  - 5.0.100-rc.2.20479.15 - C:\Program Files\dotnet\sdk\5.0.100-rc.2.20479.15
  - 5.0.402 - C:\Program Files\dotnet\sdk\5.0.402
  - 6.0.100-preview.7.21379.14 - C:\Program Files\dotnet\sdk\6.0.100-preview.7.21379.14
  - 6.0.100-rc.1.21458.32 - C:\Program Files\dotnet\sdk\6.0.100-rc.1.21458.32
  - 6.0.100 - C:\Program Files\dotnet\sdk\6.0.100
```

Figure 1-15. *Maui-check checking for JDK, VS2022, and Android SDKs*

The tool is community supported and open source; the source can be found at *https://github.com/Redth/dotnet-maui-check*.

Maui-check looks for:

- OpenJdk/AndroidSDK

- .NET 6 SDK

- .NET MAUI/iOS/Android workloads and packs

- .NET MAUI Templates

- Workload Resolver .sentinel files for .NET and Visual Studio Windows/Mac

We'll dive deeper into MAUI in Chapter 6 of this book.

Wrapping Up

In this introductory chapter, we reviewed .NET roadmap and its history. I hope this chapter gave you a sense of what .NET 6 is about and made you eager to dive deeper into the latest release of .NET. The different concepts that we have touched upon in this chapter will be explored further in the rest of the book. We will take a closer look at .NET tooling with the command line interface; we will explore desktop development in WPF, WinForms, and the Windows App SDK. We will learn about building powerful web applications that run on the client with Blazor and how to build cross-platform mobile apps with MAUI.

While not an exhaustive list of everything .NET 6 offers, we have selected the most important parts of .NET 6. .NET 6 is a big and important release; it brings a plethora of new features and new paradigms to the framework. Consequent chapters in this book will cover many of those and go into much more detail. Before we dive into all the feature goodness, let's take a look under the hood in *Chapter* 2 and explore the various runtimes and extensibility packs.

CHAPTER 2

Runtimes and Desktop Packs

.NET 6 runs everywhere, from Windows to the Web, Linux, and mobile and embedded devices. But how? How do they manage to get the same code to run and behave in (mostly) the same way not only across platforms but also across CPU architectures? The secret is in the underlying architecture of .NET 6.

There have been numerous iterations in Microsoft's cross-platform strategy. We've seen shared projects in Xamarin, where the code gets compiled into each platform; we have had portable class libraries where the libraries supported the lowest common denominator of all the selected platforms and more recently we had .NET Standard libraries. But why all these different approaches? It's actually quite simple. .NET on one platform was not exactly the same as .NET on another platform. We've had .NET, Mono, .NET Compact Framework, .NET Micro Framework, etc.

Fixing the splintering of .NET versions was one of the core promises of .NET Core; it took a bit longer than expected but we are finally getting really close to one .NET. No matter what platform you are running on, if your application is running on .NET 6, you can use .NET 6 class libraries and share them over all supported platforms.

.NET 6 Architecture

A very big step on the road to .NET unification was taken in .NET 5, by closing a big gap in missing APIs compared to the classic .NET Framework Microsoft that was able to serve the .NET API surface as an abstraction layer. This means that, as developers, we don't have to worry about what platform we're running on or if certain .NET features will work or even compile on the platform we're running on. Figure 2-1 shows Microsoft's view on .NET architecture.

© Nico Vermeir 2022

N. Vermeir, *Introducing .NET 6*, https://doi.org/10.1007/978-1-4842-7319-7_2

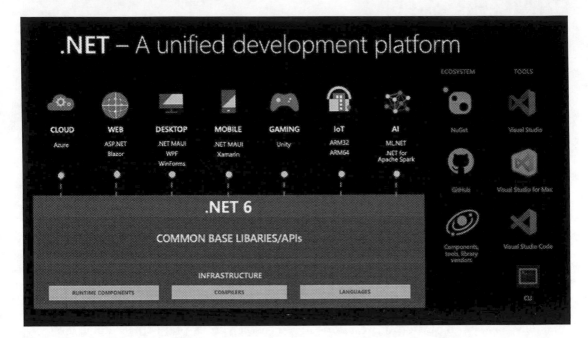

Figure 2-1. *.NET unification*

What the image portraits is the .NET abstraction layer. We write the same .NET code everywhere, but depending on the compile target, a different compiler will be used. When executing a .NET application, a different runtime may be used depending on the platform it is being executed on. Let's take a command line application, for example, a command line has no UI so no platform-specific code to render screens is necessary, meaning that the same CLI application can run on Windows, Linux, and macOS. When compiling this application, the default .NET 6 compiler will be used, resulting in one executable. Running this executable on Windows will be handled by the common language runtime, CoreCLR. On macOS and Linux, however, this will be handled by Mono, completely transparent to developers and users.

Runtimes

The .NET languages are managed languages, meaning that code you write in C# gets compiled down to intermediate language. Once your code gets executed, that intermediate language is compiled into machine code by the just in time compiler, or JIT. That JIT is part of the common language runtime, or CLR.

When writing .NET code, we don't program against an operating system; the system APIs in C# don't target Windows/Linux/macOS directly; instead, they target the API surface of the common language runtime called CoreFX. CoreFX is the newer name of what used to be the Base Class Library or BCL. It includes the `System.*` namespaces that we use all the time to call platform or framework APIs. The CLR calls into the operating system's APIs via CoreFX to perform the tasks requested by the developer. In this way, the CLR functions as an abstraction layer, enabling cross-platform code.

The CLR also gives us memory management, keeping track of objects in memory and releasing them when they are no longer needed. This garbage collection is part of the runtime and is what makes .NET languages managed, compared to unmanaged languages like C and C++ where you must do your own memory management.

.NET 6 contains two default runtimes. Depending on the platform you are running your code on, it will be executed by either CoreCLR or Mono.

The .NET 6 runtimes are open source and available at `https://github.com/dotnet/runtime`.

CoreCLR

The CoreCLR is the .NET 6 version of the classic CLR. It is the common language runtime used for running .NET code on Windows. No matter if it is a desktop application, web application, or console app, if any of these run on Windows, they will use the CoreCLR.

Mono

Mono started as an open-source project to bring .NET and its languages to Linux. Mono was based on the publication of the .NET open standard. The first version of Mono was released in 2004. The maintainers of the Mono open-source project were a small company called Ximian. Ximian and thus Mono were acquired by Novell, Novell was acquired by Attachmate, and the future of Mono seemed very dark. Some people from Ximian formed a new company called Xamarin. Xamarin continued the work on Mono, eventually releasing a mobile cross-platform framework based on Mono. Microsoft became the owner of the Mono project after acquiring Xamarin in 2016.

Mono currently ships as part of .NET 6; it is the default runtime when not running on a Windows-based operating system.

WinRT

The Windows Runtime, or WinRT, is the runtime used for Universal Windows Platform Applications, or UWP. UWP was originally meant to deliver a "build once, run on all Windows 10 devices." These devices included computers, tablets, smartphones, Xbox, Hololens, and embedded devices. WinRT applications can be built using C# or C++ and XAML. WinRT is not a runtime in the strict sense of the word. It's more like an interface on top of the Win32 API.

Managed Execution Process

The managed execution process is the process that is followed to get from code to a running application. It consists of three steps.

Figure 2-2. *Managed execution process*

First step is compiling to the Microsoft Intermediate Language, or MSIL. For this, we will need a compiler that can compile the language we're writing our code in to intermediate language.

The second step is compiling the MSIL code into native code. There are two ways to do this.

The first one is using the Just-In-Time, or JIT compiler. The JIT compiler is supplied by the runtime, making JIT compilation possible on different architectures and operating system. If there is a .NET runtime on the platform, there is a JIT compiler. JIT compilation is not a one-shot process; it happens continuously as your application is being used; this is by design to keep in mind that not all code in the MSIL will end up being called. By JIT compiling on the go, the runtime limits the number of resources your application is using. Once a piece of MSIL is compiled into native code, it is stored in memory and does not need to recompile if the application is running.

The second way to compile MSIL into native code is doing it ahead of time (AOT) using .NET's ahead-of-time compiler called CoreRT. Ahead of time compilation means that the full set of MSIL instructions get translated into native code before anything is being executed, usually during installation of software. In .NET AOT compilation is handled by a tool called the native image generator, or Ngen. Ngen compiles all MSIL in an assembly into native code; that native code gets persisted on disk so that when a user launched your application, there is no more JIT compilation, resulting in a faster application.

Figure 2-3. Ahead-of-time compilation

An important step in the compilation step of the managed execution process for both JIT and AOT is code verification. Code verifications makes sure that the code being compiled into native is safe; it protects the system from malicious behavior in software. The compiler takes the MSIL and treats it as unsafe by default. It will verify that the MSIL was correctly generated, that no memory locations can be accessed that shouldn't be accessed, that all type references are compatible, and so on. Note that this verification can be disabled by system administrator.

The final step in the managed execution process is running the code. This is where the operating system takes the native code, either from the AOT compiler or from the JIT compiler, and executes the instructions. While the application is being executed, the runtime will trigger services like garbage collection, code verification, and so on.

Desktop Packs

.NET 6 furthers Microsoft's cross-platform, open-source journey that they started in 2014. While it all started with cloud and Web, we now have support for Windows desktop applications written in WPF or WinForms. But since Windows is not cross-platform and both WinForms and WPF are too integrated in Windows to make it cross-platform, there had to be a solution to make those frameworks work while still maintaining the cross-platform mindset. To get the Windows only assemblies into the framework, they would have to either make .NET tied into one operating system again, or make different flavors of .NET, or put those assemblies into packs that can be optionally added to an application. That third option is exactly what they did. Figure 2-2 shows how the .NET 6 architecture is layered to have a common base library called CoreFX but can still have specific targets.

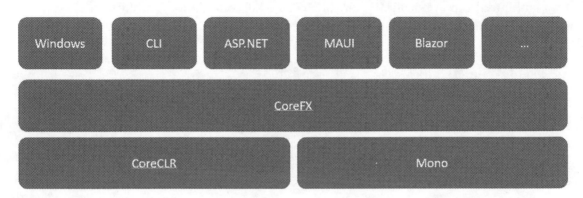

Figure 2-4. *.NET 6 layered architecture*

On the image we can clearly see that .NET is still very much cross-platform, but should we want to add Windows-only code, for example, we can by referencing a specific .NET implementation through a Target Framework Moniker, or TFM.

Listing 2-1 shows setting the Target Framework Moniker or TFM to .NET 6 with Windows support and the UseWPF tag in the csproj file that adds support for WPF in a .NET 6 project.

Listing 2-1. Adding WPF support

```
<Project Sdk="Microsoft.NET.Sdk">

  <PropertyGroup>
    <OutputType>WinExe</OutputType>
    <TargetFramework>net6.0-windows</TargetFramework>
    <Nullable>enable</Nullable>
    <UseWPF>true</UseWPF>
  </PropertyGroup>

</Project>
```

For comparison, Listing 2-2 shows the project file for a .NET 6 WinForms project.

Listing 2-2. Adding WinForms support

```
<Project Sdk="Microsoft.NET.Sdk">

  <PropertyGroup>
    <OutputType>WinExe</OutputType>
    <TargetFramework>net6.0-windows</TargetFramework>
    <UseWindowsForms>true</UseWindowsForms>
  </PropertyGroup>

</Project>
```

The default TFM for .NET 6 is net6.0. Referencing that TFM means you will get access to all the common, cross-platform APIs. However, should you have the need to have platform-specific APIs, like, for example, the notification system on Android or iOS, you can use OS-specific Target Framework Monikers. In general if you are building a class library or an ASP.NET project, net6.0 should suffice. For other types of projects, .NET 6 includes the following TFMs:

- net6.0

- net6.0-Android

- net6.0-ios

- net6.0-macos

- net6.0-maccatalyst

- **net6.0-tvos**

- net6.0-Windows

Creating a new WPF or WinForms project will automatically set the TFM to net6.0-windows.

The WPF and WinForms project templates include a reference to Microsoft.WindowsDesktop.App.WPF or Microsoft.WindowsDesktop.App.WinForms. These are called Desktop Packs.

In the solution explorer, you can find the desktop pack under Dependencies, Frameworks, as shown in Figure 2-3.

```
▲  ⬚ Dependencies
    ▷  📊 Analyzers
    ▲  ⬚ Frameworks
        ▷  📦 Microsoft.NETCore.App
        ▲  📦 Microsoft.WindowsDesktop.App.WPF
              📁 Accessibility
              📁 Microsoft.Win32.Registry.AccessControl
              📁 Microsoft.Win32.SystemEvents
              📁 PresentationCore
              📁 PresentationFramework
              📁 PresentationFramework.Aero
              📁 PresentationFramework.Aero2
              📁 PresentationFramework.AeroLite
              📁 PresentationFramework.Classic
              📁 PresentationFramework.Luna
              📁 PresentationFramework.Royale
              📁 PresentationUI
              📁 ReachFramework
              📁 System.CodeDom
              📁 System.Configuration.ConfigurationManager
              📁 System.Diagnostics.EventLog
              📁 System.Diagnostics.PerformanceCounter
              📁 System.DirectoryServices
              📁 System.IO.Packaging
              📁 System.Printing
              📁 System.Resources.Extensions
              📁 System.Security.Cryptography.Pkcs
              📁 System.Security.Cryptography.ProtectedData
              📁 System.Security.Cryptography.Xml
              📁 System.Security.Permissions
              📁 System.Threading.AccessControl
              📁 System.Windows.Controls.Ribbon
              📁 System.Windows.Extensions
              📁 System.Windows.Input.Manipulations
              📁 System.Windows.Presentation
              📁 System.Xaml
              📁 UIAutomationClient
              📁 UIAutomationClientSideProviders
              📁 UIAutomationProvider
              📁 UIAutomationTypes
              📁 WindowsBase
```

Figure 2-5. *The WPF Desktop pack*

While the `net6.0-windows` TFM is sufficient to get access to the native Windows APIs, it does not contain the specific logic to render WinForms via GDI+ or WPF via DirectX. That logic is contained in the desktop packs. We go over how WinForms and WPF work in more detail in Chapter 4 of this book.

Wrapping Up

While .NET 6 is an easy-to-use and very developer-friendly framework, there is a lot going on under the hood. It has a layered architecture with several runtimes, a complex three-step compilation process, and even different ways of compiling. All of this complexity is hidden pretty well for us developers; we don't have to worry that our application will select the Mono runtime on Linux; that is all taken care of for us. However, it is still important to have an idea of what is going on under the hood.

Besides making .NET easy to use, Microsoft had a big challenge with maintaining the cross-platform dream while still being able to provide access to platform-native APIs. Not only for new applications written in new technologies but also for more mature frameworks like WPF and WinForms. Multiple extensions of .NET 6 were created to solve this. We can use these extensions by targeting the correct Target Framework Moniker. Add the desktop packs to this and the cross-platform, native story with full legacy support is complete.

CHAPTER 3

Command Line Interface

.NET 6 ships with an extensive set of command line interface (CLI) tools. The toolset allows us to develop, build, run, test, and execute .NET applications on multiple platforms. The .NET 6 CLI ships as part of the .NET 6 SDK.

In this chapter, we will go over the most commonly used commands in the CLI. We will learn about creating projects, restoring dependencies, and even compiling and deploying applications. You will see that what we do from Visual Studio is not magic of the editor but it just triggers these command line tools.

Table 3-1 shows an overview of the basic commands included with the .NET 6 CLI. The complete CLI documentation can be found at `https://docs.microsoft.com/en-us/dotnet/core/tools/`.

© Nico Vermeir 2022
N. Vermeir, *Introducing .NET 6*, https://doi.org/10.1007/978-1-4842-7319-7_3

Table 3-1. *Basic CLI commands*

Command	Explanation
New	Create a new project using a project template
Restore	Restore dependencies to the project
Build	Compile the project
Publish	Outputs the binaries of an application to a folder for deployment
Run	Execute the application
Test	Run automated tests included in the project
Vstest	Superseded by `test`
Pack	Packages the project as a NuGet package
Migrate	Migrates old .NET Core 2 projects to newer SDK-style projects
Clean	Cleans project output
Sln	Lists or modifies the project in a solution
Help	Shows more information on a command
Store	Deploys assemblies to the runtime package store

Besides basic commands, there are also commands that can directly modify a project. Table 3-2 lists the project modification commands.

Table 3-2. *Project modification commands*

Command	Explanation
Add package	Adds NuGet package to the project
Add reference	Adds project reference to the project
Remove package	Removes NuGet package from the project
Remove reference	Removes project reference from the project
List reference	Lists project references

We also have some more advanced commands at our disposal. Table 3-3 lists the advanced commands with a short description.

Table 3-3. *Advanced .NET CLI commands*

Command	Explanation
Nuget delete	Deletes or unlists a package from a NuGet server
Nuget locals	Clears or lists local NuGet resources
Nuget push	Pushes a package to a NuGet server and lists it
Msbuild	Builds a project and all dependencies

The .NET CLI manages more than just projects. We can use it to install extra tools; an example of this is shown in Chapter 6 with *maui-check*, which is a tool that verifies that everything is installed correctly to start doing mobile development with .NET. Table 3-4 shows the available commands to manage tools in .NET.

Table 3-4. *Commands for .NET tools*

Command	Explanation
Tool install	Installs a .NET tool
Tool list	Lists all installed tools
Tool update	Updates a tool to the latest version
Tool restore	Installs all tools referenced in a manifest file
Tool run	Runs a tool
Tool uninstall	Removes a tool from the system

Dotnet New

The `dotnet new` command can create a new project, configuration file or solution, based on a template.

Listing 3-1 shows the help for the command as a reference.

Listing 3-1. Help page for dotnet new

```
dotnet new --help
Usage: new [options]

Options:
  -h, --help                        Displays help for this command.
  -l, --list <PARTIAL_NAME>         Lists templates containing the specified
                                    template name. If no name is specified, lists
                                    all templates.
  -n, --name                        The name for the output being created. If no
                                    name is specified, the name of the output
                                    directory is used.
  -o, --output                      Location to place the generated output.
  -i, --install                     Installs a source or a template package.
  -u, --uninstall                   Uninstalls a source or a template package.
  --interactive                     Allows the internal dotnet restore command to
                                    stop and wait for user input or action (e.g.,
                                    to complete authentication).
  --add-source, --nuget-source      Specifies a NuGet source to use during
                                    install.
  --type                            Filters templates based on available types.
                                    Predefined values are "project" and "item".
  --dry-run                         Displays a summary of what would happen if
                                    the given command line were run if it would
                                    result in a template creation.
  --force                           Forces content to be generated even if it
                                    would change existing files.
  -lang, --language                 Filters templates based on language and
                                    specifies the language of the template
                                    to create.
  --update-check                    Check the currently installed template
                                    packages for updates.
  --update-apply                    Check the currently installed template
                                    packages for update, and install the updates.
  --search <PARTIAL_NAME>           Searches for the templates on NuGet.org.
```

--author \<Author\>	Filters the templates based on the template author. Applicable only with --search or --list | -l option.
--package \<PACKAGE\>	Filters the templates based on NuGet package ID. Applies to --search.
--columns \<COLUMNS_LIST\>	Comma separated list of columns to display in --list and --search output. The supported columns are language, tags, author, type.
--columns-all	Display all columns in --list and --search output.
--tag \<TAG\>	Filters the templates based on the tag. Applies to --search and --list.
--no-update-check	Disables checking for the template package updates when instantiating a template.

Help can also be requested per project type. Listing 3-2 shows the output for dotnet new wpf -help, for example.

Listing 3-2. Help for WPF

```
WPF Application (C#)
Author: Microsoft
Description: A project for creating a .NET WPF Application
Options:
  -f|--framework  The target framework for the project.
                      netcoreapp3.0    - Target netcoreapp3.0
                      netcoreapp3.1    - Target netcoreapp3.1
                      net5.0           - Target net5.0
                      net6.0           - Target net6.0
                  Default: net6.0

  --langVersion   Sets langVersion in the created project file
                  text - Optional
```

--no-restore   If specified, skips the automatic restore of the project
                    on create.
                    bool - Optional
                    Default: false

--nullable   Whether to enable nullable reference types for this project.
                    bool - Optional
                    Default: true

WPF is one of the available templates in .NET 6. For a complete list of all available templates on your machine, you can run dotnet new --list or dotnet new -l.

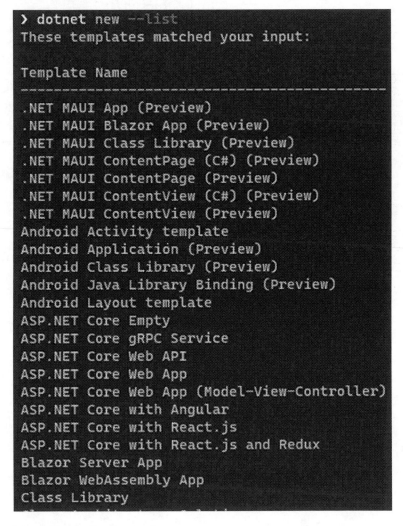

```
> dotnet new --list
These templates matched your input:


Template Name
------------------------------------------------
.NET MAUI App (Preview)
.NET MAUI Blazor App (Preview)
.NET MAUI Class Library (Preview)
.NET MAUI ContentPage (C#) (Preview)
.NET MAUI ContentPage (Preview)
.NET MAUI ContentView (C#) (Preview)
.NET MAUI ContentView (Preview)
Android Activity template
Android Application (Preview)
Android Class Library (Preview)
Android Java Library Binding (Preview)
Android Layout template
ASP.NET Core Empty
ASP.NET Core gRPC Service
ASP.NET Core Web API
ASP.NET Core Web App
ASP.NET Core Web App (Model-View-Controller)
ASP.NET Core with Angular
ASP.NET Core with React.js
ASP.NET Core with React.js and Redux
Blazor Server App
Blazor WebAssembly App
Class Library
```

Figure 3-1. *List of installed templates*

This list can be extended by installing other templates, either manually or through the command line. Third parties can provide their own templates as well. Let's say, for example, we want to create an Uno app through the command line (https://platform.uno/). I have the Uno SDK installed on my machine, but not the dotnet new templates. According to their docs, I can create a new Uno project using dotnet new unoapp. Figure 3-1 shows the result.

```
> dotnet new unoapp -o MyApp
The list of templates was synchronized with the Optional SDK Workloads.
No templates found matching: 'unoapp'.
To list installed templates, run 'dotnet new --list'.
To search for the templates on NuGet.org, run 'dotnet new unoapp --search'.
```

Figure 3-2. *Trying to create a new project without template*

Looking at the documentation for dotnet new, we can see that there's an --install flag that *"Installs a source or a template pack."* From the Uno docs, we can find a command to download and install their template pack. Figure 3-2 shows the templates after installing.

```
> dotnet new -i Uno.ProjectTemplates.Dotnet
The following template packages will be installed:
   Uno.ProjectTemplates.Dotnet

Success: Uno.ProjectTemplates.Dotnet::4.0.9 installed the following templates:
Template Name                                    Short Name             Language
----------------------------------------------   --------------------   --------
Cross-Platform App (Prism)                       unoapp-prism           [C#]
Cross-Platform Library                           unolib                 [C#]
Cross-Platform UI Tests Library                  unoapp-uitest          [C#]
Cross-Runtime Library                            unolib-crossruntime    [C#]
Multi-Platform App                               unoapp                 [C#]
Multi-Platform App (net6)                        unoapp-net6            [C#]
Multi-Platform App (WinUI)                       unoapp-winui           [C#]
Multi-Platform App net6 (WinUI)                  unoapp-winui-net6      [C#]
Uno Platform WebAssembly Head for Xamarin.Forms  wasmxfhead             [C#]
```

Figure 3-3. *Output after installing the Uno templates*

Let's try the dotnet new command again.

```
> dotnet new unoapp -o MyApp
The list of templates was synchronized with the Optional SDK Workloads.
The template "Cross-Platform App" was created successfully.
```

Figure 3-4. *Successfully created a new Uno project through the command line*

Since the templates have been installed on my machine, dotnet new knows what to do. It inflates the template into a new project and puts it in the directory my command line is currently set in. the -o parameter stands for Output; dotnet new will use this as the name for both the folder and the project it's creating.

Templates are distributed using NuGet infrastructure and thus are packaged as NuGet packages. The default install location of these templates on Windows is %USERPROFILE%\.templateengine\dotnetcli\.

An interesting option in dotnet new is the dry-run option. Figure 3-4 shows the output if we try to create a new WPF project with the --dry-run flag.

```
> dotnet new wpf -o WpfDemo --dry-run
The list of templates was synchronized with the Optional SDK Workloads.
File actions would have been taken:
  Create: ./App.xaml
  Create: ./App.xaml.cs
  Create: ./AssemblyInfo.cs
  Create: ./WpfDemo.csproj
  Create: ./MainWindow.xaml
  Create: ./MainWindow.xaml.cs

Processing post-creation actions...
Action would have been taken automatically:
  Restore NuGet packages required by this project.
```

Figure 3-5. *Dry-run output*

Dry-run lists all the actions that would have happened if the command was run without --dry-run. It didn't actually do anything; the command just lists what would have happened.

Creating new projects through inflating a template is handled by a component called the .NET Core Templating Engine. It's an open source piece of software, available at https://github.com/dotnet/templating.

Dotnet Restore

The dotnet restore command restores dependencies and tools of a project. It uses the information in the project's projectfile (*.csproj in case of a C#-based project). This command usually does not need to be executed explicitly; it gets triggered from the following:

- dotnet new
- dotnet build
- dotnet build server
- dotnet run
- dotnet test
- dotnet publish
- dotnet pack

Should you still want to do dotnet restore manually for whatever reason, you can stop it being called from the above commands by using the --no-restore option like so:

Listing 3-3. Creating a new project without restoring packages

```
dotnet new wpf -o WpfDemo --no-restore
```

Being able to prevent package restore and call it whenever we need it gives us the flexibility needed to setup a fine-grained build pipeline. More on build and release pipelines further in this chapter.

Listing 3-4 shows the help on dotnet restore.

Listing 3-4. dotnet restore help

```
Usage:
  dotnet [options] restore [<PROJECT | SOLUTION>...]

Arguments:
  <PROJECT | SOLUTION>  The project or solution file to operate on. If a file
  is not specified, the command will search the current directory for one.

Options:
  -s, --source <SOURCE>          The NuGet package source to use for
                                 the restore.

  --packages <PACKAGES_DIR>      The directory to restore packages to.
  --use-current-runtime          Use current runtime as the target
                                 runtime.

  --disable-parallel             Prevent restoring multiple projects
                                 in parallel.
```

--configfile <FILE>	The NuGet configuration file to use.
--no-cache	Do not cache packages and http requests.
--ignore-failed-sources	Treat package source failures as warnings.
-f, --force	Force all dependencies to be resolved even if the last restore was successful. This is equivalent to deleting project.assets.json.
-r, --runtime <RUNTIME_IDENTIFIER>	The target runtime to restore packages for.
--no-dependencies	Do not restore project-to-project references and only restore the specified project.
-v, --verbosity <LEVEL>	Set the MSBuild verbosity level. Allowed values are q[uiet], m[inimal], n[ormal], d[etailed], and diag[nostic].
--interactive	Allows the command to stop and wait for user input or action (e.g., to complete authentication).
--use-lock-file	Enables project lock file to be generated and used with restore.
--locked-mode	Don't allow updating project lock file.
--lock-file-path <LOCK_FILE_PATH>	Output location where project lock file is written. By default, this is 'PROJECT_ROOT\packages.lock.json'.
--force-evaluate	Forces restore to reevaluate all dependencies even if a lock file already exists.
-?, -h, --help	Show command line help.

Dotnet restore needs a project to restore; it either finds this implicitly in the folder the command line is currently set in, through a project path can be passed explicitly or through a solution file.

Before we can build an application, we first need to do a dotnet restore. This will generate a *project.assets.json* file that dotnet build needs. That file contains a complete configuration for dotnet build; it configures project path and name, referenced libraries, target frameworks, and so on. Listing 3-5 shows an example of the project.assets.json.

Listing 3-5. project.assets.json example

```
{
  "version": 3,
  "targets": {
    "net6.0": {}
  },
  "libraries": {},
  "projectFileDependencyGroups": {
    "net6.0": []
  },
  "packageFolders": {
    "C:\\Users\\myUser\\.nuget\\packages\\": {},
    "C:\\Program Files (x86)\\Microsoft Visual Studio\\Shared\\
    NuGetPackages": {},
    "C:\\Program Files (x86)\\Microsoft\\Xamarin\\NuGet\\": {},
    "C:\\Program Files\\dotnet\\sdk\\NuGetFallbackFolder": {}
  },
  "project": {
    "version": "1.0.0",
    "restore": {
      "projectUniqueName": "C:\\Projects\\Apress\\cli\\CliDemo\\CliDemo.
      csproj",
      "projectName": "CliDemo",
      "projectPath": "C:\\Projects\\Apress\\cli\\CliDemo\\CliDemo.csproj",
      "packagesPath": "C:\\Users\\myUser\\.nuget\\packages\\",
      "outputPath": "C:\\Projects\\Apress\\cli\\CliDemo\\obj\\",
      "projectStyle": "PackageReference",
```

```
    "fallbackFolders": [
      "C:\\Program Files (x86)\\Microsoft Visual Studio\\Shared\\
      NuGetPackages",
      "C:\\Program Files (x86)\\Microsoft\\Xamarin\\NuGet\\",
      "C:\\Program Files\\dotnet\\sdk\\NuGetFallbackFolder"
    ],
    "configFilePaths": [
      "C:\\Users\\myUser\\AppData\\Roaming\\NuGet\\NuGet.Config",
      "C:\\Program Files (x86)\\NuGet\\Config\\Microsoft.VisualStudio.
      FallbackLocation.config",
      "C:\\Program Files (x86)\\NuGet\\Config\\Microsoft.VisualStudio.
      Offline.config",
      "C:\\Program Files (x86)\\NuGet\\Config\\Xamarin.Offline.config"
    ],
    "originalTargetFrameworks": [
      "net6.0"
    ],
    "sources": {
      "C:\\Program Files (x86)\\Microsoft SDKs\\NuGetPackages\\": {},
      "https://api.nuget.org/v3/index.json": {}
    },
    "frameworks": {
      "net6.0": {
        "targetAlias": "net6.0",
        "projectReferences": {}
      }
    },
    "warningProperties": {
      "warnAsError": [
        "NU1605"
      ]
    }
  },
  "frameworks": {
    "net6.0": {
      "targetAlias": "net6.0",
```

```
    "imports": [
      "net48"
    ],
    "assetTargetFallback": true,
    "warn": true,
    "frameworkReferences": {
      "Microsoft.NETCore.App": {
        "privateAssets": "all"
      }
    },
    "runtimeIdentifierGraphPath": "C:\\Program Files\\dotnet\\
    sdk\\6.0.100\\RuntimeIdentifierGraph.json"
      }
    }
  }
}
```

You can find this file in your project's obj folder after dotnet restore should you want to take a look.

NuGet.config

Dotnet restore can take a nuget.config file into account. A nuget.config file can set different settings per project; it's an XML file with one `<configuration>` top-level node.

Listing 3-6 shows an example of a nuget.config file.

Listing 3-6. nuget.config example

```
<?xml version="1.0" encoding="utf-8"?>
<configuration>
    <config>
        <!-- Set default install location for packages -->
        <add key="repositoryPath" value="%HOME%/Packages" />
    </config>
```

```xml
    <packageRestore>
        <add key="enabled" value="True" />
        <add key="automatic" value="True" />
    </packageRestore>

    <!-- Specify package sources used for this project -->
    <packageSources>
        <add key="NuGet official package source" value="https://api.nuget.
        org/v3/index.json" />
    </packageSources>

    <!-- Set Microsoft as trusted signer -->
    <trustedSigners>
        <author name="microsoft">
            <certificate fingerprint="3F9001EA83C560D712C24CF213C3D31
            2CB3BFF51EE89435D3430BD06B5D0EECE" hashAlgorithm="SHA256"
            allowUntrustedRoot="false" />
            <certificate fingerprint="AA12DA22A49BCE7D5C1AE64CC1F3D89
            2F150DA76140F210ABD2CBFFCA2C18A27" hashAlgorithm="SHA256"
            allowUntrustedRoot="false" />
        </author>
        <repository name="nuget.org" serviceIndex="https://api.nuget.org/
        v3/index.json">
            <certificate fingerprint="0E5F38F57DC1BCC806D8494F4F90FBC
            EDD988B46760709CBEEC6F4219AA6157D" hashAlgorithm="SHA256"
            allowUntrustedRoot="false" />
            <certificate fingerprint="5A2901D6ADA3D18260B9C6DFE2133C9
            5D74B9EEF6AE0E5DC334C8454D1477DF4" hashAlgorithm="SHA256"
            allowUntrustedRoot="false" />
            <owners>microsoft;aspnet;nuget</owners>
        </repository>
    </trustedSigners>
</configuration>
```

The config file can contain a config section with:

- dependencyVersion

- globalPackagesFolder

- repositoryPath

- defaultPushSource

- proxy settings

  - http_proxy

  - http_proxy.user

  - http_proxy.password

  - no_proxy

- signatureValidationMode

The config file can also control binding redirects. Binding redirects trick .NET into believing an assembly is actually another one, for example, if one specific NuGet package needs an older version of another package, we can trick the compiler into thinking package v3.5 is actually package v2.0. NuGet can set those redirects in your projects automatically. We can control this behavior through the ⟨bindingRedirects⟩ section.

NuGet.config can contain instructions on automatic restore of packages during builds; this is enabled by default but can be disabled by setting automatic to false in the ⟨packageRestore⟩ section.

If the nuget.config file is at solution level of a code base, we can control whether or not the packages themselves are included in source control by setting disableSourceControlIntegration in the ⟨solution⟩ section.

Probably the most used section in nuget.config is the ⟨packageSources⟩ section. This is used to add extra package sources where NuGet can look for packages, besides nuget.org. It can come in handy if you have an own private package feed, for example, Azure DevOps Artifact Feeds. Should one of those feeds need credentials, you can set those through ⟨packageSourceCredentials⟩ or through API keys via ⟨apikeys⟩. Besides explicitly defining package sources, we can also explicitly disable them through ⟨disabledPackageSource⟩.

There are other interesting but less used sections available. Table 3-5 shows a complete overview for completeness.

Table 3-5. *Overview of NuGet.config sections*

Element	Description
<config>	General configuration
<bindingRedirects>	Sets whether or not NuGet handles automatic redirects
<packageRestore>	Controls if package restore is enabled and automatic on build
<solution>	Enables/disables source control integration of the solution file
<packageSource>	Adds extra NuGet package sources to restore packages from
<trustedSigners>	Sets trusted package authors, with their signature and repository feeds
<fallbackPackageFolders>	Points to folders that act as a local, offline cache for packages
<packageManagement>	Allows projects to use the older packages.config instead of PackageReference

Dotnet Build

Dotnet build builds (what a shock!) your project and all of its dependencies. It's a straightforward command with a limited set of options. Listing 3-7 shows its options.

Listing 3-7. Options for dotnet build

```
Usage:
  dotnet [options] build [<PROJECT | SOLUTION>...]

Arguments:
  <PROJECT | SOLUTION>  The project or solution file to operate on. If a
  file is not specified, the command will search the current directory
  for one.

Options:
  --use-current-runtime                Use current runtime as the target
                                       runtime.
```

-f, --framework <FRAMEWORK>	The target framework to build for. The target framework must also be specified in the project file.
-c, --configuration <CONFIGURATION>	The configuration to use for building the project. The default for most projects is 'Debug.'
-r, --runtime <RUNTIME_IDENTIFIER>	The target runtime to build for.
--version-suffix <VERSION_SUFFIX>	Set the value of the $(VersionSuffix) property to use when building the project.
--no-restore	Do not restore the project before building.
--interactive	Allows the command to stop and wait for user input or action (e.g., to complete authentication).
-v, --verbosity <LEVEL>	Set the MSBuild verbosity level. Allowed values are q[uiet], m[inimal], n[ormal], d[etailed], and diag[nostic].
--debug	
-o, --output <OUTPUT_DIR>	The output directory to place built artifacts in.
--no-incremental	Do not use incremental building.
--no-dependencies	Do not build project-to-project references and only build the specified project.
--nologo	Do not display the startup banner or the copyright message.
--sc, --self-contained	Publish the .NET runtime with your application so the runtime doesn't need to be installed on the target machine. The default is 'true' if a runtime identifier is specified.

`--no-self-contained`	Publish your application as a framework-dependent application. A compatible .NET runtime must be installed on the target machine to run your application.
`-a, --arch <arch>`	The target architecture.
`--os <os>`	The target operating system.
`-?, -h, --help`	Show command line help.

Dotnet build triggers the same workflow as *Build Solution* does in Visual Studio; whenever you click *Build Solution* in Visual Studio, it launches dotnet build under the hood. It takes your code and its dependencies and compiles it into DLLs, executables, symbols, and so on.

Before we can build an application, we need to make sure that all dependencies are restored. This can be done by running `dotnet restore` which we've seen earlier in this chapter. However, we don't have to run dotnet restore every time before building a project; it runs implicitly when executing dotnet build. Unless we use `dotnet build --no-restore`.

Dotnet build uses msbuild to do the actual compiling of the code. MSBuild options can be passed in through parameters like -l for logging. MSBuild can be called directly from the dotnet tool by using `dotnet msbuild <arguments>`. We won't dive into the msbuild options in this book. The `dotnet build` command is basically the same as `msbuild -restore` although the output looks different.

Two important parameters for the dotnet build command are configuration and runtime. Configuration specifies the configuration used for this build, while the runtime parameter specifies what version of the .NET runtime we're building against.

The default configurations in .NET are Release and Debug. If we don't specify a configuration, the Debug configuration will be used by default. Depending on the selected configuration, the build output will by default appear in *bin\<config>\net6.0*. These configurations differ in the way they optimize code for either debugging purposes or performance. Listing 3-8 shows how we can switch configurations.

Listing 3-8. Running a build in the Release configuration

```
dotnet build -c release
```

Runtimes are specified using a runtime identifier (RID). RIDs are used to define on the type of system architecture the application will run. An application needs to be compiled differently for a 64-bit Intel processor compared to a 64-bit ARM processor and for the different operating systems and their versions. An RID follows the pattern as shown in Listing 3-9.

Listing 3-9. RID pattern

```
<os>.<version>-<architecture>-<additional>
```

For example, let's build an application for use on ARM64, which is an architecture that Windows can run on and try to run the application. Figure 3-6 shows the build and the attempt to run the application.

```
> dotnet build -r win-arm64
Microsoft (R) Build Engine version 17.0.0+c9eb9dd64 for .NET
Copyright (C) Microsoft Corporation. All rights reserved.

  Determining projects to restore...
  All projects are up-to-date for restore.
C:\Program Files\dotnet\sdk\6.0.100\Sdks\Microsoft.NET.Sdk\targets\Microsoft.NET.Sdk.targets(1110,5): warning NETSDK1179: One of '--se
' is used. [C:\Projects\Apress\WinUi\review\ConsoleApp1\ConsoleApp1\ConsoleApp1.csproj]
  ConsoleApp1 -> C:\Projects\Apress\WinUi\review\ConsoleApp1\ConsoleApp1\bin\Debug\net6.0\win-arm64\ConsoleApp1.dll

Build succeeded.

C:\Program Files\dotnet\sdk\6.0.100\Sdks\Microsoft.NET.Sdk\targets\Microsoft.NET.Sdk.targets(1110,5): warning NETSDK1179: One of '--se
' is used. [C:\Projects\Apress\WinUi\review\ConsoleApp1\ConsoleApp1\ConsoleApp1.csproj]
    1 Warning(s)
    0 Error(s)

Time Elapsed 00:00:01.08
nico_@NOCTIS  C:\Projects\Apress\WinUi\review\ConsoleApp1\ConsoleApp1
> .\bin\Debug\net6.0\win-arm64\ConsoleApp1.exe
Program 'ConsoleApp1.exe' failed to run: The specified executable is not a valid application for this OS platform.At line:1 char:1
+ .\bin\Debug\net6.0\win-arm64\ConsoleApp1.exe
+ ~~~~~~~~~~~~~~~~~~~~~~~~~~~~~~~~~~~~~~~~~~~~~~.
At line:1 char:1
+ .\bin\Debug\net6.0\win-arm64\ConsoleApp1.exe
+ ~~~~~~~~~~~~~~~~~~~~~~~~~~~~~~~~~~~~~~~~~~~~~~
    + CategoryInfo          : ResourceUnavailable: (:) [], ApplicationFailedException
    + FullyQualifiedErrorId : NativeCommandFailed
```

Figure 3-6. *Running an ARM application on x64*

The .NET runtime contains a runtime.json file. In this file is a runtime graph; it specifies what operating systems and what versions/architectures are available or what the fallback is. Listing 3-10 shows an example entry from runtime.json.

Listing 3-10. Example entry in runtime.json

```
"alpine.3.13": {
  "#import": [
    "alpine.3.12"
  ]
}
```

Listing 3-10 shows the entry for Alpine Linux, a lightweight Linux distribution. The entry specifies Alpine version 3.13 but imports 3.12; when .NET tries to restore NuGet packages for a project targeting Alpine Linux, it will try to find packages targeting Alpine 3.13. Should there be a package that does not target this version, it will look for a fallback to Alpine 3.12 support. The complete runtime.json file can be found on GitHub `https://github.com/dotnet/runtime/blob/main/src/libraries/Microsoft.NETCore.Platforms/src/runtime.json`.

Listing 3-11. dotnet runtimes

Listing 3-11 lists the most common runtimes for .NET:

- Windows Portable

  - win-x64

  - win-x86

  - win-arm

  - win-arm64

- Windows 7/Windows Server 2008 R2

  - win7-x64

  - win7-x86

- Windows 8.1/Windows Server 2012 R2

  - win81-x64

  - win81-x86

  - win81-arm

- Windows 10/Windows Server 2016

  - win10-x64

  - win10-x86

  - win10-arm

  - win10-arm64

- Linux Portable

  - linux-x64

  - linux-musl-x64

  - linux-arm

  - linux-arm64

- Red Hat Enterprise Linux

  - rhel-x64

  - rhel.6-x64

- MacOS Portable

  - osx-x64 (Minimum OS version is macOS 10.12 Sierra.)

- macOS 10.x

  - osx.10.10-x64

  - osx.10.11-x64

  - osx.10.12-x64

  - osx.10.13-x64

  - osx.10.14-x64

  - osx.10.15-x64

- macOS 11.x

  - osx.11.0-x64

  - osx.11.0-arm64

Chapter 2 of this book dives deeper into runtimes, platforms, and extensibility packs.

Dotnet Publish

Dotnet publish takes the compiled application and its dependencies and publishes them to the file system, ready for deployment either through a webserver or application setup through an MSI or setup file, ...

Listing 3-12. Dotnet publish options

Usage:
```
  dotnet [options] publish [<PROJECT | SOLUTION>...]
```

Arguments:
```
  <PROJECT | SOLUTION>  The project or solution file to operate on. If a file
  is not specified, the command will search the current directory for one.
```

Options:
```
  --use-current-runtime            Use current runtime as the target
                                   runtime.

  -o, --output <OUTPUT_DIR>        The output directory to place the
                                   published artifacts in.

  --manifest <MANIFEST>            The path to a target manifest
                                   file that contains the list of
                                   packages to be excluded from the
                                   publish step.

  --no-build                       Do not build the project before
                                   publishing. Implies --no-restore.

  --sc, --self-contained           Publish the .NET runtime with your
                                   application so the runtime doesn't
                                   need to be installed on the target
                                   machine.
                                   The default is 'true' if a runtime
                                   identifier is specified.

  --no-self-contained              Publish your application as a
                                   framework-dependent application.
                                   A compatible .NET runtime must be
                                   installed on the target machine to
                                   run your application.
```

--nologo	Do not display the startup banner or the copyright message.
-f, --framework <FRAMEWORK>	The target framework to publish for. The target framework has to be specified in the project file.
-r, --runtime <RUNTIME_IDENTIFIER>	The target runtime to publish for. This is used when creating a self-contained deployment. The default is to publish a framework-dependent application.
-c, --configuration <CONFIGURATION>	The configuration to publish for. The default for most projects is 'Debug'.
--version-suffix <VERSION_SUFFIX>	Set the value of the $(VersionSuffix) property to use when building the project.
--interactive	Allows the command to stop and wait for user input or action (e.g., to complete authentication).
--no-restore	Do not restore the project before building.
-v, --verbosity <LEVEL>	Set the MSBuild verbosity level. Allowed values are q[uiet], m[inimal], n[ormal], d[etailed], and diag[nostic].
-a, --arch <arch>	The target architecture.
--os <os>	The target operating system.
-?, -h, --help	Show command line help.

Running dotnet publish will compile the application and publish the output to a specific directory. The output will contain the DLLs, a *.deps.json* file listing all the project dependencies, a *.runtime.json* file that specifies the runtime for the application, and the dependencies for the application. Just like with dotnet build, this command also runs dotnet restore implicitly, and just like with dotnet build, dotnet restore also calls into msbuild, passing the parameters through.

Dotnet publish comes with a plethora of options; however, most of those are just pass-through to the dotnet build command that gets called when publishing. Those parameters have already been discussed when talking about dotnet build, so let us focus on the dotnet deploy specific ones.

--framework, or -f, deploys the application for a specific target framework. Note that the target framework moniker (TFM) needs to be specified in the project file. If we specify multiple frameworks, we will get output for all of these different frameworks with one deploy command. Listing 3-13 lists the TFMs for .NET 6.

Listing 3-13. Target framework monikers for .NET 6

- net6.0
- net6.0-android
- net6.0-ios
- net6.0-macos
- net6.0-maccatalyst
- net6.0-tvos
- net6.0-windows

Listing 3-14 shows how the target framework is specified in the project file.

Listing 3-14. Specifying .NET 6 as target framework

```
<Project Sdk="Microsoft.NET.Sdk">

  <PropertyGroup>
    <OutputType>Exe</OutputType>
    <TargetFramework>net6.0</TargetFramework>
  </PropertyGroup>

</Project>
```

Listing 3-14 comes from a command line-type application. It specifies .NET 6 as target framework; this is not an OS-specific TFM so this application will run everywhere .NET 6 is supported (Windows, Linux, MacOS, ...). Projects can specify multiple TFMs by changing the *TargetFramework* tag to the plural *TargetFrameworks*.

Listing 3-15. Specifying multiple target frameworks

```
<Project Sdk="Microsoft.NET.Sdk">

  <PropertyGroup>
    <OutputType>Exe</OutputType>
    <TargetFrameworks>net6.0;net45</TargetFrameworks>
  </PropertyGroup>

</Project>
```

Listing 3-15 targets both .NET 6 and .NET 4.5. If we were to build this project, we would get two output folders, one for each target platform containing a binary compiled for that specific platform.

-p:PublishSingleFile=true gives you a single file as output. This single file executable is a self-extracting archive containing all dependencies and libraries for your application. At first run, it extracts everything in a directory based on version number and name of the application. Every new launch of the application will launch from that folder, meaning that the first run will be slower since the extracting needs to happen first. Having a single file makes it easier to distribute applications. Publishing as a single file works since .NET Core 3.0; if you're targeting older versions, you'll get compiler errors. Figure 3-7 shows the differences in publishing single file or not.

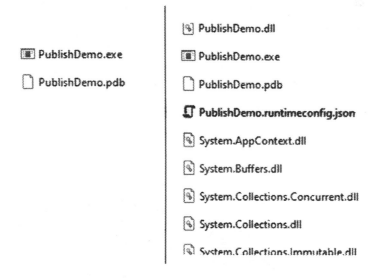

Figure 3-7. *Publishing single file (left) or default (right)*

`--self-contained` Self-contained applications include the .NET runtime your application specifies so that it doesn't need to be installed on the target machines. This eliminates the risk of having to install multiple versions of the .NET runtime on a machine, potentially causing conflicts. Shipping the .NET runtime with your application greatly simplifies installation, but it does come with a warning. Software contains bugs, especially in complex software like .NET; these bugs can show up pretty late in their lifespan and potentially cause severe security issues. Companies like Microsoft are usually quite fast to fix those security issues and push out an update. If you are packaging a specific .NET runtime version with your app, it is up to you as application developer to follow up on those .NET updates and update your application with the new version of the .NET runtime when needed. In other words, you are responsible for replacing vulnerable .NET binaries in your application.

`--no-self-contained` does not ship the .NET runtime with the application. In this case, the application relies on the version of the .NET runtime installed on the user's machine.

Dotnet Run

Dotnet run runs your application. It builds the application using dotnet build and launches the application.

Listing 3-16. Documentation on dotnet run

```
Usage:
  dotnet [options] run [[--] <additional arguments>...]]

Options:
  -c, --configuration <CONFIGURATION>   The configuration to run for.
                                        The default for most projects is
                                        'Debug'.
  -f, --framework <FRAMEWORK>           The target framework to run for.
                                        The target framework must also be
                                        specified in the project file.
  -r, --runtime <RUNTIME_IDENTIFIER>    The target runtime to run for.
```

--project <project>	The path to the project file to run (defaults to the current directory if there is only one project).
-p, --property <property>	Properties to be passed to MSBuild.
--launch-profile <launch-profile>	The name of the launch profile (if any) to use when launching the application.
--no-launch-profile	Do not attempt to use launchSettings.json to configure the application.
--no-build	Do not build the project before running. Implies --no-restore.
--interactive	Allows the command to stop and wait for user input or action (e.g., to complete authentication).
--no-restore	Do not restore the project before building.
--sc, --self-contained	Publish the .NET runtime with your application so the runtime doesn't need to be installed on the target machine. The default is 'true' if a runtime identifier is specified.
--no-self-contained	Publish your application as a framework-dependent application. A compatible .NET runtime must be installed on the target machine to run your application.
-v, --verbosity <LEVEL>	Set the MSBuild verbosity level. Allowed values are q[uiet], m[inimal], n[ormal], d[etailed], and diag[nostic].
-a, --arch <arch>	The target architecture.
--os <os>	The target operating system.
-?, -h, --help	Show command line help.

Dotnet run executes the binaries in the bin/<config>/<TFM> folder. This is where the output of the build command is put. In case of .NET 6, this could be /bin/<Configuration>/net6.0. Other frameworks can be specified by using the --framework parameter. A configuration can be specified by using the --configuration parameter. Listing 3-17 shows a complete example of a dotnet run command.

Listing 3-17. Running a .NET 6 application using CLI

```
dotnet run --configuration Release --framework net6.0 --project
.\CliDemo.csproj
```

Dotnet Test

Dotnet test is used to run unit tests included in a project.

Listing 3-18. dotnet test documentation (shortened for brevity)

```
Usage:
  dotnet [options] test [<PROJECT | SOLUTION>...]

Arguments:
  <PROJECT | SOLUTION>  The project or solution file to operate on. If a file
  is not specified, the command will search the current directory for one.

Options:
  -s, --settings <SETTINGS_FILE>        The settings file to use when
                                        running tests.
  -t, --list-tests                      List the discovered tests instead
                                        of running the tests.
  -e, --environment <NAME="VALUE">      Sets the value of an environment
                                        variable.
                                        Creates the variable if it does not
                                        exist and overrides if it does
                                        This will force the tests to be run
                                        in an isolated process.
                                        This argument can be specified
                                        multiple times to provide multiple
                                        variables.
```

Dotnet test commands trigger a dotnet build after which it executes any unit tests it finds. It supports any test framework that has support for .NET 6, for example, MSTest, NUnit, XUnit, etc. Every test that was run by the tool will print its result; after all tests are run, the dotnet test command will return to either 0 (all tests successful) or 1 (at least one test failed). Figure 3-8 shows an example output of dotnet test.

```
> dotnet test
  Determining projects to restore...
  All projects are up-to-date for restore.
  You are using a preview version of .NET. See: https://aka.ms/dotnet-core-preview
  You are using a preview version of .NET. See: https://aka.ms/dotnet-core-preview
  CliDemo -> C:\Projects\Apress\cli\CliDemo\bin\Debug\net6.0\CliDemo.dll
  CliDemo.UnitTests -> C:\Projects\Apress\cli\CliDemo.UnitTests\bin\Debug\net6.0\CliDemo.UnitTests.dll
Test run for C:\Projects\Apress\cli\CliDemo.UnitTests\bin\Debug\net6.0\CliDemo.UnitTests.dll (.NETCoreApp,Version=v
6.0)
Microsoft (R) Test Execution Command Line Tool Version 16.10.0-preview-20210317-02
Copyright (c) Microsoft Corporation.  All rights reserved.

Starting test execution, please wait...
A total of 1 test files matched the specified pattern.
  Failed Test3 [18 ms]
  Stack Trace:
    at CliDemo.UnitTests.Tests.Test3() in C:\Projects\Apress\cli\CliDemo.UnitTests\UnitTest1.cs:line 27


Failed!  - Failed:     1, Passed:     4, Skipped:     0, Total:     5, Duration:  - CliDemo.UnitTests.dll (net6.0)
```

Figure 3-8. *Example output of dotnet test*

In the screenshot, you can see that four tests passed, while one failed. The tests in this sample project are written using NUnit; dotnet test automatically picks up on this and uses the correct adapter. Should it not find the correct adapter, or you want to use a custom one, you can use the `--test-adapter-path` option of the dotnet test command. The custom adapter needs to be named **.TestAdapter.dll* for it to be picked up by the .NET CLI tooling. Figure 3-6 also shows that the first step in running the test command is verifying if dependencies need to be restored or if the project needs to be compiled.

After fixing the failing unit test, we get the result shown in Figure 3-9.

```
Starting test execution, please wait...
A total of 1 test files matched the specified pattern.

Passed!  - Failed:     0, Passed:     5, Skipped:     0, Total:     5, Duration:  - CliDemo.UnitTests.dll (net6.0)
```

Figure 3-9. *Passing all unit tests*

Other often used options in dotnet test are:

- --configuration same as with dotnet build and dotnet deploy, sets the configuration to be used.

- --collect enables data collection, for example, code coverage.

- --framework sets the framework used for the test host. This does not set the framework your application is built against; it's only the framework version that the test host is using.

Using the CLI in GitHub Actions

In case you're wondering why you would ever use command line functions when you have a perfectly good, very powerful IDE experience, you've come to the right place. The .NET CLI is mostly used in CI/CD pipelines. We'll dive deeper in the nitty-gritty of CI/CD in Chapter 7 of this book; for now just remember that it is a tool chain that builds, tests, and deploys applications automatically, for example, on every source code push on specific branches. GitHub Actions is one example of a cloud-based CI/CD toolchain that developers can leverage. Other examples are Azure DevOps or Jenkins. In this example, we'll use GitHub Actions. The different steps required to make a GitHub Action build and deploy a .NET 6 application are defined in a YAML file. If you don't know YAML, it's a data language that is often used for configuration files. It has a minimal syntax, based on indentation instead of brackets like JSON or element tags like XML.

GitHub Actions are available from the top menu on a GitHub Repository as shown in Figure 3-10.

🖳 Xavalon / XamlStyler

<> Code   ⓘ Issues 51   ⌥ Pull requests 4   ⊙ Actions   ⬚ Wiki   ⓘ Security   ⮑ Insights   ⚙ Settings

Figure 3-10. *GitHub Actions*

Listing 3-19 shows a simple example of a GitHub Actions YAML file.

Listing 3-19. Building a .NET 6 application through GitHub Actions

```
Name: Net6Demo

on:
  push:
    branches: [ main ]
  pull_request:
    branches: [ main ]
```

```
env:
  PROJECTFILE_PATH: './src/Net6Demo.Api/Net6Demo.Api.csproj'
  PROJECT_PATH: './src/Net6Demo.Api/'
  DOTNET_VERSION: '6.0'
  CONFIG: Release

jobs:
  build:

    runs-on: ubuntu-latest

    steps:
    - uses: actions/checkout@v2

    - name: Setup .NET 6
      uses: actions/setup-dotnet@v1
      with:
        dotnet-version: ${{ env.DOTNET_VERSION }}

    - name: Install dependencies
      run: dotnet restore ${{ env.PROJECTFILE_PATH }}

    - name: Build
      run:  |
        dotnet build ${{ env.PROJECTFILE_PATH }} -c ${{ env.CONFIG }} -
        no-restore
        dotnet publish ${{ env.PROJECTFILE_PATH }} -c ${{ env.CONFIG }}
```

Let's go over the top-level blocks first. The first block, 'name', specifies the name for this specific GitHub Action.

'on' specifies the triggers. In this case the action will get triggered whenever a new commit happens on the main branch or when a pull request against the main branch is created.

'env' registers variables that can be used throughout the YAML file, to prevent duplicate hard-coded values.

'jobs' is where the magic happens; in this example, we have a 'build' job. This job will compile our application and publish the output, ready for a deploy job to pick it up and push it to a server.

'build' has two blocks. The first one 'runs on' specified the operating system that will be used for the build. Pipelines, like GitHub Actions or Azure DevOps, are run on, usually virtual, machines. Those machines have a specific operating system installed and have a piece of software called an agent. This agent reports the machine's status to the build service and can accept build requests. Once a request comes in, it downloads all the different tasks and starts executing the request. The GitHub Actions agent takes the YAML file, downloads the tasks needed, and performs them. GitHub Actions provides agents on Windows, Linux, and MacOS. They also provide an option to host your own agent on your own machines.

'steps' contain all the steps needed to compile the application. This is quite a simple setup. Listing 3-20 shows the extracted steps from the complete file in Listing 3-19.

Listing 3-20. Steps in a GitHub Action

```
steps:
- uses: actions/checkout@v2

- name: Setup .NET 6
  uses: actions/setup-dotnet@v1
  with:
    dotnet-version: ${{ env.DOTNET_VERSION }}

- name: Install dependencies
  run: dotnet restore ${{ env.PROJECTFILE_PATH }}

- name: Build
  run:  |
    dotnet build ${{ env.PROJECTFILE_PATH }} --c ${{ env.CONFIG }}
    --no-restore
    dotnet publish ${{ env.PROJECTFILE_PATH }} -c ${{ env.CONFIG }}
```

The first step in the action only has a 'uses' statement. 'uses' specifies a specific task to be used for this step. In this case, it specifies '*actions/checkout@v2*'; this means that the agent will look for an action called checkout and download version 2 of this action. This specific one will perform a *git checkout* command against the main branch, as defined earlier in the YAML file, of our current GitHub repository.

The 'Setup .NET 6' step will download the *actions/setup-dotnet/@v1* task and pass in the environment variables we've defined earlier. This task will then setup the specified version of the .NET SDK and install it on the machine where the agent is hosted.

The final two steps use .NET CLI commands that we've described earlier in this chapter. First, we will restore the dependencies using *dotnet restore*. I like to do the restore separately from the build command. When a task failed, we can search for the reason in the task logs; by splitting the restore and build task, we limit the log size we potentially need to look through.

In the 'Build' step, we use dotnet build in Release configuration; we prevent restoring dependencies with the --no-restore flag since that happened in the previous step. And finally we use dotnet deploy to create our artifacts.

This specific action only builds the application and creates artifacts ready for deployment. The actual deployment of the artifacts is usually defined separately and is very dependent on the environment you want to deploy to.

Other Commands

This chapter has described the most common basic commands in the .NET CLI tooling. There are plenty more commands, like add and remove. Add and remove are used for adding or removing both NuGet packages and project references. Figure 3-11 shows adding the Entity Framework NuGet package using the CLI.

```
> dotnet add package Microsoft.EntityFrameworkCore
  Determining projects to restore...
  Writing C:\Users\nico_\AppData\Local\Temp\tmp39CD.tmp
info : Adding PackageReference for package 'Microsoft.EntityFrameworkCore' into project 'C:\Projects\Apress\cli\Cli
Demo\CliDemo.csproj'.
info :    GET https://api.nuget.org/v3/registration5-gz-semver2/microsoft.entityframeworkcore/index.json
info :    OK https://api.nuget.org/v3/registration5-gz-semver2/microsoft.entityframeworkcore/index.json 131ms
info : Restoring packages for C:\Projects\Apress\cli\CliDemo\CliDemo.csproj...
info : Package 'Microsoft.EntityFrameworkCore' is compatible with all the specified frameworks in project 'C:\Proje
cts\Apress\cli\CliDemo\CliDemo.csproj'.
info : PackageReference for package 'Microsoft.EntityFrameworkCore' version '5.0.5' added to file 'C:\Projects\Apre
ss\cli\CliDemo\CliDemo.csproj'.
info : Committing restore...
info : Generating MSBuild file C:\Projects\Apress\cli\CliDemo\obj\CliDemo.csproj.nuget.g.props.
info : Writing assets file to disk. Path: C:\Projects\Apress\cli\CliDemo\obj\project.assets.json
log  : Restored C:\Projects\Apress\cli\CliDemo\CliDemo.csproj (in 154 ms).
```

Figure 3-11. *Adding a NuGet package through the command line*

Figure 3-12 shows adding a project reference to a .NET 6 class library using the command line.

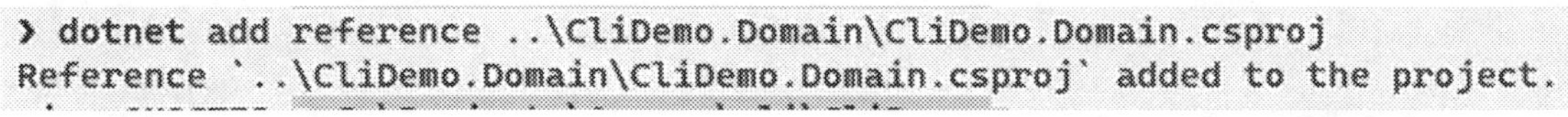

```
> dotnet add reference ..\CliDemo.Domain\CliDemo.Domain.csproj
Reference `..\CliDemo.Domain\CliDemo.Domain.csproj` added to the project.
```

Figure 3-12. *Adding a project reference through the command line*

Some frameworks, extension, etc. come with their own command line-based tool; Entity Framework, for example, ships with a CLI tool, for example, to create migrations or update a database. These tools are managed with the `dotnet tool` command. Dotnet tool can install tools, list all the installed tools, update or restore them, run them, and uninstall them.

Wrapping Up

In this chapter, we have gone over the most common parts of the extensive CLI tooling that is included with .NET 6. We as developers use these tools more than we realize, since they are the magic behind the buttons and shortcut keys in Visual Studio. Knowing what the capabilities are, and how to find the different options, is important knowledge, not only to have an idea of what is going on under the hood of Visual Studio but also to be able to define build and release pipelines.

CHAPTER 4

Desktop Development

I often get the question if there is still use in learning desktop technologies like WPF or WinForms. My answer is always the same: of course there is! There has been a big movement toward the Web the past few years, which definitely makes sense in regard to ease of deployment and installation. No need to juggle MSI files around, making sure every client computer has the correct version of .NET installed, finding out what version of the software a customer is using, and so on. With web applications, we install the software on a server, and all of our users just use their browsers to use the application. So why are native apps (both desktop and mobile apps) still a thing? The answer is simple, performance and capabilities. The Web, for now, does not have the same level of access to peripherals and operating system as a native app does. As for performance, let's look at the way an operating system renders its applications. Rendering happens in steps, layer by layer. A WPF application, for example, will render its main window followed by the controls on that specific window; the whole rendering of an application is optimized to draw the user interface as fast as possible to not make the user feel like the application is hanging. If we apply that same logic to a web browser, you'll understand that the browser's main window and controls like the back and forward buttons, favorite bar, extension icons, and so on are rendered first. Once everything is on the screen, the browser will start interpreting and rendering the HTML, so the actual user interface of your web application is last to render. Another major difference is threading, JavaScript is single-threaded, so it's not possible to schedule heavy work on a separate thread. The advice there is to have a server handle the heavy lifting and make your frontend wait for the response, which is a very valid argument, except for applications that need real-time heavy processing, like the software stock brokers use, for example. Every millisecond of delay caused by a request going over the network can cost them money. A native desktop application, running on a powerful client computer, can handle these calculations with ease.

© Nico Vermeir 2022

N. Vermeir, *Introducing .NET 6*, https://doi.org/10.1007/978-1-4842-7319-7_4

.NET 6 comes with multiple choices for desktop development, WPF, WinForms, Windows App SDK, CLI, Blazor Desktop, and MAUI. In this chapter, we'll take a look at these options, except for Blazor Desktop, and we will discuss that option in the Blazor chapter of this book.

WinAPI

Win32 and Win64, depending on the OS and CPU architecture, are the APIs in Windows that allow applications to run. The API is responsible for everything going on in Windows, from rendering applications and access to the operating system to installation/configuration and so on. It's the engine under the hood of Windows. Without WinAPI, we simply wouldn't be able to run applications on Windows. WinAPI is a native C/C++ API, meaning we'd need to write applications in those languages to leverage the WinAPI API set.

With WinAPI, we can build applications that have incredible performance, because we are in an unmanaged world. Languages like C# and Java, for example, are managed languages, meaning that there is a runtime taking care of recovering and managing memory. Unmanaged code, like C or C++, runs much closer to the metal, leaving the responsibility of reclaiming memory to the developer but gaining performance in return. But this performance comes with a price. It takes longer to develop these types of applications, and since they are unmanaged they are more prone to memory-related bugs. Listing 4-1 shows an example of the C++ code needed to simply draw an empty window on screen. Feel free to copy, compile, and run the code in Listing 4-1 if you have a C++ environment setup, and you will notice that it just works but shows an empty screen.

Listing 4-1. Drawing an empty window with Win32

```
#ifndef UNICODE
#define UNICODE
#endif

#include <windows.h>

LRESULT CALLBACK WindowProc(HWND hwnd, UINT uMsg, WPARAM wParam, LPARAM
lParam);
```

```
int WINAPI wWinMain(HINSTANCE hInstance, HINSTANCE, PWSTR pCmdLine, int
nCmdShow)
{
    // Register the window class.
    const wchar_t CLASS_NAME[]  = L"Sample Window Class";

    WNDCLASS wc = { };

    wc.lpfnWndProc   = WindowProc;
    wc.hInstance     = hInstance;
    wc.lpszClassName = CLASS_NAME;

    RegisterClass(&wc);

    // Create the window.

    HWND hwnd = CreateWindowEx(
        0,                              // Optional window styles.
        CLASS_NAME,                     // Window class
        L"Learn to Program Windows",    // Window text
        WS_OVERLAPPEDWINDOW,            // Window style

        // Size and position
        CW_USEDEFAULT, CW_USEDEFAULT, CW_USEDEFAULT, CW_USEDEFAULT,

        NULL,       // Parent window
        NULL,       // Menu
        hInstance,  // Instance handle
        NULL        // Additional application data
        );

    if (hwnd == NULL)
    {
        return 0;
    }

    ShowWindow(hwnd, nCmdShow);
```

```
    // Run the message loop.
    MSG msg = { };
    while (GetMessage(&msg, NULL, 0, 0))
    {
        TranslateMessage(&msg);
        DispatchMessage(&msg);
    }

    return 0;
}

LRESULT CALLBACK WindowProc(HWND hwnd, UINT uMsg, WPARAM wParam,
LPARAM lParam)
{
    switch (uMsg)
    {
    case WM_DESTROY:
        PostQuitMessage(0);
        return 0;

    case WM_PAINT:
        {
            PAINTSTRUCT ps;
            HDC hdc = BeginPaint(hwnd, &ps);

            // All painting occurs here, between BeginPaint and EndPaint.
            FillRect(hdc, &ps.rcPaint, (HBRUSH) (COLOR_WINDOW+1));
            EndPaint(hwnd, &ps);
        }
        return 0;
    }

    return DefWindowProc(hwnd, uMsg, wParam, lParam);
}
```

WinForms

WinForms was introduced in 2002 as part of the initial release of .NET. It was meant to be the successor of the very popular Visual Basic 6. WinForms provided the same graphical editor that allowed developers to drag and drop a user interface onto a canvas, specifying anchor points to specify resizing behavior.

WinForms is a managed wrapper around Win32, enabling .NET as an option to create Windows applications.

Within Win32 is an API set responsible for drawing 2D vector graphics and formatted text on the screen; this API is called GDI+ (or simply GDI on Windows versions older than Windows XP). GDI+ stands for Graphics Device Interface. It is an abstraction layer between applications and the graphics hardware. WinForms relies heavily on GDI+ to perform its rendering. As .NET developers, we usually don't come into direct contact with GDI+; instead, we use the abstractions provided by WinForms and let the framework handle all the low-level drawing code. Before .NET 6, WinForms was strictly using GDI+ for drawing on the screen, which made development easier as it creates an abstraction of the graphical device; while this made development easier, it also slowed down performance because of the abstraction overhead. To solve this, the WinForms team opted to use the classic GDI in specific cases, for example, when rendering brushes.

Let's explore WinForms. From Visual Studio 2022, start a new project and select WinForms as project template. Give it a good name and let the project generate. Building a user interface in WinForms is usually done through the designer surface in Visual Studio; the designer generates C# code that is used to actually draw all elements on screen. We can write the C# directly should we need to, but the designer greatly simplifies creating complex screens. To open the designer, double-click Form1.cs in the solution explorer.

Figure 4-1. *The WinForms designer*

Figure 4-2 shows the basic layout of a new WinForms project in .NET 6.

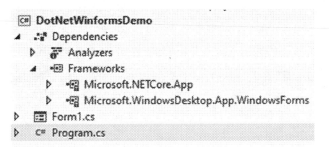

Figure 4-2. *A new .NET 6 WinForms project*

In the Frameworks section, you'll notice an entry for .NET, *Microsoft.NETCore.App*, and another reference called *Microsoft.WindowsDesktop.App.WindowsForms*. This is the desktop pack needed to be able to run and develop Windows native desktop applications with .NET 6. More information on extensibility packs can be found in Chapter 2 of this book. Program.cs contains the entry point of our application. Listing 4-2 shows the default Program class.

Listing 4-2. Default Program class

```
internal static class Program
{
    /// <summary>
    ///  The main entry point for the application.
    /// </summary>
    [STAThread]
    static void Main()
    {
        ApplicationConfiguration.Initialize();
        Application.Run(new Form1());
    }
}
```

Program is a static class; just like any other .NET 6 project, it is the starting point of our application.

STAThread

First thing to note here is the STAThread attribute. STA stands for single-threaded apartment; to understand what this does, we need to make a sidestep into the world of the apartment model process, but before we get into that we need to make sure we've got the meaning of a few concepts right.

> *Process*: A set of resources, code, data, and virtual memory

> *Thread*: Code that is executed within a process in a linear way

An application typically has one process that can contain one or more threads. Creating multiple threads within a process allows our application to execute code in parallel; do keep in mind that running code in parallel does not automatically guarantee an increase in performance. Multithreading can be hard to get right and comes with its own set of challenges like thread safety, preventing deadlocks and race conditions.

Component Object Model, or COM, enables application to open up their functionality to other applications in an API-like manner, by generating wrappers that can be called in other application. Windows exposes COM wrappers, for example, for the file and folder dialogs or message boxes.

WinForms relies on the COM wrappers exposed by Windows, and COM runs in a process with a single thread (the UI thread); however, new threads can be created from that point on. This is needed, for example, when you need to execute a long-running operation and you want to prevent the UI from freezing.

The final concept we need to know is the *apartment*. An apartment is a group of COM objects in a process. Every COM object lives in exactly one apartment, meaning that the methods on a COM object can only be called from a thread that belongs to the same apartment; should any other thread need to call into that COM object, it needs to pass through a proxy.

The WinForms process contains a single thread for rendering the UI; to render the UI, it needs to call into COM wrappers, which means that the COM wrappers and the single thread in our application's process need to belong to the same apartment. Since apartments come in two flavors, single-threaded and multithreaded, and we only have one thread, we need a single-threaded apartment. However, we are building a C# application; C# applications ever since .NET Framework 2.0 by default use a multithreaded apartment. That's why the *STAThread* attribute is set on the *Program* class, to indicate that this application needs a single-threaded apartment.

WinForms Startup

To keep the Program class clean and tidy, some configuration is abstracted away since .NET 6. The `Initialize` method that you can see in Program.cs, or Listing 4-2, that is called on `ApplicationConfiguration` calls three configuration methods, shown in Listing 4-3.

Listing 4-3. The configuration calls in Initialize

```
Application.SetHighDpiMode(HighDpiMode.SystemAware);
Application.EnableVisualStyles();
Application.SetCompatibleTextRenderingDefault(false);
```

DPI Mode

After the *STAThread* attribute, we see some default configuration being set, starting with high DPI mode. DPI, or dots per inch, specifies how many pixels a screen can render on a one inch line; nowadays, the term DPI is often used together with PPI, pixels per inch. Strictly speaking, DPI is a term used for printers and PPI for screens, but DPI seems to be the term most often used in both contexts. So in short, the higher the DPI of a monitor, the more pixels can be placed upon the screen. So why does this matter? Let's compare two surfaces with different DPI values and draw a rectangle of 8 by 2 pixels on them.

Figure 4-3. *Comparing different DPI*

Figure 4-3 shows the same rectangle but drawn on surfaces of the same physical size, but with different DPI values; notice that the higher the DPI of a surface is, the smaller the objects drawn on that surface seem to appear. Operating systems, including mobile operating systems, solve this problem by implementing logical pixels per inch. It's sort of a virtual screen that is laid over the actual screen; this technique exists to ensure that applications look the same across different screens; aspect ratios are a different problem of course; but that's beside the point here.

So what was the problem with WinForms applications? Windows tried to make sure that an application looked the same size on every monitor; in a multi-monitor setup that combines high DPI monitors with normal DPI monitors, this means that applications will be "zoomed in" if you will, instead of being scaled natively. This results in a blurry, pixelated image. We can simulate this in Windows by changing the scale factor in the display settings, shown in Figure 4-4.

73

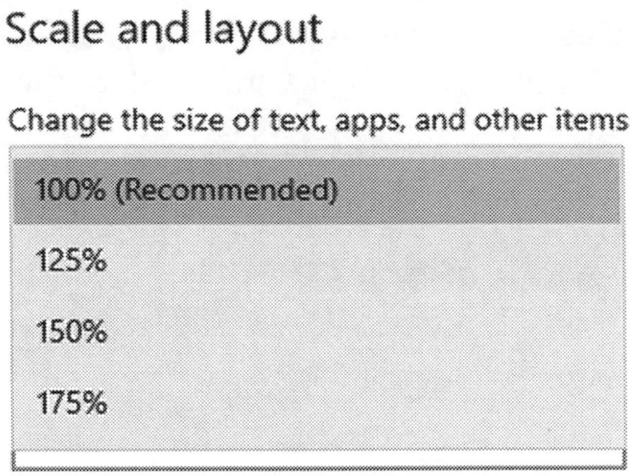

Scale and layout
Change the size of text, apps, and other items
100% (Recommended)
125%
150%
175%

Figure 4-4. *Display scale settings in Windows*

Figures 4-5 and 4-6 show the difference in application sharpness when high DPI support is switched off in a WinForms application. The screenshots were taken on 175% size.

Form1
Show Messagebox
Is this text sharp?
OK

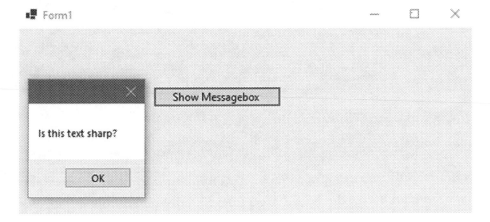

Figure 4-5. *A sharp looking application*

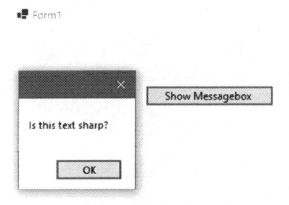

Figure 4-6. *The same application at a different scale factor*

Notice that Figure 4-6 shows a very blurry experience, not what you want to see on an expensive, fancy 4k ultrawide monitor is it? To fix this, Microsoft updated the GDI API with multiple modes for high DPI. The work on high DPI mode started in .NET Core 3 and kept improving with each release.

- DPI Unaware – this is the "old" behavior; applications assume 100% scaling at 96 DPI; this will result in the blurry applications that are demonstrated in Figure 4-6.

- System DPI Aware – apps will scale according to the DPI of the main monitor at the time of login into Windows. This can still result in blurry applications on the other monitors, but the application will look great on the main monitor.

- Per Monitor DPI Aware – this enables applications to update their rendering according to the DPI of the monitor they are currently on. These applications can update immediately when moved to a monitor with a different DPI; this does require developers to test their UI at different DPI settings.

- Mixed Mode DPI Aware – in mixed mode, we can set one of the above three modes on every top-level window, meaning that we can have different application windows behave differently on different monitors.

DPI mode in a WinForms application can be set in the app.config file, through an API call or via a static method that needs to be called at startup. The default template in .NET 6 includes setting the DPI mode to System Aware through the static method, which is now the recommended way of setting the DPI mode. Depending on what version of Windows your application is running on, you can have three or four modes.

- Unaware

- Unaware GDI Scaled

- System Aware

- Per Monitor

- Per Monitor v2

Most of these match perfectly on the list of modes supported in the GDI+ API, but what about Per Monitor v2? This is a mode that only works on Windows 10 version 1607 and later. Per Monitor v2 extends the Per Monitor option into the non-client areas, meaning that title bars and scroll bars, for example, will keep DPI scaling in mind as well. It also extends scaling events to child windows while Per Monitor limits this for parent windows only.

Responding to Scale Events

WinForms provides some events, helper methods, and properties to allow us to react to DPI changes and update the UI where needed.

- DpiChanged – an event that fires when the DPI is changed for the monitor the form is currently on.

- DpiChangedAfterParent – an event that fires when the parent control or form changed DPI from code after receiving a DpiChanged event.

- DpiChangedBeforeParent – an event that fires when the parent control or form changed DPI from code before receiving a DpiChanged event.

- LogicalToDeviceUnits – a helper method that converts a logical size to device units, keeping the current DPI in mind, and returns a `System.Drawing.Size` object.

- ScaleBitmapLogicalToDevice – a helper method that scales a `System.Drawing.Bitmap` to device units after a DPI change.

- DeviceDpi – a property that gets the current DPI value for the monitor the form is currently displayed on. This property comes in as a parameter on a DpiChanged event.

Listing 4-4 shows an example of a form that uses some of these events and properties to show a form that displays DPI information. If you still have the designer window open from the first part of this chapter, you can press F7 to switch to the code behind. From there we can add an eventhandler to the `DpiChanged` event, shown here in the constructor. From that eventhandler, we update the text on a label that we dropped on the form using the designer.

Listing 4-4. Reacting to DPI changes

```
public partial class DpiForm : Form
{
    public DpiForm()
    {
        InitializeComponent();
        DpiLabel.Text = $"Current DPI: {DeviceDpi}";

        DpiChanged += OnDpiChanged;
    }

    private void OnDpiChanged(object sender, DpiChangedEventArgs e)
    {
        DpiLabel.Text = $"DPI changed from {e.DeviceDpiOld} to
        {e.DeviceDpiNew}";
    }
}
```

Figure 4-7 shows the result of the form when it starts up.

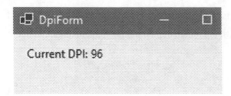

Figure 4-7. *Form displaying the current DPI*

If we set High DPI mode to DpiUnaware and change the scaling of the monitor, you'll notice that the form seems to zoom in; it will get blurry but the text in the label will remain the same. This means that the system still calculates the size according to 96 DPI, instead of the new value. Figure 4-8 shows this result.

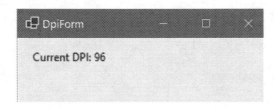

Figure 4-8. *Result when scaling set to 175%*

After setting High DPI mode to PerMonitorV2, we expect the DPI to change when we adjust scaling, and it does exactly that, but we get a new problem as shown in Figure 4-9.

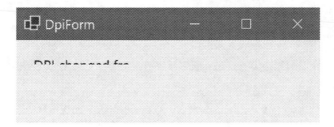

Figure 4-9. *Result after changing scaling*

You'll notice that the text we do see is rendered sharp; however, the label didn't resize, so our text is being cut off. This is because the WinForms designer, by default, sets autoscale mode to Font. However, our font size is not changing; our scale factor is. We can solve this by changing the autoscale mode as shown in Listing 4-5; Figure 4-10 shows the result.

Listing 4-5. Setting autoscale mode to DPI instead of font

```
public DpiForm()
{
    InitializeComponent();
    DpiLabel.Text = $"Current DPI: {DeviceDpi}";
    AutoScaleMode = AutoScaleMode.Dpi;
    DpiChanged += OnDpiChanged;
}

private void OnDpiChanged(object sender, DpiChangedEventArgs e)
{
    DpiLabel.Text = $"DPI changed from {e.DeviceDpiOld} to
    {e.DeviceDpiNew}";
}
```

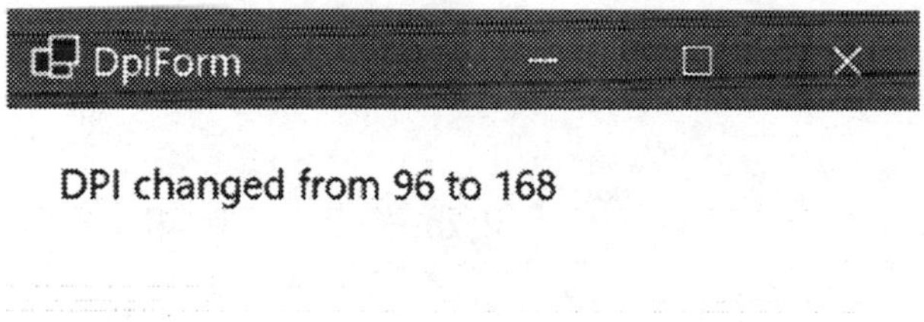

Figure 4-10. *Result after changing autoscale mode*

Visual Styles

Let's continue with the startup calls; the next step is `Application.EnableVisualStyles`.

EnableVisualStyles simply prepares all the colors, fonts, and other visual elements in the theme of the current operating system. Let's take a form with a label, datepicker, and a button as shown in Figure 4-11.

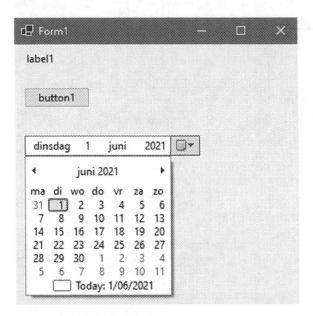

Figure 4-11. *Form with default controls*

The elements on this form automatically take the styling of Windows 10, the operating system the application was running on when taking this screenshot. We can disable loading the visual styles by replacing the call to Initialize with Listing 4-3 and commenting out `Application.EnableVisualStyles` method we get the result from Figure 4-12.

Figure 4-12. *Same application without Windows 10 theme*

The application still runs, but visually it looks very old; that is because all the controls fallback to their default look and feel. `Application.EnableVisualStyles` will keep the user's preference in mind; if it runs on a Windows system with visual styles disabled, it will respect this setting and load the application without visual styles.

Text Rendering

The next call in our WinForms application's startup cycle is `Application.SetCompatibl eTextRenderingDefault(false)`.

Before I can explain what `SetCompatibleTextRenderingDefault` does, we'll need to take a small history lesson. Back in .NET Framework version older than .NET 2.0, text was rendered using GDI+ and its Graphics class. From .NET Framework 2.0 onward, this was switched to GDI and the TextRenderer class. TextRenderer fixed a number of problems with performance and localization. Because WinForms prides itself on backward compatibility, we had two different ways text on WinForms controls could be rendered, and they were visually different. To fix this, the

SetCompatibleTextRenderingDefault method was introduced, and when the bool value is set to true, all text will be rendered using the old Graphics class in the GDI+ library. The default WinForms template passes false as parameter so that text in our applications is rendered using TextRenderer in GDI instead of Graphic in GDI+. The only time this parameter needs to be true is when you're migrating an old .NET Framework 1.0 or 1.1 app to a newer version, and even then it might be worth seeing how many controls and logic need to be changed to just make the app run on GDI.

The Message Loop

The final call before our application appears on screen is Application.Run(new Form1()).

The Run method starts what's called the message loop. A Windows desktop application needs a loop where it handles user events. The application exits once the loop exits, and this can be done programmatically by calling Exit() to terminate the application or ExitThread() to terminate the current thread, which will exit the application only if no other foreground threads are running. Applications can be exited manually by the user clicking the close button, pressing ALT-F4 or any other way to close an application on Windows. The Run method takes in a form as parameter; this form will be the startup form of the application. The message loop will end once this form is closed, effectively exiting the application.

The Form Designer

Building a form is usually done through the form designer. The designer is a visual canvas where controls can be dropped from the toolbox and laid out. Doing this visually makes for a powerful and fast developer loop. Figure 4-13 shows dropping a button from the toolbox onto the designer surface.

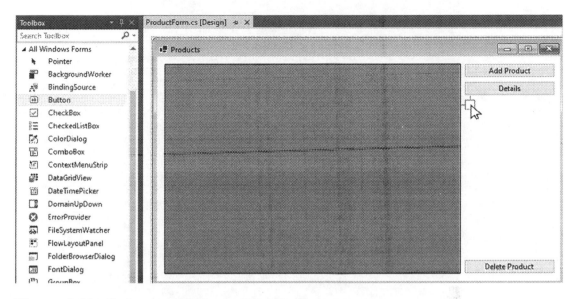

Figure 4-13. *Dropping a button onto the designer*

Feel free to double-click a form to open the designer and play around with the toolbox. Drop some components, move some controls around, and have a look at the properties. You'll notice that the designer tries to help you by snapping the controls to align with the margins of the other controls to make for a consistent layout. Once a control is placed, we can use the properties window (F4 is the shortcut key to open the properties for the selected control) to set different properties and hook up event handlers. For example, click on the dropdown for BackColor and try some different values. You will notice that the designer reacts immediately to your changes.

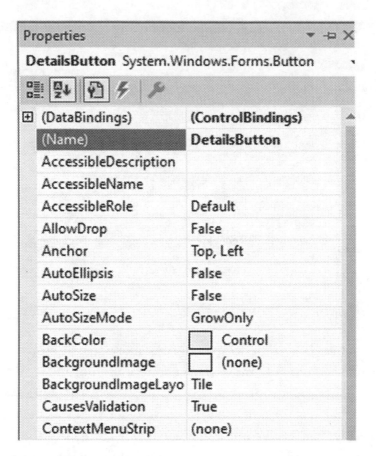

Figure 4-14. *Properties window*

Responding to Events

There are a few different ways to make a button react to a click. The fastest way is to double click on the button in the designer; this will generate a click event handler in the code behind of the form. Double-clicking any control will hook up an event handler to the default event for that control; click event for buttons, textchanged for textboxes, selectionchanged for combobox, and so on. Should we want to hook up another event, we can do this through the events pane in the properties window, found behind the lightning icon that can be seen in Figure 4-14. Look for the event you need and double-click the space beside it, as shown in Figure 4-15.

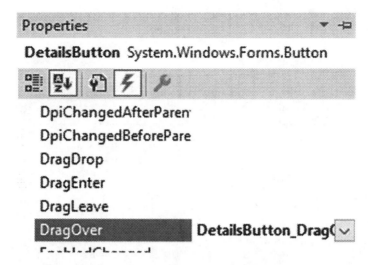

Figure 4-15. *Hooking up an event through the properties window*

Another way is to do programmatically as shown in Listing 4-6.

Listing 4-6. Programmatically reacting to a button getting focus

```
public ProductForm()
{
    InitializeComponent();
    DetailsButton.DragOver += DetailsButton_DragOver;
}

private void DetailsButton_DragOver(object sender, EventArgs e)
{

}
```

Once our design looks good in the designer, it's time to see what it actually looks like on screen. The first results are very good, until we resize the window.

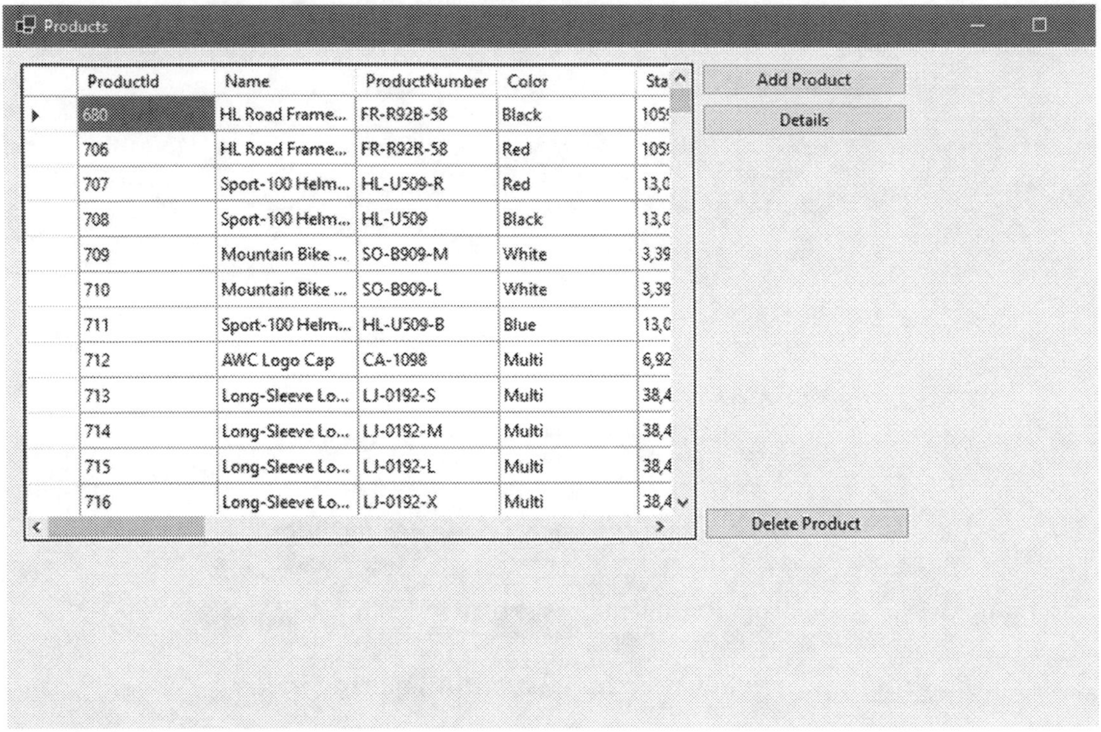

Figure 4-16. *Resized window*

Looks like our application is not very responsive yet. Making controls resized in WinForms is done through anchors; anchor is a property set on every control that determines what border is anchored to the side of the form.

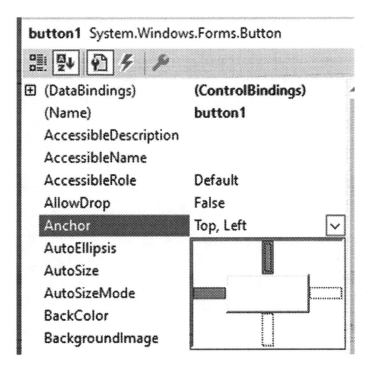

Figure 4-17. *Anchoring a button to the left and top*

After applying the correct anchor points, which is all anchor points in this case, we can make the form behave like Figure 4-18.

	ProductId	Name	ProductNumber	Color	StandardCost	ListPrice	Size	Weight	ProductCategory	ProductModel
►	680	HL Road Frame...	FR-R92B-58	Black	1059,3100	1431,5000	58	1016,04	18	6
	706	HL Road Frame...	FR-R92R-58	Red	1059,3100	1431,5000	58	1016,04	18	6
	707	Sport-100 Helm...	HL-U509-R	Red	13,0863	34,9900			35	33
	708	Sport-100 Helm...	HL-U509	Black	13,0863	34,9900			35	33
	709	Mountain Bike ...	SO-B909-M	White	3,3963	9,5000	M		27	18
	710	Mountain Bike ...	SO-B909-L	White	3,3963	9,5000	L		27	18
	711	Sport-100 Helm...	HL-U509-B	Blue	13,0863	34,9900			35	33
	712	AWC Logo Cap	CA-1098	Multi	6,9223	8,9900			23	2
	713	Long-Sleeve Lo...	LJ-0192-S	Multi	38,4923	49,9900	S		25	11
	714	Long-Sleeve Lo...	LJ-0192-M	Multi	38,4923	49,9900	M		25	11
	715	Long-Sleeve Lo...	LJ-0192-L	Multi	38,4923	49,9900	L		25	11
	716	Long-Sleeve Lo...	LJ-0192-X	Multi	38,4923	49,9900	XL		25	11
	717	HL Road Frame...	FR-R92R-62	Red	868,6342	1431,5000	62	1043,26	18	6
	718	HL Road Frame...	FR-R92R-44	Red	868,6342	1431,5000	44	961,61	18	6
	719	HL Road Frame...	FR-R92R-48	Red	868,6342	1431,5000	48	979,75	18	6
	720	HL Road Frame...	FR-R92R-52	Red	868,6342	1431,5000	52	997,90	18	6
	721	HL Road Frame...	FR-R92R-56	Red	868,6342	1431,5000	56	1016,04	18	6
	722	LL Road Frame ...	FR-R38B-58	Black	204,6251	337,2200	58	1115,83	18	9
	723	LL Road Frame ...	FR-R38B-60	Black	204,6251	337,2200	60	1124,90	18	9
	724	LL Road Frame ...	FR-R38B-62	Black	204,6251	337,2200	62	1133,98	18	9
	725	LL Road Frame ...	FR-R38R-44	Red	187,1571	337,2200	44	1052,33	18	9
	726	LL Road Frame ...	FR-R38R-48	Red	187,1571	337,2200	48	1070,47	18	9
	727	LL Road Frame ...	FR-R38R-52	Red	187,1571	337,2200	52	1088,62	18	9
	728	LL Road Frame ...	FR-R38R-58	Red	187,1571	337,2200	58	1115,83	18	9
	729	LL Road Frame ...	FR-R38R-60	Red	187,1571	337,2200	60	1124,90	18	9
	730	LL Road Frame ...	FR-R38R-62	Red	187,1571	337,2200	62	1133,98	18	9
	731	ML Road Frame...	FR-R72R-44	Red	352,1394	594,8300	44	1006,97	18	16
	732	ML Road Frame...	FR-R72R-48	Red	352,1394	594,8300	48	1025,11	18	16
	733	ML Road Frame...	FR-R72R-52	Red	352,1394	594,8300	52	1043,26	18	16

Figure 4-18. *Form that resizes using anchor points*

Figure 4-19 shows the used anchor points for every control.

ProductId	Name	ProductNumber	Color	StandardCost	ListPrice	Size	Weight	ProductCategory	ProductModelI...
680	HL Road Frame ...	FR-R92B-58	Black	1059.3100	1431.5000	58	1016.04	18	6
706	HL Road Frame...	FR-R92R-58	Red	1059.3100	1431.5000	58	1016.04	18	6
707	Sport-100 Helm...	HL-U509-R	Red	13.0863	34.9900			35	33
708	Sport-100 Helm...	HL-U509	Black	13.0863	34.9900			35	33
709	Mountain Bike ...	SO-B909-M	White	2.3963	9.5000	M		27	18
710	Mountain Bike ...	SO-B909-L	White	2.3963	9.5000	L		27	18
711	Sport-100 Helm...	HL-U509-B	Blue	13.0863	34.9900			35	33
712	AWC Logo Cap	CA-1098	Multi	6.9223	8.9900			23	2
713	Long-Sleeve Lo...	LJ-0192-S	Multi	38.4923	49.9900	S		25	11
714	Long-Sleeve Lo...	LJ-0192-M	Multi	38.4923	49.9900	M		25	11
715	Long-Sleeve Lo...	LJ-0192-L	Multi	38.4923	49.9900	L		25	11
716	Long-Sleeve Lo...	LJ-0192-X	Multi	38.4923	49.9900	XL		25	11
717	HL Road Frame...	FR-R92R-62	Red	868.6342	1431.5000	62	1043.26	18	6
718	HL Road Frame..	FR-R92R-44	Red	868.6342	1431.5000	44	961.61	18	6
719	HL Road Frame..	FR-R92R-48	Red	868.6342	1431.5000	48	979.75	18	6
720	HL Road Frame..	FR-R92R-52	Red	868.6342	1431.5000	52	997.90	18	6
721	HL Road Frame..	FR-R92R-56	Red	868.6342	1431.5000	56	1016.04	18	6
722	LL Road Frame ...	FR-R38B-58	Black	204.6251	337.2200	58	1115.83	18	9
723	LL Road Frame ...	FR-R38B-60	Black	204.6251	337.2200	60	1124.90	18	9
724	LL Road Frame ...	FR-R38B-62	Black	204.6251	337.2200	62	1133.98	18	9
725	LL Road Frame ...	FR-R38R-44	Red	187.1571	337.2200	44	1052.33	18	9
726	LL Road Frame ...	FR-R38R-48	Red	187.1571	337.2200	48	1070.47	18	9
727	LL Road Frame ...	FR-R38R-52	Red	187.1571	337.2200	52	1088.62	18	9
728	LL Road Frame ...	FR-R38R-58	Red	187.1571	337.2200	58	1115.83	18	9
729	LL Road Frame ...	FR-R38R-60	Red	187.1571	337.2200	60	1124.90	18	9
730	LL Road Frame ...	FR-R38R-62	Red	187.1571	337.2200	62	1133.98	18	9
731	ML Road Frame...	FR-R72R-44	Red	352.1394	594.8300	44	1006.97	18	16
732	ML Road Frame...	FR-R72R-46	Red	352.1394	594.8300	48	1025.11	18	16
733	ML Road Frame...	FR-R72R-52	Red	352.1394	594.8300	52	1043.26	18	16

Buttons: Add Product, Details, Delete Product

Figure 4-19. *Anchor points on the form*

The grid that is on the form in Figures 4-18 and 4-19 is the DataGridView. The classic DataGrid control has not been ported from .NET Framework; DataGridView is based on DataGrid and extends it, for example, in the data sources it accepts. Listing 4-7 shows a simple example of setting data to the DataGridView named ProductsDataGrid.

Listing 4-7. Setting data to a DataGridView

```
private async void ProductForm_Load(object sender, EventArgs e)
{
    var ctx = new AdventureWorksContext();
    var products = await ctx.Products.ToListAsync();
    ProductsDataGrid.DataSource = products;
}
```

We're using an Entity Framework datacontext to easily get to our data. Once data is loaded, we assign it to the DataGridView's DataSource property, and that is all that's needed to show the data in the grid.

Let's add the possibility to add new products to the dataset; Listing 4-8 shows a first attempt at this.

Listing 4-8. Add new products to the dataset

```
public partial class ProductForm : Form
{
    private List<Product> _products;

    public ProductForm()
    {
        InitializeComponent();
    }

    private async void ProductForm_Load(object sender, EventArgs e)
    {
        AdventureWorksContext ctx = new ();
        _products = await ctx.Products.ToListAsync();
        ProductsDataGrid.DataSource = _products;
    }

    private void AddProductButton_Click(object sender, EventArgs e)
    {
        _products.Add(new Product());
    }
}
```

The click event handler is triggered when the *Add Product* button is clicked; nothing seems to happen however. Should you set a breakpoint in the event handler, you'll notice that the event is triggered and new products are added to the list but that change is not reflected in the UI. That is because in WinForms the UI is not reactive; it does not monitor every property to see if it might need to update; instead, it waits for an event that tells it what property has changed. Listing 4-9 shows a working example.

Listing 4-9. Working databinding

```
public partial class ProductForm : Form
{
    private BindingList<Product> _products;

    public ProductForm()
    {
        InitializeComponent();
    }

    private async void ProductForm_Load(object sender, EventArgs e)
    {
        AdventureWorksContext ctx = new();

        List<Product> products = await ctx.Products.ToListAsync();
        _products = new BindingList<Product>(products);
        ProductsDataGrid.DataSource = _products;
    }

    private void AddProductButton_Click(object sender, EventArgs e)
    {
        _products.Add(new Product());
    }
}
```

Only one thing changed; the List<Product> has changed into a
BindingList<Product>; a BindingList triggers an event whenever the data in the list
changes, allowing our UI to respond to that change.

WPF

Windows Presentation Foundation, WPF for short, is the spiritual successor of
WinForms. It was known under the codename "Avalon" and was announced in .NET
Framework 3.0 timeframe. WPF relies on DirectX for its rendering, compared to
WinForm's GDI. The biggest difference between WinForms and WPF is the UI, while
there still is a graphical designer, it no longer generates C# code to build its UI but
instead generates eXtended Application Markup Language, or XAML.

WPF was ported from the classic .NET Framework to .NET Core 3.0. After the initial port, a new visual designer was created and has evolved with every release of .NET.

After creating a new WPF project with .NET 6, we end with the solution as shown in Figure 4-20.

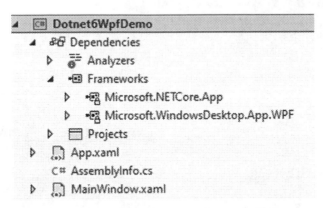

Figure 4-20. *A blank WPF project*

That is a very lightweight project structure; it contains only three files! And we can even remove AssemblyInfo should we want to. AssemblyInfo contains theming information for our WPF application. It sets the ThemeInfo assembly attribute; this attribute specifies if there is an assembly containing resource definitions for the controls used in your application. Resource definitions include templates, styles, and colors. The ThemeInfoattribute takes two parameters, a theme-specific dictionary location and a generic dictionary location. Resource dictionaries in XAML are comparable to CSS files in web development; they contain style definitions, converters, and so on. The ThemeInfo resource dictionary locations can be set to one of three values.

- ExternalAssembly

- None

- SourceAssembly

External assemblies live outside of your code base. WPF will search for assemblies according to a naming convention. For example, take an application called *DotnetSixWpf.* If we want to place theming in a separate assembly, we can name that assembly, or assemblies, *DotnetSixWpf.Dark.dll* or *DotnetSixWpf.Light.dll,* for example, to define dark and light themes. The names of your themes are whatever you want them to be, but the naming of the assembly needs to be *<assembly>.<themename>*.

SourceAssembly refers to resource dictionaries that are included within your application. In our project, we need to have a *themes* folder where WPF will look for our style definitions.

WPF Startup

Moving on to App.xaml, this file is the starting point of our application. You'll notice that it consists of two files, App.xaml and App.xaml.cs. The xaml file and the code behind code file are both the same partial class. When compiling, the XAML code gets transformed into C# code; this is very important to know because if you change the namespace or class name in the code behind, you'll also need to change it on the XAML side of things.

Listing 4-10. Default App.xaml in WPF

```
<Application x:Class="Dotnet6WpfDemo.App"
             xmlns="http://schemas.microsoft.com/winfx/2006/xaml/
             presentation"
             xmlns:x="http://schemas.microsoft.com/winfx/2006/xaml"
             xmlns:local="clr-namespace:Dotnet6WpfDemo"
             StartupUri="MainWindow.xaml">
    <Application.Resources>

    </Application.Resources>
</Application>
```

Listing 4-10 shows the XAML part of App.xaml. The important part here is the StartupUri; this property sets the first window to show when launching the application. You'll notice that the code behind of App.xaml is quite empty. That is because the bootstrapping and launching of the WPF application is done in the generated App class that combines both the XAML and the code parts. You can inspect this file by going to your project in Windows Explorer and take a look in the obj folder.

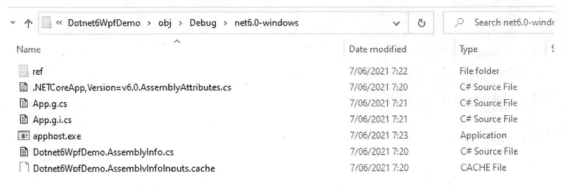

Figure 4-21. *Generated files on disk*

Every file in this folder that has `.g.` in its filename has been generated by the compiler. Listing 4-11 shows the generated App.g.cs file, the actual starting point of the application.

Listing 4-11. Generated application startup code

```
public partial class App : System.Windows.Application {

    /// <summary>
    /// InitializeComponent
    /// </summary>
    [System.Diagnostics.DebuggerNonUserCodeAttribute()]
    [System.CodeDom.Compiler.GeneratedCodeAttribute("PresentationBuild
    Tasks", "6.0.0.0")]
    public void InitializeComponent() {

        #line 5 "..\..\..\App.xaml"
        this.StartupUri = new System.Uri("MainWindow.xaml", System.
        UriKind.Relative);

        #line default
        #line hidden
    }
```

```
/// <summary>
/// Application Entry Point.
/// </summary>
[System.STAThreadAttribute()]
[System.Diagnostics.DebuggerNonUserCodeAttribute()]
[System.CodeDom.Compiler.GeneratedCodeAttribute("PresentationBuild
Tasks", "6.0.0.0")]
public static void Main() {
        Dotnet6WpfDemo.App app = new Dotnet6WpfDemo.App();
        app.InitializeComponent();
        app.Run();
    }
}
```

Even in the generated startup code, there is not a lot going on; you will notice the StartupUri property being set to the value that was defined in App.xaml. Next to that there is the Main method that every application in .NET 6 has as a starting point. Main initializes our App class and calls its Run method; that method is part of WPF's Application base class. It contains the logic for creating the window wrapper and creates the first window to be shown. The application base class also contains some virtual methods that can be overridden for configuring lifecycle events; some examples of these methods are OnActivated, OnDeactivated, OnLoadCompleted, OnExit, OnStartup, OnSessionEnding, and OnNavigated.

XAML Layout

Moving on to MainWindow. MainWindow also consists of two files, just like the App class. Building your UI in a WPF application can be done quite similar to WinForms; WPF also has a graphical designer, for example. Visual Studio by default shows the XAML editor when opening a XAML file. We can switch to the designer by pressing *shift-F7* or selecting *Design* on the bottom left of Visual Studio.

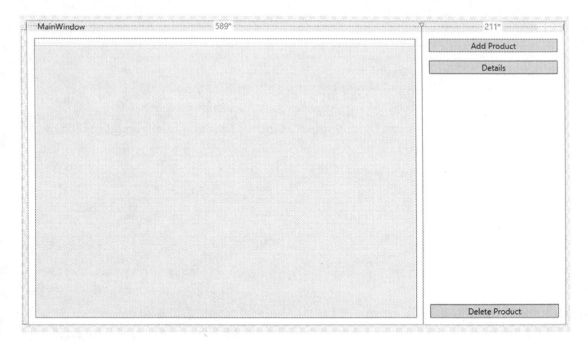

Figure 4-22. *WPF graphical designer*

As you can see in Figure 4-22, it allows us to drag and drop controls from the toolbox and position them in a very graphical way, just like with WinForms. Figure 4-23 shows the running application; don't worry about the logic to get data in the datagrid; we're only looking at the design in this example.

ProductId	Name	ProductNumber	Color	StandardCost	ListPrice	Size
680	HL Road Frame - Black, 58	FR-R92B-58	Black	1059.3100	1431.5000	58
706	HL Road Frame - Red, 58	FR-R92R-58	Red	1059.3100	1431.5000	58
707	Sport-100 Helmet, Red	HL-U509-R	Red	13.0863	34.9900	
708	Sport-100 Helmet, Black	HL-U509	Black	13.0863	34.9900	
709	Mountain Bike Socks, M	SO-B909-M	White	3.3963	9.5000	M
710	Mountain Bike Socks, L	SO-B909-L	White	3.3963	9.5000	L
711	Sport-100 Helmet, Blue	HL-U509-8	Blue	13.0863	34.9900	
712	AWC Logo Cap	CA-1098	Multi	6.9223	8.9900	
713	Long-Sleeve Logo Jersey, S	LJ-0192-S	Multi	38.4923	49.9900	S
714	Long-Sleeve Logo Jersey, M	LJ-0192-M	Multi	38.4923	49.9900	M
715	Long-Sleeve Logo Jersey, L	LJ-0192-L	Multi	38.4923	49.9900	L
716	Long-Sleeve Logo Jersey, XL	LJ-0192-X	Multi	38.4923	49.9900	XL
717	HL Road Frame - Red, 62	FR-R92R-62	Red	868.6342	1431.5000	62
718	HL Road Frame - Red, 44	FR-R92R-44	Red	868.6342	1431.5000	44
719	HL Road Frame - Red, 48	FR-R92R-48	Red	868.6342	1431.5000	48
720	HL Road Frame - Red, 52	FR-R92R-52	Red	868.6342	1431.5000	52
721	HL Road Frame - Red, 56	FR-R92R-56	Red	868.6342	1431.5000	56
722	LL Road Frame - Black, 58	FR-R38B-58	Black	204.6251	337.2200	58
723	LL Road Frame - Black, 60	FR-R38B-60	Black	204.6251	337.2200	60
724	LL Road Frame - Black, 62	FR-R38R-62	Black	204.6251	337.2200	62

Figure 4-23. *The application*

It really does look very similar to the WinForms version, so why does WPF even exist if it's just a copy of WinForms? Because it really is not a copy of WinForms. The designer was created to make it easier for WinForms developers to cross over to WPF, but if you blindly follow the way you are used to doing things, you will not get very performant generated code. That brings us to another big difference between WinForms and WPF, the WinForms designer generated C# or Visual Basic code, and the WPF designer generates XAML code. XAML is an XML-based language that allows us to define layouts in a nested way, similar to HTML. Listing 4-12 shows the XAML code that was generated by using the designer.

Listing 4-12. Generated XAML code

```
<Window
    x:Class="Dotnet6WpfDemo.MainWindow"
    xmlns="http://schemas.microsoft.com/winfx/2006/xaml/presentation"
    xmlns:x="http://schemas.microsoft.com/winfx/2006/xaml"
    xmlns:d="http://schemas.microsoft.com/expression/blend/2008"
    xmlns:mc="http://schemas.openxmlformats.org/markup-compatibility/2006"
```

```
Title="MainWindow"
Width="800"
Height="450"
mc:Ignorable="d">
<Grid>
    <Grid.ColumnDefinitions>
        <ColumnDefinition Width="589*" />
        <ColumnDefinition Width="211*" />
    </Grid.ColumnDefinitions>
    <DataGrid x:Name="ProductsDataGrid" Margin="10,10,10,10" />
    <Button
        Grid.Column="1"
        Width="191"
        Margin="0,10,0,0"
        HorizontalAlignment="Center"
        VerticalAlignment="Top"
        Content="Add Product" />
    <Button
        Grid.Column="1"
        Width="191"
        Margin="0,43,0,0"
        HorizontalAlignment="Center"
        VerticalAlignment="Top"
        Content="Details" />
    <Button
        Grid.Column="1"
        Width="191"
        Margin="0,404,0,0"
        HorizontalAlignment="Center"
        VerticalAlignment="Top"
        Content="Delete Product" />
    <Button
        Grid.Column="1"
        Width="0"
        Margin="350,228,0,0"
```

```
        HorizontalAlignment="Left"
        VerticalAlignment="Top"
        Content="Button" />

    </Grid>
</Window>
```

XAML works with layout containers; one of those is the grid. A grid can get divided into rows and columns; elements in a grid get placed in a certain row and a certain column. The height of the rows and the width of the columns can be set in three ways. We can hardcode it in pixels, for example, `<ColumnDefinition Width="150" />` creates a column that is 150 pixels wide. We can make the column size itself automatically by using `<ColumnDefinition Width="Auto" />`. Or we can use star notation to make a column by either taking up all available space or dividing all available space over a set of columns relatively as shown in Listing 4-13.

Listing 4-13. Relative sizing of columns

```
<Grid.ColumnDefinitions>
    <ColumnDefinition Width="1*" />
    <ColumnDefinition Width="2*" />
</Grid.ColumnDefinitions>
```

In Listing 4-13, we see two columns defined using star notation. In total we get 3, meaning that the available space will be divided into three equal parts. The first column will get one part, hence 1*. The second column will get two parts, hence 2*.

If we go back to Listing 4-12, we will see that the columns of that grid are defined as **589*** and **211***. That is because of the designer; I have created those columns by clicking in the designer. What happens is that the grid is divided up into 800 columns, 589 for the first column and 211 for the second column. This can be greatly simplified by changing the column definitions to Listing 4-14. Keep in mind that this will change the width ratio between the different columns. Always verify the result when changing values in XAML.

Listing 4-14. Simplified columndefinitions

```
<Grid.ColumnDefinitions>
    <ColumnDefinition Width="3*" />
    <ColumnDefinition Width="1*" />
</Grid.ColumnDefinitions>
```

This can also be done from the designer; if you select the grid, its sizings become visible and can be adjusted as shown in Figure 4-24.

Figure 4-24. *Changing grid layout from the designer*

The next optimalization is easily spotted if we try to resize the form; notice what happens to the delete button.

ProductId	Name	ProductNumber	Color	StandardCost	ListPrice	Size	We
680	HL Road Frame - Black, 58	FR-R92B-58	Black	1059.3100	1431.5000	58	10'
706	HL Road Frame - Red, 58	FR-R92R-58	Red	1059.3100	1431.5000	58	10'
707	Sport-100 Helmet, Red	HL-U509-R	Red	13.0863	34.9900		
708	Sport-100 Helmet, Black	HL-U509	Black	13.0863	34.9900		
709	Mountain Bike Socks, M	SO-B909-M	White	3.3963	9.5000	M	
710	Mountain Bike Socks, L	SO-B909-L	White	3.3963	9.5000	L	
711	Sport-100 Helmet, Blue	HL-U509-B	Blue	13.0863	34.9900		
712	AWC Logo Cap	CA-1098	Multi	6.9223	8.9900		
713	Long-Sleeve Logo Jersey, S	LJ-0192-S	Multi	38.4923	49.9900	S	
714	Long-Sleeve Logo Jersey, M	LJ-0192-M	Multi	38.4923	49.9900	M	
715	Long-Sleeve Logo Jersey, L	LJ-0192-L	Multi	38.4923	49.9900	L	
716	Long-Sleeve Logo Jersey, XL	LJ-0192-X	Multi	38.4923	49.9900	XL	
717	HL Road Frame - Red, 62	FR-R92R-62	Red	868.6342	1431.5000	62	10.
718	HL Road Frame - Red, 44	FR-R92R-44	Red	868.6342	1431.5000	44	96'
719	HL Road Frame - Red, 48	FR-R92R-48	Red	868.6342	1431.5000	48	97!
720	HL Road Frame - Red, 52	FR-R92R-52	Red	868.6342	1431.5000	52	99'
721	HL Road Frame - Red, 56	FR-R92R-56	Red	868.6342	1431.5000	56	10'
722	LL Road Frame - Black, 58	FR-R38B-58	Black	204.6251	337.2200	58	11'
723	LL Road Frame - Black, 60	FR-R38B-60	Black	204.6251	337.2200	60	11'

Add Product

Details

Figure 4-25. *Delete button is not responsive*

As you can see, the button does not respond nicely to resizing the form. Listing 4-15 shows the XAML for this specific button.

Listing 4-15. XAML for the delete button

```
<Button
    Grid.Column="1"
    Width="191"
    Margin="0,404,0,0"
```

```
HorizontalAlignment="Center"
VerticalAlignment="Top"
Content="Delete Product" />
```

The button is vertically aligned to the top, meaning that it will appear as close to the top of its parent as it is allowed. The margin property pushed the button down from the top. Margin takes four values, respectively, left, top, right, and bottom. Do take care not to mix this order up with the order in CSS, which is different! By setting the VerticalAligment to Bottom, we can force the button down; by using the bottom margin, we can push it back up a bit to align with the datagrid. Figure 4-26 shows the improved responsiveness.

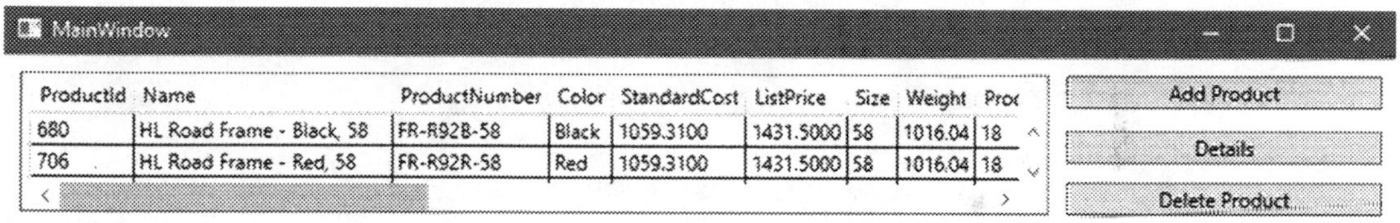

Figure 4-26. *Delete button stays in relative place after resizing*

Listing 4-16 shows the new XAML.

Listing 4-16. Improved XAML for the button

```
<Button
    Grid.Column="1"
    Margin="10"
    HorizontalAlignment="Stretch"
    VerticalAlignment="Bottom"
    Content="Delete Product" />
```

One last thing to improve is the XAML for the other two buttons; just like with the delete product button, their positioning is done with absolute values. What we could do is use a StackPanel within our Grid. A StackPanel is a container that will take all its children and stack them in a vertical or horizontal list, giving the exact outcome we need for the two top buttons. However, every time you think of nesting containers, think twice. WPF has a layouting cycle; the grid will start calculating the size of every row, every column. If we place a StackPanel in Row index 0, column index 1, it will start calculating the sizing of the grid; if it reaches the StackPanel, it will need to do a new layout cycle on the Grid because of the relative sizing of the panel, resulting in lower performance of the application. In other words, try to prevent nesting of layout containers as much as possible, even if it means more manual XAML work. The problem we're facing can be fixed easily by adding extra rows to our grid. Listing 4-17 shows the full XAML code for the grid.

Listing 4-17. Full responsive XAML

```
<Grid>
    <Grid.ColumnDefinitions>
        <ColumnDefinition Width="3*" />
        <ColumnDefinition />
    </Grid.ColumnDefinitions>
    <Grid.RowDefinitions>
        <RowDefinition Height="Auto" />
        <RowDefinition Height="Auto" />
        <RowDefinition Height="*" />
    </Grid.RowDefinitions>

    <DataGrid
        x:Name="ProductsDataGrid"
        Grid.Row="0"
        Grid.RowSpan="3"
        Grid.Column="0"
        Margin="10,10,0,10" />
    <Button
        Grid.Row="0"
        Grid.Column="1"
        Margin="10"
        HorizontalAlignment="Stretch"
        VerticalAlignment="Top"
        Content="Add Product" />
    <Button
        Grid.Row="1"
        Grid.Column="1"
        Margin="10"
```

```
        HorizontalAlignment="Stretch"
        VerticalAlignment="Top"
        Content="Details" />
    <Button
        Grid.Row="2"
        Grid.Column="1"
        Margin="10"
        HorizontalAlignment="Stretch"
        VerticalAlignment="Bottom"
        Content="Delete Product" />
</Grid>
```

Looking at the rowdefinitions, you will notice three rows. The top two have height set to Auto; the third one takes on all available space. This combined with the correct VerticalAlignments and some margins results in exactly the layout we want, including responsiveness. A small extra performance optimalization could be to give the top two rows an absolute value. Those rows exist solely to contain one button each; if there is absolutely no reason for the buttons to grow in height, we can set the row height to a fixed value so that the layout cycle doesn't need to calculate the height.

Visual Tree

The WPF designer includes some tools to speed up the process of developing a UI. Figure 4-27 shows the toolbar in the title bar of a WPF application running in debug.

Figure 4-27. *Visual Tree toolbar*

Much like the DOM in HTML, WPF builds a visual tree of elements that are created in a window. That visual tree can be inspected and even adjusted at runtime. Listing 4-18 shows a generic method that can be used to find ancestors of a certain type; these methods will traverse the visual tree in search for the specific type.

Listing 4-18. Finding a parent in the visual tree

```
public static T FindParentOfType<T>(this DependencyObject element) where T
: DependencyObject
{
    DependencyObject parentElement = element;
    do
    {
        parentElement = VisualTreeHelper.GetParent(parentElement);
        T parent = parentElement as T;

        if (parent != null)
          {
                return parent;
          }
    } while (parentElement != null);

    return null;
}
```

This example uses the VisualTreeHelper to traverse the visual tree in search for a specific type. Being able to inspect and traverse the visual tree from code gives us a great flexibility. No matter what control or part of the UI we are in, we can always find specific control instances. This allows us to create dynamic views where classic databinding, where you need to know everything up front, would not suffice.

Back to the toolbar, the *Select Element* on the toolbar allows us to select an element in the running application and inspect its runtime values, much like the developer tools in a browser. First select the *Select Element* button on the toolbar, select an element in the running application, and switch back to Visual Studio. In Visual Studio is a *Live Visual Tree* pane; it might be collapsed by default. If you can't find it, use the Search box in the title bar to search for *Live Visual Tree*. In the Live Visual Tree pane, we can see the actual current visual tree. Right-clicking an element and selecting Show Properties will open the Live Property Explorer pane showing the properties of the selected element. The properties that are not calculated by WPF can be changed here and will impact the running application. Do note that your changes here will not automatically reflect in your XAML code. These are great tools to find the exact values you need, or debugging a visual issue while running your application, but it is not a real-time editor.

Figure 4-28. *Inspecting the visual tree*

We can even use the toolbar to show us the layout adorners like margins and paddings of a selected element, as demonstrated in Figure 4-29. By toggling the layout adorners, we can inspect the margins and paddings of selected elements, again very similar to what you might be used to from browser developer tools.

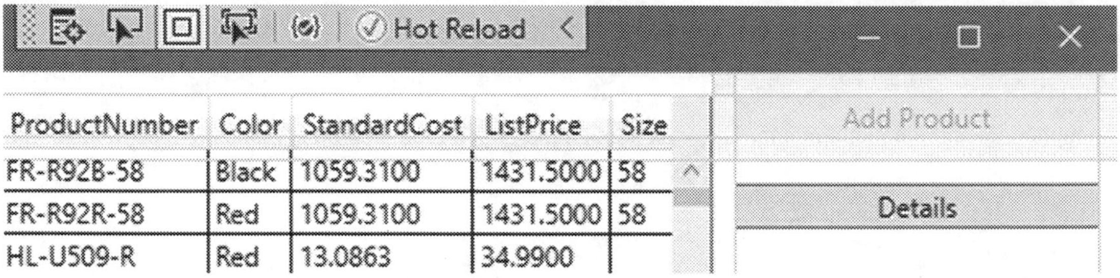

Figure 4-29. *Layout adorners for the selected button*

The Hot Reload check in the toolbar shows that we can edit our XAML and save it, and the changes will be reflected in the running application without restarting it. We will dive deeper into Hot Reload later in this chapter.

Data Binding

One of the greatest strengths of XAML is its binding framework. XAML bindings allow us to bind UI properties to C# properties so that the UI updates whenever the property changes, or vice versa. In the example, we've been using so far the items in the datagrid loaded in a WinForms style of working, as demonstrated in Listing 4-19.

Listing 4-19. Loading the datagrid

```
public partial class MainWindow : Window
{
    private List<Product> _products;

    public MainWindow()
    {
        InitializeComponent();
        Loaded += OnLoaded;
    }
```

```
    private async void OnLoaded(object sender, RoutedEventArgs e)
    {
        AdventureWorksContext ctx = new();

        _ products = await ctx.Products.ToListAsync();
        ProductsDataGrid.ItemsSource = _products;
    }

    private void AddProductButton_Click(object sender, EventArgs e)
    {
        _products.Add(new Product());
    }
}
```

While this does work, it does not use any binding. Converting this is as simple as turning the private field into a public property and remove setting the itemssource manually.

Listing 4-20. Ready for binding

```
public partial class MainWindow : Window
{
    public List<Product> Products { get; set; }

    public MainWindow()
    {
        InitializeComponent();
        DataContext = this;
        Loaded += OnLoaded;
    }

    private async void OnLoaded(object sender, RoutedEventArgs e)
    {
        AdventureWorksContext ctx = new();

        Products = await ctx.Products.ToListAsync();
    }
```

```
    private void AddProductButton_Click(object sender, EventArgs e)
    {
        Products.Add(new Product());
    }
}
```

A very important line that has snuck in here is DataContext = this. This line tells the binding framework in what instance it can resolve its bindings; in this case, we set it to the code behind of the window. Now we just need to set the binding statement in the datagrid.

Listing 4-21. Setting a binding in XAML

```
<DataGrid
    x:Name="ProductsDataGrid"
    Grid.Row="0"
    Grid.RowSpan="3"
    ItemsSource="{Binding Products}"
    Grid.Column="0"
    Margin="10,10,0,10" />
```

That should do it! However, when we run the application, you'll notice that the datagrid is still empty. Did we miss something? Are bindings broken in .NET 6? Do not worry; this is a result of the order in which things are happening and a result of the fact that we aren't notifying the UI of a change yet.

The binding framework is not constantly monitoring its bound properties for changes; this would really tear down any performance. Instead, it listens to property changed events coming from its datacontext. To fire these events, we need to implement the INotifyPropertyChanged interface. Listing 4-22 shows the changes to make it work.

Listing 4-22. Implementing INotifyPropertyChanged

```
public partial class MainWindow : Window, INotifyPropertyChanged
    {
        private List<Product> _products;

        //INotifyPropertyChanged member
        public event PropertyChangedEventHandler PropertyChanged;
```

```
public List<Product> Products
{
    get => _products;
    set
    {
        if (value == _products)
        {
            return;
        }

        _products = value;
        PropertyChanged?.Invoke(this, new PropertyChangedEventArgs
        (nameof(Products)));
    }
}
```
...

The INotifyPropertyChanged interface contains one member, the PropertyChanged event. We fire this in the set method of the Products property. By firing this event, we notify the datagrid that its data has changed and that it needs to refresh its UI. We dive deeper into XAML, binding, and the MVVM design pattern in Chapter 6 of this book. Chapter 6 handles MAUI, Microsoft's cross-platform framework.

Windows App SDK

As we have seen, there are different ways of building desktop applications for Windows. Each platform, being it WinForms or WPF, comes with its own specific way of interacting with the operating system. Back when .NET 6 was in its planning phase, a new project was announced by Microsoft under the name *Project Reunion*. Project Reunion promised to unify the way desktop applications were build and were interacting with the operating system. Eventually Project Reunion got renamed to the Windows App SDK.

The Windows App SDK is a set of components, tools, and a unified API that can be used to build applications for Windows 10 and Windows 11. The Windows App SDK does not replace any frameworks; it's more of an add-on, something that complements current frameworks to provide a more consistent way of working.

The Windows App SDK consists of several features.

Table 4-1. *Windows App SDK features*

Feature	Description
WinUI 3	The UI components for building Windows applications
DWriteCore	Cleartype text rendering using a device-independent text layout system
MRT core	Manage translations and images in multiple languages and scales
App instancing	Control over applications being able to run multiple instances of themselves
Rich activation	Launch your app through a URI or from another app
Power management	Inspect how your app affects the device's power usage
App windows management	Create and manage app windows
Push notifications	Send rich push notifications from Azure to your app
Deployment	Deploy the Windows App SDK runtime with your app

The easiest way to get started with the Windows App SDK is by downloading and installing the Visual Studio 2022 extension from `https://aka.ms/windowsappsdk/stable-vsix-2022-cs`. This extension will install the WinUI project templates in Visual Studio.

Besides the extension, we also need the *Universal Windows Platform*, *.NET Desktop,* and *Desktop Development with C++* workloads installed from the Visual Studio Installer.

Building a Windows App SDK application

From Visual Studio, we create a new solution. In the project type selection window, we can filter on WinUI. The WinUI 3 templates contain the references to the Windows App SDK. The SDK is fully wired up and ready to go.

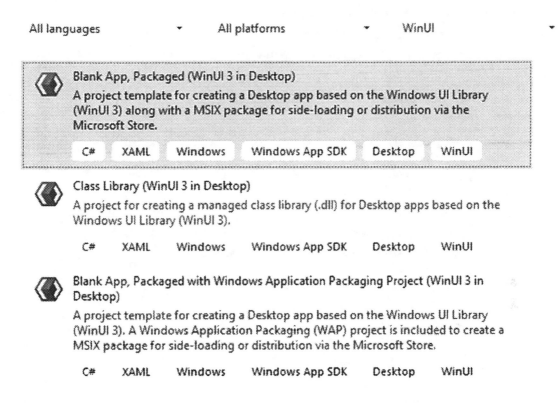

Figure 4-30. *WinUI templates*

There are two types of WinUI applications, packaged applications and unpackaged applications. Unpackaged applications result in an executable that we ourselves are responsible for to put into an installer; these types of applications are used when installing through an MSI or setup.exe wizard. Packaged applications on the other hand are fully prepared to be installed using MSIX. MSIX is Microsoft's packaging format; it is **an easy way for users to install, update, and uninstall applications on their system. The** biggest advantage to MSIX is that every application installed through MSIX works with a sandboxed registry and a sandboxed filesystem, meaning if we uninstall the application, all traces of it are effectively removed from the system. This prevents the slowing down of computers because of registry keys that keep floating around.

There are two app templates, one packaged with MSIX and one packaged with MSIX using a Windows Application Packaging (WAP) project. The second type will generate a solution with two projects. The second project is only there to configure and generate the MSIX file using the package manifest. This is mostly there for backward compatibility reasons since the WAP projects have been around ever since MSIX was introduced with UWP.

111

As you might have seen, there is no template for creating unpackaged apps. An unpackaged app can be created by selecting the packaged app without WAP template and adding the WindowsPackageType setting with value None to the project file. For this example, we will use the Blank App, Packaged project type, without a WAP project. Select the template and create a new solution. Figure 4-31 shows the generated project.

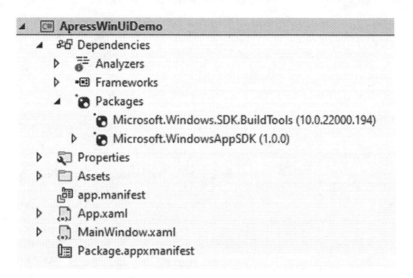

Figure 4-31. *Packaged Windows App SDK project*

The dependencies clearly show the reference to the Windows App SDK. The *Package.appxmanifest* is used for setting app preferences, like preferred orientation, the icons to be shown in the Microsoft Store should we want to publish our application there, and package versioning. The *app.manifest* file is an XML file that contains some startup settings. Listing 4-23 shows the default content.

Listing 4-23. app.manifest file

```
<?xml version="1.0" encoding="utf-8"?>
<assembly manifestVersion="1.0" xmlns="urn:schemas-microsoft-com:asm.v1">
  <assemblyIdentity version="1.0.0.0" name="ApressWinUiDemo.app"/>

  <application xmlns="urn:schemas-microsoft-com:asm.v3">
    <windowsSettings>
      <!-- The combination of below two tags have the following effect:
          1) Per-Monitor for >= Windows 10 Anniversary Update
          2) System < Windows 10 Anniversary Update
```

```
    -->
    <dpiAware xmlns="http://schemas.microsoft.com/SMI/2005/
    WindowsSettings">true/PM</dpiAware>
    <dpiAwareness xmlns="http://schemas.microsoft.com/SMI/2016/
    WindowsSettings">PerMonitorV2, PerMonitor</dpiAwareness>
   </windowsSettings>
  </application>
</assembly>
```

Those DPI values sure look familiar; they are the same values we have set back when we were talking about WinForms.

Let's have a look at MainWindow.xaml. It looks very similar to what we had in WPF, so how do we know we really are using the Windows App SDK with WinUI 3? Figure 4-32 shows what the namespaces for a button in XAML; on the left is the WinUI 3 project we just created, while on the right is a .NET 6 WPF application.

```
<StackPanel                              <StackPanel
    HorizontalAlignment="Center"              HorizontalAlignment="Center"
    VerticalAlignment="Center"                VerticalAlignment="Center"
    Orientation="Horizontal">                 Orientation="Horizontal">
    <Button x:Name="myButton" Click·          <Button x:Name="myButton" Click
</StackP│ Microsoft.UI.Xaml.Controls.Button │  </StackPa│ System.Windows.Controls.Button │
.ndow>                                    lindow>
```

Figure 4-32. *WinUI 3 namespaces vs. WPF namespaces*

Every control in WinUI 3 lives in the *Microsoft.UI.Xaml.Controls* namespace. With this, we have confirmation that we are using the controls from the WinUI 3 library, coming from the Windows App SDK NuGet package. No longer do we need to wait for a Windows update whenever a bug is found in a control or when new controls are announced. Thanks to WinUI 3, the controls are now shipped out of band with Windows, through NuGet.

Using Windows APIs with Windows App SDK

An often-requested feature for WinUI was access to the Windows APIs, for example, to set the title in the window's title bar or to automatically center a window when launching. This functionality has been released with the Windows App SDK. Listing 4-24 shows how we can use the Windows App SDK to get a reference to the AppWindow object for the current window. This code can be copied directly in the code behind of any WinUI window, for example, the default MainWindow in the project template.

Listing 4-24. Getting a reference to AppWindow

```
private AppWindow GetAppWindowForCurrentWindow()
{
    IntPtr hWnd = WinRT.Interop.WindowNative.GetWindowHandle(window);
    WindowId myWndId = Win32Interop.GetWindowIdFromWindow(hWnd);
    return AppWindow.GetFromWindowId(myWndId);
}
```

Thanks to the Windows App SDK, we get access to the Windows Runtime, or WinRT, interop capabilities. We first fetch a pointer to where the window lives in memory (*window* is the name given to the window element in XAML). With that pointer we can grab the window ID, and finally with that ID we can fetch the actual AppWindow instance.

Now that we have an AppWindow instance we can start using it to manipulate the window. Listing 4-25 shows the code to set a title in the titlebar and to resize the window into a square of 500 by 500 pixels.

Listing 4-25. Manipulating the AppWindow

```
private void myButton_Click(object sender, RoutedEventArgs e)
{
    AppWindow appWindow = GetCurrentAppWindow();
    if (appWindow != null)
    {
        appWindow.Title = "Hello Windows App SDK!";
        appWindow.Resize(new SizeInt32(500, 500));
    }
}
```

This code replaces the button's event handler that was in MainWindow when it was created. When we run this and click the button, you will see the title change, and the window will resize to the result in Figure 4-33.

Figure 4-33. *AppWindow after manipulation*

This was just one example of how we can use the Windows App SDK. The full set of documentation can be found at `https://docs.microsoft.com/en-us/windows/apps/windows-app-sdk/`.

Packaging

Once your application is ready to be shipped, we can package it as an MSIX. Make sure to verify the *Packaging* tab *in Package.appxmanifest*. Before we can create our MSIX, we need to select a certificate to sign our application. MSIX requires this to prevent attacks on the user's system through altered software. The toolchain does allow us to create a test certificate, but I would strongly advice to get a real trusted certificate to sign your applications. For now, for the sake of this demo, a self-signed certificate will suffice. Click on the *Choose Certificate* option and select *Create*. This will create a self-signed certificate and add it to your project as a **.pfx* file. Figure 4-34 shows the certificate window.

Figure 4-34. *Selecting a certificate for signing*

This certificate will now be used to sign your application before packaging it as an MSIX. But certificates only work when they are trusted by the machine they are used on. Navigate to the *pfx* file in Windows Explorer and double-click it. This will launch the *Certificate Import Wizard*. Select Local Machine as store location in step 1. The certificate's filename in step 2 should already be filled in with your pfx file. In step 3 you are asked to select a password; this is optional and can be left blank. In the final step we will select the certificate store ourselves and browse to Trusted Root Certificate Authorities.

Figure 4-35. *Selected the trusted root authorities*

Select Next and Finish to import the certificate into your Trusted Root Authority.

A quick but very important sidenote. We have just imported a self-signed certificate into our Trusted Root store of our machine. This is not the way certificates are meant to be used, and we are potentially opening up our machine for malicious software. Keep this in mind and remove the certificate from your store as soon as possible.

Once everything is in order, right-click the project and select *Pack*.

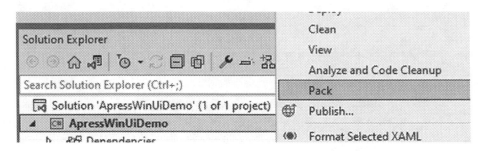

Figure 4-36. *Pack option in Visual Studio*

Once Visual Studio is done packaging your application, you will find an MSIX file in your project's *bin\<cpu architecture>\Release\net6.0-windows10.0.19041.0\win10-x86\ AppPackages\ApressWinUiDemo_1.0.0.0_x86_Test*.

Double-click the MSIX file and an installer will popup. If you did everything correctly, the installer will say that this is a trusted app, which means that the certificate that was used for signing the application is trusted by your machine. Figure 4-37 shows the installer.

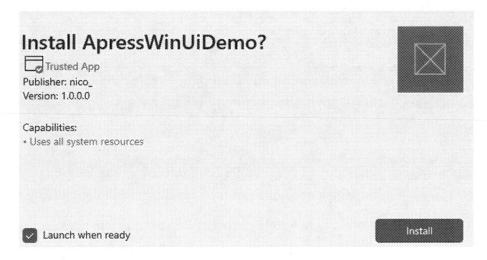

Figure 4-37. *Installing an MSIX packaged application*

After installing, the application will show up in the list of installed applications on your Windows installation. Remember, this application is using sandboxed registry and filesystem, so uninstalling it shouldn't leave a trace behind.

Migrating to .NET 6

The basics of migrating an existing desktop application to .NET 6 is straightforward, of course depending on the complexity of the application. Migration comes in six steps.

1. Run the portability analyzer.

2. Migrate to PackageReference.

3. Update to .NET 4.8.

4. Switch the desktop project to .NET 6.

5. Switch any class libraries to .NET 6.

6. Run the application and test thoroughly.

First step is usually running a Visual Studio extension called "Portability Analyzer." The documentation can be found at `https://docs.microsoft.com/en-us/dotnet/standard/analyzers/portability-analyzer`. This extension will scan your code base and generate a report that gives an overview of how portable your code is and what assemblies are compatible with which version of .NET. The report in Excel looks like in Figure 4-38.

Submission Id	9dc5e5ba-6787-4f45-b531-28ea68cccbd5		
Description			
Targets	.NET + Platform Extensions,Version=v5.0,.NET,Version=v5.0		
Assembly Name	**Target Framework**	**.NET + Platform**	**.NET,Version**
Pixelator, Version=1.0.3.0, Culture=neutral, P .NETFramework,Version=v4.0,Profile		100	100
Pixelator.Logging, Version=1.0.0.0, Culture=n .NETFramework,Version=v4.0,Profile		100	100
API Catalog last updated on	Friday, May 14, 2021		
See 'https://aka.ms/dotnet-portabilityanalyzer' to learn how to read this table			

Figure 4-38. *Portability Analyzer*

I've used a demo application that was built in WinForms with .NET 4.0; in the analyzer settings, I've checked .NET 5 as target framework. The analyzer tells me that my application is 100% compatible with .NET 5; since .NET 6 is the successor of .NET 5, it should work just fine. Do keep in mind that all this analyzer does is checking if the framework APIs you use and and the references you have are compatible with the selected target framework. It does not compile, run, or test your application in any way.

The next step in the porting process is moving away from the old packages.config file to PackageReference. NuGet references used to be stored in an xml file called packages.config in older versions of .NET. After a while those referenced moved to a section in the csproj file called PackageReference. Migration to PackageReference is straightforward in Visual Studio; right-click references and select *Migrate packages. config to PackageReference*.

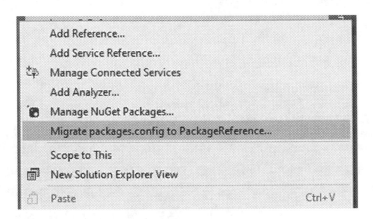

Figure 4-39. *Migrating to PackageReference*

Visual Studio will uninstall all NuGet packages from the project; remove the packages.config and reinstall the NuGet packages in PackageReference. After migration it will show an HTML report detailing any compatibility issues. Don't forget to build your application after this step to make sure all packages are restored from the NuGet package feed. Make sure that your NuGet packages have the correct version installed. You might need to update some to have .NET 6 support.

After upgrading to PackageReference, the next step is to update your application to the latest version of the classic .NET Framework, .NET 4.8. Upgrading to .NET 4.8 first will bring you closer to "the new .NET" that started with .NET Core. This is done easily from the properties of each project, as shown in Figure 4-40.

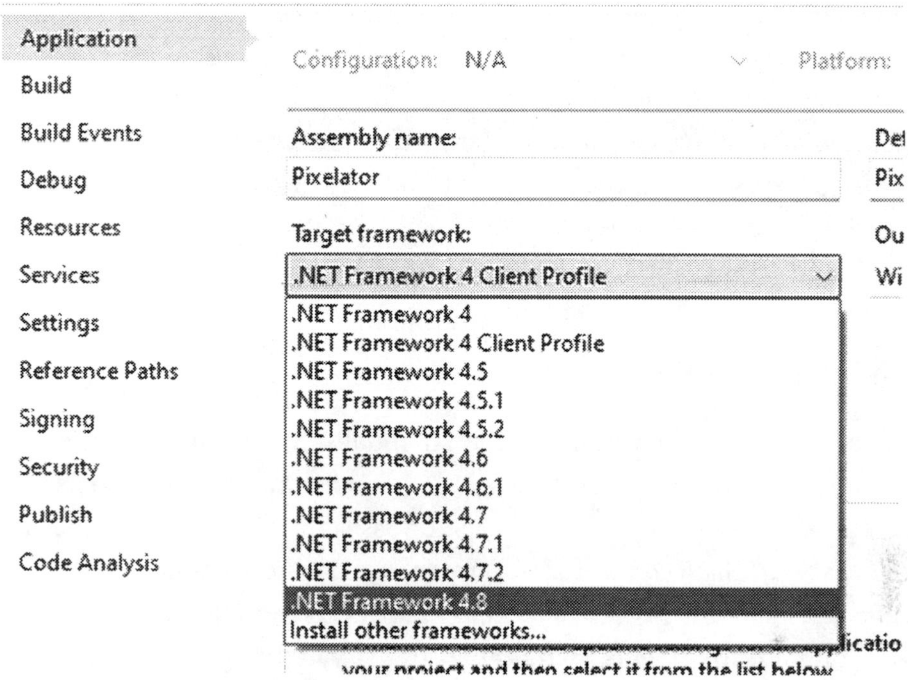

Figure 4-40. *Updating to .NET 4.8*

If you don't see the .NET Framework 4.8 option, you need to download and install the .NET Framework 4.8 SDK from this link `https://dotnet.microsoft.com/en-us/download/visual-studio-sdks`. Make sure your application still compiles and runs after this step.

With that, we're finally ready for the big migration! There's quite an easy trick to move an application to .NET 6.

- Create a new .NET 6 application of the same type (WPF, WinForms, Class Library, etc.) as the project you're trying to migrate.

- Copy the csproj of the new project to the location of the old project.

- Rename the new csproj to have the same name as the csproj of the old application.

- Open in Visual Studio, recreate the references, and add the NuGet packages again.

And that's it! Because of the new project structure since .NET Core, it's as easy as replacing the csproj with a .NET 6 version. There is one more step after migrating all projects within your solution: test every single button, textbox, and flow in your application. No matter how insignificant the code seems, or whether or not it compiles, test everything! For example, `Process.Start("https://www.apress.com")` might seem like a very trivial piece of code that couldn't break, but it does. Since .NET Core, this no longer works and crashes the application.

Upgrade Assistant

There is an alternative to doing the migration manually. Microsoft has created a command line tool called Upgrade Assistant. It basically does the same steps as described above but automatically. The upgrade assistant is open source and can be found at *https://github.com/dotnet/upgrade-assistant*. Upgrading a project using the upgrade assistant is as easy as calling `upgrade assistant upgrade .\Pixelator.csproj`. The upgrade assistant is a wizard that guides you through the process step by step, allowing you to skip whatever step you want or see more details.

```
1. [Complete] Back up project
2. [Complete] Convert project file to SDK style
3. [Next step] Clean up NuGet package references
4. Update TFM
5. Update NuGet Packages
6. Add template files
7. Update source code
     a. Apply fix for UA0002: Types should be upgraded
     b. Apply fix for UA0012: 'UnsafeDeserialize()' does not exist
8. Move to next project

Choose a command:
   1. Apply next step (Clean up NuGet package references)
   2. Skip next step (Clean up NuGet package references)
   3. See more step details
   4. Select different project
   5. Configure logging
   6. Exit
> 1
[07:18:42 INF] Applying upgrade step Clean up NuGet package references
[07:18:42 INF] Adding package reference: Microsoft.DotNet.UpgradeAssistant.Extensions.Default.Analyzers, Version=0.2.233
091
[07:18:44 WRN] No version of Microsoft.CSharp found that supports ["net48"]; leaving unchanged
[07:18:44 WRN] No version of System.Data.DataSetExtensions found that supports ["net48"]; leaving unchanged
[07:18:44 INF] Upgrade step Clean up NuGet package references applied successfully
Please press enter to continue...
```

Figure 4-41. *Upgrade assistant*

Just like with the manual process, test every single nook and cranny of your application after migrating to .NET 6!

Wrapping Up

The desktop remains a very important platform to this day. Microsoft knows this and provides us as developers with several options for building great desktop experiences. Classic frameworks like WinForms and WPF have received updates to bring them in the modern era, with support for high-DPI monitors. Tools like the Windows App SDK unify the API surface of Windows so that we have a common way of interacting with Windows, no matter the desktop framework we are using. In this chapter, we have explored all three options. We have seen that each of the three options has its own strengths and that there is no best option.

CHAPTER 5

Blazor

Blazor, the new kid on the block in the web frontend world since 2018. It understandably gets compared to the likes of Angular, React, and Vue all the time, but it is a whole other beast. For starters, Blazor is not JavaScript based; it is .NET based.

Blazor, in its pure web form, has two flavors. There is Blazor Server and Blazor WebAssembly. No matter what version you prefer, the development experience is the same; you use C# and HTML to build your frontend application. But, haven't we tried this before? Wasn't there something called Silverlight that also let us build frontend web applications with C#? There sure was, but Silverlight was based on a plugin system that was Windows only; it could never survive in this day and age where so much of what we do on the Internet happens on mobile devices or on non-Windows devices. Blazor manages to bring us .NET to the web frontend using only open web standards. No plugins are required; Blazor applications run in the same secure sandbox as JavaScript-based frameworks but with added flexibility, depending on your choice of Blazor flavor.

Blazor WebAssembly

Blazor WebAssembly is the version of Blazor that comes the closest to JavaScript frameworks like Angular and React in that the code is executed in the user's browser instead of on a server. This is however not done by transpiling C# code into JavaScript in a TypeScript kind of way; instead, Blazor makes use of WebAssembly, an open web standard that defines a binary code format for running applications in the browser sandbox. In other words, WebAssembly is a platform that can run applications. WebAssembly, or Wasm, became a W3C recommendation in December 2019. One of the main objectives of Wasm was getting better, even near-native, performance out of web applications. While JavaScript is definitely a powerful language, it still lacks the performance, features, and maturity from the more enterprise-ready managed languages like C# and Java.

125

© Nico Vermeir 2022
N. Vermeir, *Introducing .NET 6*, https://doi.org/10.1007/978-1-4842-7319-7_5

After Wasm was officially a supported standard in the most common browsers, someone at Microsoft decided to see if they could get .NET to run on that new platform. After a while, a proof of concept was ready and demoed using a stripped down version of Mono. This proof of concept turned into a development team; the development team turned the demo into a product.

Blazor Wasm is evolving fast, but it is also limited by WebAssembly itself in some ways. The current version of Wasm doesn't allow direct manipulation of the DOM and has no multithreading. Both limitations are being addressed in future versions of WebAssembly.

Creating a Blazor Wasm Project

.NET 6 comes with default templates for Blazor Wasm applications. Figure 5-1 shows the second step in the wizard where we can provide additional information.

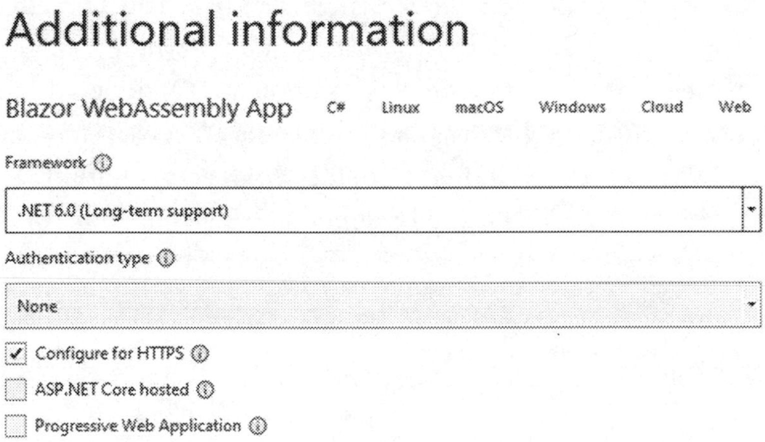

Figure 5-1. *Blazor Wasm template wizard*

The template can be configured in multiple ways. First there are some built-in authentication types like single user accounts or the Microsoft Identity Platform. Choosing one of these options will adjust the template with boilerplate code that enables either local users or users to log in using their Microsoft account. More information on the built-in security can be found at https://docs.microsoft.com/en-us/aspnet/core/blazor/security/?view=aspnetcore-6.0. Configure for HTTPS is checked by default and sets the configuration so that the application only responds to HTTPS requests.

The second option allows you to host your application in an ASP.NET Core project. By default, a Blazor Wasm project can be a static hosted web application; by adding a server-side component, we still maintain the exact same Blazor client project, but we get extra server-side capabilities. Since Blazor Wasm cannot connect directly to a database, we usually need an API in some form to feed data to the app; in .NET, this is usually an ASP.NET WebAPI. By making your Blazor app ASP.NET Core hosted, you automatically get your WebAPI and Wasm application in one application. Project-wise you will get three projects, the Blazor Wasm client project, the ASP.NET Core server project, and a shared project that can share classes between both. Only the Server project needs to be deployed. Since that project has a reference to the Blazor client project, it will automatically include it in the artifacts that get deployed onto the web server. Figure 5-2 shows a diagram to illustrate the relation between client, server, and shared.

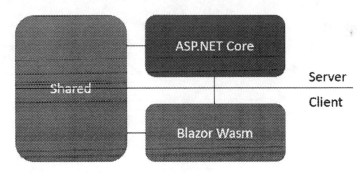

Figure 5-2. *Blazor client/server architecture*

Blazor Progressive Web Apps

The final option in the project wizard is Progressive Web Application. A Progressive Web Application, or PWA, is a web application that can install itself like a native application. Meaning that it will get an icon and when launched will not show any browser controls anymore, but it will still be "just" a web application. By checking the option in the project wizard, the template will include a *manifest.json* file. This file enables browsers to install web applications as a PWA. Listing 5-1 shows the default *manifest.json* included with a new created project. You will find the *manifest.json* in the Blazor client project under the *wwwroot* folder.

Listing 5-1. Default manifest file for a Blazor Wasm app

```
{
  "name": "BlazorWasmDemo",
  "short_name": "BlazorWasmDemo",
  "start_url": "./",
  "display": "standalone",
  "background_color": "#ffffff",
  "theme_color": "#03173d",
  "prefer_related_applications": false,
  "icons": [
    {
      "src": "icon-512.png",
      "type": "image/png",
      "sizes": "512x512"
    },
    {
      "src": "icon-192.png",
      "type": "image/png",
      "sizes": "192x192"
    }
  ]
}
```

As you can tell, it consists of meta information that the operation system needs to be able to make it look like the web application is installed on the OS. If we launch this application in a browser that supports PWA installation, you will see an icon lighting up allowing us to install the PWA as an app. Figure 5-3 shows the browser option in Microsoft Edge once it detects a manifest.json file. The exact look might be different depending on your browser and browser version.

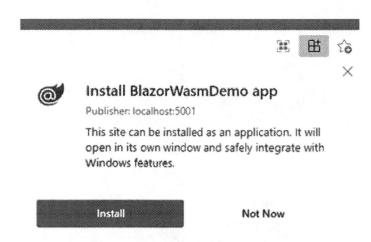

Figure 5-3. *Installing a web app as PWA*

Besides a *manifest.json* file, there's also a service worker added to the project. Service workers are JavaScript code that acts like a proxy between the application and the network. Service workers enable offline access to web applications by caching data and fetching updated data once the network is available.

More information on building a Blazor-based PWA, including the manifest file and service workers, can be found at `https://docs.microsoft.com/en-us/aspnet/core/blazor/progressive-web-app?view=aspnetcore-6.0&tabs=visual-studio`.

Exploring the Blazor Client Project

Figure 5-4 shows a default Blazor WASM client project loaded in Visual Studio.

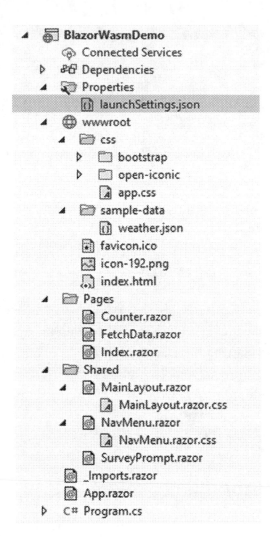

Figure 5-4. *A Blazor WASM project*

Blazor makes use of the Razor framework that made its debut in ASP.NET MVC. If you have done ASP.NET MVC before, you will recognize a lot of things, but there are some Blazor-specific things in there as well.

Listing 5-2 shows the content of the counter page.

Listing 5-2. Counter page in the default Blazor template

```
@page "/counter"

<h1>Counter</h1>
```

```
<p role="status">Current count: @currentCount</p>

<button class="btn btn-primary" @onclick="IncrementCount">Click me</button>

@code {
    private int currentCount = 0;

    private void IncrementCount()
    {
        currentCount++;
    }
}
```

Razor is a framework that mixes HTML and .NET code. It allows us to declare variables and bind them to HTML elements or trigger .NET methods from HTML elements.

In Razor, an @ sign signals the start of a .NET statement. An example of this is @page "/counter" at the top of the page. Page is an attribute; instead of using square brackets, we use the @ sign again to set this attribute to the counter page. In case of the page attribute, it is used for Blazor's navigation service. This page can now be accessed through https://the-webapps-url/counter.

The @code directive specifies the code block for this specific page; those code blocks are scoped to the page they are declared in. The sample code declares a private field called currentCount in a normal C# way. That field is bound to in HTML by prefixing it with an @ sign, <p role="status">Current count: @currentCount</p>.

This page also demonstrates updating a data field by calling a method. The HTML button specifies an @onclick event. This type of event is different from the HTML/JavaScript combination you might be used to because of the @ sign. Once again, this signals a .NET statement, in this case calling a method that is declared within this page. The IncrementCount method increases the integer field with 1, immediately updating the UI as a result.

The interesting part here is that the page is not updated through a server callback but rather through updating the DOM; this can be seen in most browser's dev tools (F12). Looking at the visual tree in dev tools, they often mark the elements that are changing. Figure 5-5 shows this for the counter page right after clicking the button for the fifth time.

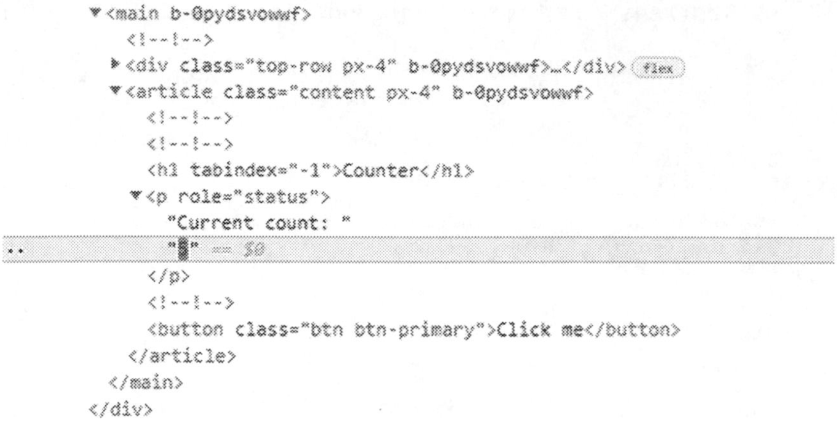

```
▼<main b-0pydsvowwf>
    <!--!-->
  ▶<div class="top-row px-4" b-0pydsvowwf>…</div>  flex
  ▼<article class="content px-4" b-0pydsvowwf>
      <!--!-->
      <!--!-->
      <h1 tabindex="-1">Counter</h1>
    ▼<p role="status">
        "Current count: "
        "█" == 50
      </p>
      <!--!-->
      <button class="btn btn-primary">Click me</button>
    </article>
  </main>
</div>
```

Figure 5-5. *Updating the DOM after a button click*

As you can see, only one element is marked, so only one small part of the page is changing. This results in fast web applications that feel more native than, for example, ASP.NET MVC applications that often rely on page reloads and server callbacks.

Blazor in .NET 6

To see how .NET 6 handles Blazor projects, let's start at the beginning. As usual a Blazor app starts at Program.cs, shown in Listing 5-3.

Listing 5-3. Program class of a Blazor WASM application

```
using BlazorWasmDemo;
using Microsoft.AspNetCore.Components.Web;
using Microsoft.AspNetCore.Components.WebAssembly.Hosting;

var builder = WebAssemblyHostBuilder.CreateDefault(args);
builder.RootComponents.Add<App>("#app");
builder.RootComponents.Add<HeadOutlet>("head::after");

builder.Services.AddScoped(sp => new HttpClient { BaseAddress = new
Uri(builder.HostEnvironment.BaseAddress) });

await builder.Build().RunAsync();
```

Blazor in .NET 6 makes use of top-level statements to trim down the size and complexity of the Program file. As you can see in Listing 5-3, there is no namespace, no class declaration, and no Main method declaration; the Main method is still there but it is hidden away as a syntactic trick; should you inspect the intermediate language, you will find the Main method there. More information on top-level statements can be found here https://docs.microsoft.com/en-us/dotnet/csharp/whats-new/tutorials/top-level-statements.

This sample application sets the App component as root component for this web application. The system uses selectors like selectors in CSS to select the correct element in the *index.html* file where to inject the components. In the default template, the *#app* selector is used. If you open the default *index.html* file in the *wwwroot* folder of your project, you will find a div with app as ID. This is the div where our Blazor application will be hosted.

The App component is listed in Listing 5-4.

Listing 5-4. Default app component

```
<Router AppAssembly="@typeof(App).Assembly">
    <Found Context="routeData">
        <RouteView RouteData="@routeData" DefaultLayout=
        "@typeof(MainLayout)" />
        <FocusOnNavigate RouteData="@routeData" Selector="h1" />
    </Found>
    <NotFound>
        <LayoutView Layout="@typeof(MainLayout)">
            <p role="alert">Sorry, there's nothing at this address.</p>
        </LayoutView>
    </NotFound>
</Router>
```

The App component is the most top-level component in a default Blazor application. It configures the router, to enable page navigation, and considers the router to be similar to a NavigationPage if you're more used to Xamarin Forms or MAUI development. The router specifies found and not found views; the not found view will be shown whenever navigation triggers an HTTP 404.

Another rootcomponent being added is the HeadOutlet. Its selector specifies that the component is added to the head section of the HTML file rather than replacing it. The component itself allows us to easily set the title of the page to be reflected in the browser's tab or title bar.

After adding the root components, we register an HTTP client as a scoped service into .NET's dependency injection framework. We are registering our services here so that we can inject them in our Blazor pages later on as we will see in a minute.

Blazor Component System

As we have seen in Listing 5-4, the App.razor component declares a Router. That Router loads MainLayout.razor. MainLayout.razor is a component that can be best viewed as the application's template. Listing 5-5 shows the default MainLayout.razor.

Listing 5-5. MainLayout.razor

```
@inherits LayoutComponentBase

<div class="page">
    <div class="sidebar">
        <NavMenu />
    </div>

    <main>
        <div class="top-row px-4">
            <a href="https://docs.microsoft.com/aspnet/" target="_blank">
            About</a>
        </div>

        <article class="content px-4">
            @Body
        </article>
    </main>
</div>
```

The layout specifies where the navigation menu lives, what the grid layout of the page is, and so on. The NavMenu element specified in MainLayout is actually another Blazor component living in our project. You can find it in the Shared folder. Blazor components can be embedded in each other in a very similar way as HTML elements are added on a page. We can even add properties to a component, mark them as Parameter with an attribute, and pass data between components this way. An example of this is included in the default template in the Shared folder. Listing 5-6 shows the SurveyPrompt property as parameter declaration.

Listing 5-6. Adding parameters to a Blazor component

```
[Parameter]
public string? Title { get; set; }
```

That parameter can be set as if it was a property on an HTML element as demonstrated in Listing 5-7.

Listing 5-7. Setting a parameter

```
<SurveyPrompt Title="How is Blazor working for you?" />
```

MainLayout also contains an @Body placeholder. This placeholder is where all our Blazor pages will be inserted into the layout of the application. Choosing what page to have as initial page is as simple as setting a page's route to "/". This is often Index.razor, as is the case in the default template. Listing 5-8 shows a snippet of the default Index.razor page.

Listing 5-8. Index.Razor's page declaration

```
@page "/"
```

```
<PageTitle>Index</PageTitle>
```

Since the url to this page is the root url of the application, this page will be initially loaded and placed on the @Body part of *MainLayout*. The PageTitle we specify here is what will go in the HeadOutlet root component we declared in *Program.cs* and will become the page title.

If we now go back to the counter page we have previously seen, you can clearly see where the navigation menu comes from and what part of the MainLayout is replaced with the code from the counter component.

Creating Blazor Pages

We have mentioned both Blazor pages and Blazor components before. Blazor pages are components with an @page directive, giving them a url for the routing system to navigate to.

Let's jump to *FetchData.razor*, starting with the attributes at the top of the file, listed in Listing 5-9.

Listing 5-9. Attributes in FetchData.razor

```
@page "/fetchdata"
@inject HttpClient Http
```

We've run into the page attribute before. As a reminder, it configures the route for this page; when navigating to https://<hostname:port>/fetchdata, we will be redirected to this page. The inject attribute is Blazor's version of dependency injection. It will search for the HttpClient type in the ServiceCollection that we've seen in Listing 5-3 and set an instance of that type to the Http member.

In Listing 5-6, we see the Razor code of the FetchData class. As mentioned before, Razor can be explained by HTML mixed C# snippets. Take the if statement for example. It is prefixed with an @ sign, signaling that a code statement will follow. The statement is followed by brackets, embedding the code between the brackets in the statement. This specific statement will prevent a potential NullReferenceException on forecasts. The code loops over the forecasts collection, but if that collection is not loaded yet, it will crash. The interesting part here is that that if statement will actually get reevaluated as soon as the forecasts collection is updated. This is because Blazor has an internal method called StateHasChanged. When this method is triggered, Blazor will re-render its current state, take a diff between the old and the new render tree, and apply that diff to the old one that is still on screen. This results in only a partial refresh of the page instead of a full page reload. StateHasChanged can be called manually by us, but Blazor calls it internally whenever a property on a component changes or when an event on a component is triggered. This results in an easy way to show a "loading" message while data is being fetched from an API.

The foreach statement loops over the forecasts collection and lists its content in an HTML table. This is a great example of how flexible Razor can mix HTML elements with .NET data. We can even call member methods, like the ToShortDateString on the DateTime struct.

Listing 5-10. Razor code

```
<h1>Weather forecast</h1>

<p>This component demonstrates fetching data from the server.</p>

@if (forecasts == null)
{
    <p><em>Loading...</em></p>
}
else
{
    <table class="table">
        <thead>
            <tr>
                <th>Date</th>
                <th>Temp. (C)</th>
                <th>Temp. (F)</th>
                <th>Summary</th>
            </tr>
        </thead>
        <tbody>
            @foreach (var forecast in forecasts)
            {
            <tr>
                <td>@forecast.Date.ToShortDateString()</td>
                <td>@forecast.TemperatureC</td>
                <td>@forecast.TemperatureF</td>
                <td>@forecast.Summary</td>
            </tr>
            }
        </tbody>
    </table>
}
```

The final part of the FetchData file is the code block. Every Razor file can contain a @code block. This contains most of the logic of a Razor component, and its lifecycle methods.

Listing 5-11. Code block in a Razor file

```
@code {
    private WeatherForecast[]? forecasts;

    protected override async Task OnInitializedAsync()
    {
        forecasts = await Http.GetFromJsonAsync<WeatherForecast[]>
        ("sample-data/weather.json");
    }

    public class WeatherForecast
    {
        public DateTime Date { get; set; }

        public int TemperatureC { get; set; }

        public string? Summary { get; set; }

        public int TemperatureF => 32 + (int)(TemperatureC / 0.5556);
    }
}
```

The most interesting part of Listing 5-11 is `OnInitializedAsync`. This is one of seven lifecycle methods of a Blazor component. The complete list of lifecycle methods is:

- OnInitialized

- OnInitializedAsync

- OnParametersSet

- OnParametersSetAsync

- OnAfterRender

- OnAfterRenderAsync

- ShouldRender

As you can see, every lifecycle event, except for ShouldRender, has both a synchronous and an asynchronous version. If you are hooking into one of the lifecycle events and you need to call an async method, you need to use the async version of the lifecycle method. We can even use both the async and the sync version of these lifecycle methods at the same time; they will both execute but there is no guarantee that they will always run or finish in the same order. OnInitialized is called after the component is done loading and all UI components are available; this is the perfect lifecycle event to load initial data from a data service. OnParametersSet is called after parameters change value, usually due to another component that updates the parameter on the current component. OnAfterRender is called after everything is done rendering, but other initializations might still be happening inside other components that we are referencing. And finally, ShouldRender is called right before rendering happens. Microsoft has a nice diagram showing the component lifecycle. I have added that diagram for your reference as Figure 5-6.

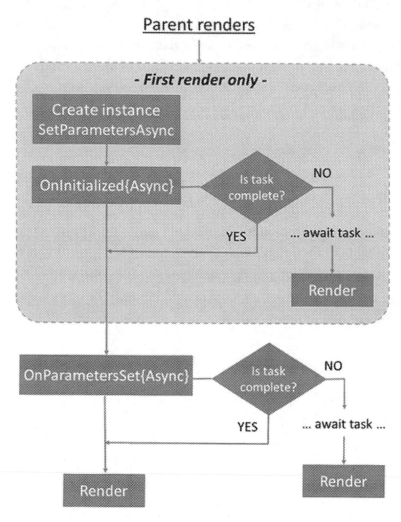

Figure 5-6. *Razor component lifecycle (Source: Microsoft)*

Running a Blazor App

So, now we know how Blazor works. But how do we go from entering a URL in our browser to a running Blazor application? Is it a plugin like Silverlight was? Do we need browsers that support Blazor? The answer is simple. Blazor is not plugin based; it runs on WebAssembly. All we need is a browser that supports Wasm, and all modern browsers do. To understand how Blazor is loaded into a browser, we need to step back and look at a basic web server. A web server in its purest form is a server that hosts a bunch of files. Those files get downloaded to the browser of someone who enters the URL that routes to your webserver. Webservers have had a form of conventions, for example, if no specific html file is specified in the URL, the server will, by default, look for *index.html* or *default.html*. Other web servers, like IIS, for example, also take this convention into account; *index.aspx* is still the startpage of an ASP.NET application. A Blazor WASM application is served as a static website; there's no need for an IIS server to make the calculations or run the .NET code. All we need is a website that can serve static content, in this case HTML, CSS, JS, and DLL files.

Figure 5-7 shows the generated files when publishing a stand-alone Blazor WASM client application without PWA support from Visual Studio. The deploy step took our wwwroot content and copied it to the output folder; it compiled our .NET code and added that to the output as well.

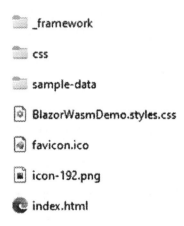

Figure 5-7. *Output after publishing a Blazor WASM application*

There is our *index.html* file! There's HTML and CSS files right there; no need to **compile or compute anything; a static file server can deliver these files to a modern** browser; the browser will spin up the WASM runtime and load in the Blazor app. We don't even need to install .NET 6 into our browser; notice that _framework folder in Figure 5-7? That contains the .NET 6 assemblies; it just ships with our application. Figure 5-8 shows part of the contents of that folder.

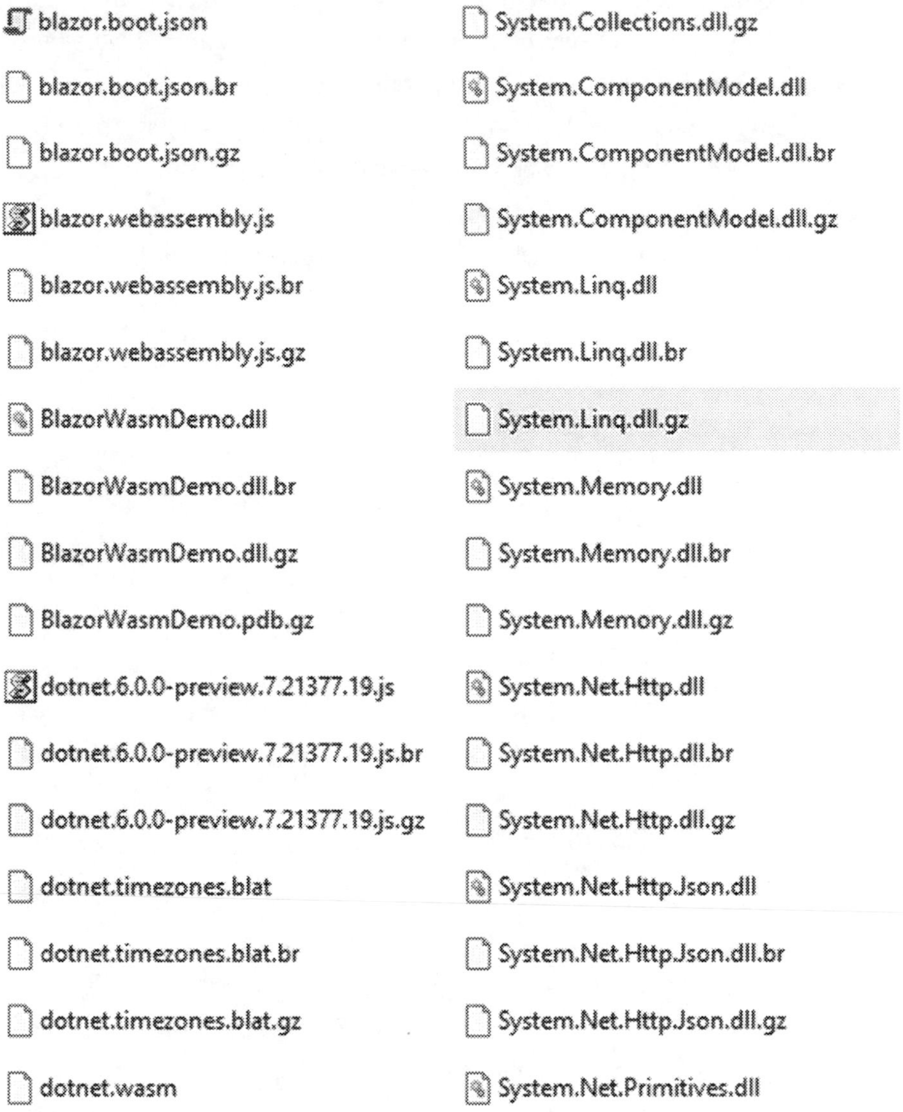

blazor.boot.json	System.Collections.dll.gz
blazor.boot.json.br	System.ComponentModel.dll
blazor.boot.json.gz	System.ComponentModel.dll.br
blazor.webassembly.js	System.ComponentModel.dll.gz
blazor.webassembly.js.br	System.Linq.dll
blazor.webassembly.js.gz	System.Linq.dll.br
BlazorWasmDemo.dll	System.Linq.dll.gz
BlazorWasmDemo.dll.br	System.Memory.dll
BlazorWasmDemo.dll.gz	System.Memory.dll.br
BlazorWasmDemo.pdb.gz	System.Memory.dll.gz
dotnet.6.0.0-preview.7.21377.19.js	System.Net.Http.dll
dotnet.6.0.0-preview.7.21377.19.js.br	System.Net.Http.dll.br
dotnet.6.0.0-preview.7.21377.19.js.gz	System.Net.Http.dll.gz
dotnet.timezones.blat	System.Net.Http.Json.dll
dotnet.timezones.blat.br	System.Net.Http.Json.dll.br
dotnet.timezones.blat.gz	System.Net.Http.Json.dll.gz
dotnet.wasm	System.Net.Primitives.dll

Figure 5-8. *_framework folder*

There are some interesting files in this folder. I have removed a lot of the files from Figure 5-8 for brevity, but the interesting ones are still there. Before we go into the actual files, notice that there are three versions of the files? That is because the output generates every file in a normal way and twice using a different type of compression. The .gz files are gzipped, while the .br files are compressed with Brotli. It is up to the server that serves our application to detect what the optimal type is for the client requesting our files.

Let's start with the actual .NET 6 runtime. As you can see, the assemblies are there, in part. All the *System.** files are part of the .NET 6 assemblies, while all of the *Microsoft.** files are specific for Blazor. When publishing a Blazor application, the framework will run a linker process. This process will remove unreachable or unused code from the generated intermediate language files, and it will remove unused binaries from the output (tree shaking). These operations are not perfect. It is very important to perform a complete end-to-end test of your application after publishing. There is a possibility that the linker was too aggressive and that your application suddenly behaves in unexpected ways. To fix this, the linker can be configured to ignore certain modules by adding nodes to the project file. The complete documentation on how to do this can be found at `https://docs.microsoft.com/en-us/dotnet/core/deploying/trim-self-contained`.

The *blazor.boot.json* file contains information about the project. It contains a list of assemblies, with hashes to prevent tampering, that need to be loaded in order for the application to start.

blazor.webassembly.js is the glue between the web world, where the HTML lives, and the native world, where .NET lives. As mentioned before, we currently cannot directly access the DOM from within the .NET Blazor code. To work around this, Microsoft created this JavaScript file. Since we cannot interact with the elements in the visual tree from within Blazor, but we can call JavaScript functions through JS Interop, this file can serve as a bridge from Blazor to the visual tree.

BlazorWasmDemo.dll contains the application code we have written.

dotnet.wasm is the native Webassembly code that contains the *instructions to load up the .NET runtime environment in the Webassembly sandbox.*

Loading a Blazor WASM application means downloading all these files and loading them into the WASM sandbox. At first sight, that might look like a lot but the Blazor team **has been hard at work to shrink .NET down as much as possible; combined with linking** and tree shaking, they managed to get a Blazor WASM application to a reasonable size when compared with other JavaScript-based SPA frameworks. Figure 5-9 shows the browser's network tab when opening a published Blazor WASM application, hosted on a static Azure website. This is an actual in-house application we are actively using and developing, so no demo application. Do keep in mind that the size on the screenshots is just for demo purposes, the actual size of your application will be different.

309 requests   9.7 MB transferred   46.6 MB resources   Finish: 7.86 s   DOMContentLoaded: 591 ms   Load: 629 ms

Figure 5-9. Launching a published Blazor WASM app

A total of 9.7 MB was downloaded; this was the first launch of that specific application. Figure 5-10 shows the same metric, but after launching the app for a second time.

Figure 5-10. *Launching the app again*

Launching the app again takes significantly less time and resources. That is because the browser caches as much as possible. There's even quite a big chance that your users won't notice the three seconds it takes to load your application. That is because there is a big difference between speed and the perception of speed. As mentioned before, the first thing loaded into the browser is the index.html file. That file contains logic to show "Loading...," while the WASM and .NET runtimes are being downloaded and started; replace that with a nice loading animation, and your application will be perceived as loading quite fast.

Blazor Server

Blazor Server is a second flavor of Blazor. It looks and feels very similar to Blazor WASM, but the big difference is in the underlying architecture. Instead of running inside web assembly, it actually runs on a server, hence the name. Blazor server uses a SignalR connection to send requests to a server that handles all the instructions and sends back changes to the DOM. Before we go any deeper, let's see what SignalR is.

SignalR

SignalR has been around for quite some years. It is a framework that allows developers to easily implement real-time communication between clients and servers. It enables server code to directly call methods on clients instead of clients having to poll for data on the server. A simple example of this is a chat application where client A pushes a new message to the server; the server then calls client B with the new message as parameter. All of this is possible due to Websockets, which is the underlying mechanism of SignalR. But it goes one step further. On platforms that don't support Websockets,

SignalR can automatically fall back to older transport protocols. Because of this fallback functionality and a load of abstractions on top of the Websockets, API SignalR has quickly gained a lot of popularity.

Thanks to SignalR we have server–client and client–server communication. By leveraging this, Microsoft built a server-based web framework that does not do page reloads; instead, they receive a piece of DOM through the SignalR connection. We can see this in action by launching the counter page of the default Blazor Server template. The project template is mostly the same as Blazor WASM, from *App.razor* to `MainLayout` down to the code of the components. Just like in Blazor WASM, when you inspect the HTML code and click the counter button, you will see that only the element containing the number is updated; the rest of the page is never reloaded.

There are a few differences in how Blazor Server launches compared to Blazor WASM. Let's start at the main entrance point of the application, *Program.cs*.

Listing 5-12. Program.cs from a Blazor Server application

```
var builder = WebApplication.CreateBuilder(args);

// Add services to the container.
builder.Services.AddRazorPages();
builder.Services.AddServerSideBlazor();
builder.Services.AddSingleton<WeatherForecastService>();

var app = builder.Build();

// Configure the HTTP request pipeline.
if (!app.Environment.IsDevelopment())
{
    app.UseExceptionHandler("/Error");
    // The default HSTS value is 30 days. You may want to change this for
        production scenarios, see https://aka.ms/aspnetcore-hsts.
    app.UseHsts();
}
```

```
app.UseHttpsRedirection();

app.UseStaticFiles();

app.UseRouting();

app.MapBlazorHub();
app.MapFallbackToPage("/_Host");

app.Run();
```

Program.cs in .NET 6 contains top-level statements once again, making for a cleaner file without a class declaration. If you've used ASP.NET MVC before, the instructions in this file might look very familiar. That is because the SignalR connection is powered by ASP.NET, so we need to bootstrap that framework as well. Similar to Blazor WASM, we start by registering services in the built-in dependency injection (DI). After registering services, we have basic boilerplate code to enable HTTPS, set up routing, and start the app.

There are two Blazor-specific calls in this file. The first one is `builder.Services.AddServerSideBlazor();`. This call registers Blazor-specific services into the DI container, services like the NavigationManager for navigation between Razor components or the IJSRuntime to enable JavaScript interop. The exact code of this method can be found on GitHub `https://github.com/dotnet/aspnetcore/blob/main/src/Components/Server/src/DependencyInjection/ComponentServiceCollectionExtensions.cs`. The second Blazor-specific call is `app.MapBlazorHub();`. This call opens the connection to the Blazor SignalR hub. A SignalR hub is a class that contains communication logic between clients and a SignalR server. In this case, the hub will contain the logic that enables receiving instructions and data from a client, generating a DOM diff and sending it back to the client. The SignalR part of Blazor Server is also open sourced on GitHub at `https://github.com/dotnet/aspnetcore/tree/main/src/Components/Server/src/BlazorPack`.

Another difference from Blazor WASM is the absence of the *index.html* page from the wwwroot folder; instead, there is a *_Host.cshtml* file in the *Pages* folder of the project. Files with the cshtml extension are ASP.NET webpages; since Blazor Server has need for a webserver that supports .NET, we can leverage the power of ASP.NET as well. The _Host.cshtml file is mostly HTML 5 with a namespace and a routing attribute. But it does contain an interesting line that impacts the entire application.

Listing 5-13. Rendering mode in Blazor Server

```
<component type="typeof(App)" render-mode="ServerPrerendered" />
```

The component tag specifies where in the host file our actual Blazor application will get rendered. The type parameter sets the startup type of the app. The render mode will specify where the application is rendered and how dynamic it can be. There are three options.

- Static: All components are rendered into static HTML, meaning that there is no connection to a Blazor SignalR server and pages have no Blazor functionality.

- Server: The webserver builds the HTML, connects to SignalR, and activates all Blazor functionality. After the server is finished with all that, the browser will receive the HTML and render everything. This is the slowest option but with the most consistent results.

- ServerPrerendered: This option uses a technique called hydration. Hydration is a known pattern in most popular SPA frameworks; it takes the best of both static and server render modes to find a middle ground between performance and functionality. Hydration is a two-step process; the first step renders static HTML which gives users the illusion of a fast page load. At this point, the page has appeared on screen but there is no Blazor functionality. In the second step, there is a piece of JavaScript in *blazor.server.js* that will open the connection to the SignalR hub and hydrate the already rendered page with functionality; the page basically re-renders invisible to the user. The *blazor.server.js* file is a file included in the *Microsoft.AspNetCore. Components.Server.dll* assembly. It gets injected in your application's output automatically.

ServerPrerendered is the default option, and looking from an end-user perspective, it is the most interesting one performance vs. functionality-wise. However, do be careful with automated tests. We have run into issues where the test runner is clicking a button before the re-rendering has taken place. The re-rendering usually happens fast, from a human perspective. Automated tests are executed by machines and can happen faster than the re-rendering.

As soon as _Host.cshtml is finished loading, we are in Blazor land. From here on out, everything works exactly the same as Blazor WASM, development-wise. Feel free to compare the code of the Razor components that are in the default templates for server and WASM projects; they are the same components. Since we've already discussed Razor components in the Blazor WASM section of this chapter, we won't go over it again.

Blazor Desktop

Back in Chapter 4, I briefly mentioned that Blazor was also available for building desktop applications. Using Blazor in WinForms or WPF applications is possible, thanks to a control called the BlazorWebView. The BlazorWebView is a component that hosts a WebView2 control, which in its turn is a component that can render HTML based on Microsoft's Edge browser. The BlazorWebView also knows how to initialize and run Blazor.

Unfortunately at the time of writing, there are no project templates available for WPF or WinForms that include the Blazor setup, so for now we will have to do it manually. For this demo, we will start from a WinForms project. The procedure for WPF is very similar so it shouldn't be a problem to follow along.

We will start with a new .NET 6-based WinForms application. Once that is created, we start by editing the project file and changing our target SDK from Microsoft.NET.Sdk to Microsoft.NET.Sdk.Razor. In the end, your project file should look like Listing 5-14.

Listing 5-14. The modified project file

```
<Project Sdk="Microsoft.NET.Sdk.Razor">

  <PropertyGroup>
    <OutputType>WinExe</OutputType>
    <TargetFramework>net6.0-windows</TargetFramework>
    <Nullable>enable</Nullable>
    <UseWindowsForms>true</UseWindowsForms>
    <ImplicitUsings>enable</ImplicitUsings>
  </PropertyGroup>

</Project>
```

Once the SDK is changed, we need to add a NuGet reference to *Microsoft. AspNetCore.Components.WebView.WindowsForms*. There is a different package for when you are following along for a WPF project; make sure to select the correct one. Figure 5-11 shows both options.

Microsoft.AspNetCore.Components.WebView.Wpf ⊘ by Microsoft, 4.92K downloads
Build WPF applications with Blazor and WebView2.
Prerelease

Microsoft.AspNetCore.Components.WebView.WindowsForms ⊘ by Microsoft, 2.91K downloads
Build Windows Forms applications with Blazor and WebView2.
Prerelease

Figure 5-11. *WPF and WinForms versions of the WebView package*

Note that at the time of writing both of these packages were still in Prerelease. That is because the Blazor Desktop efforts are part of MAUI, Microsoft's cross-platform mobile framework which we will talk about in Chapter 6. MAUI was supposed to be released together with .NET 6 but they missed that mark. Instead it will launch somewhere in 2022.

Once the NuGet package is installed, we can start adding Blazor files. We start by creating a wwwroot folder in the WinForms project and adding in an index.html and app.css. I have copied these files over from a Blazor WASM project. Next I have copied the Counter.razor component that we have seen before in this chapter. In the end, your project should look like Figure 5-12.

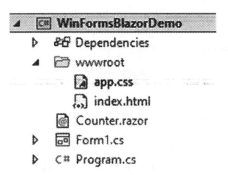

Figure 5-12. *Project structure for WinForms with Blazor*

An important step is changing the *Copy to output* property for every file in the *wwwroot* folder to *Copy if newer* as demonstrated in Figure 5-13.

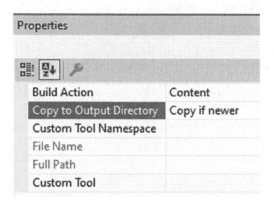

Figure 5-13. *Changing the copy to output properties*

The final step in the process is creating the `BlazorWebView` and adding it to a form. This can be done through the editor; the `BlazorWebView` will show up in the toolbox, or it can be done by code. Listing 5-15 shows adding the `BlazorWebView` by code.

Listing 5-15. Adding the BlazorWebView to a form

```
public BlazorForm()
{
    InitializeComponent();

    var serviceCollection = new ServiceCollection();
    serviceCollection.AddBlazorWebView();

    var blazor = new BlazorWebView
    {
        Dock = DockStyle.Fill,
        HostPage = "wwwroot/index.html",
        Services = serviceCollection.BuildServiceProvider(),
    };

    blazor.RootComponents.Add<Counter>("#app");
    Controls.Add(blazor);
}
```

We are adding the `BlazorWebView` from the constructor. First we create a new instance of `ServiceCollection`, which is needed for dependency injection inside the Blazor part. We call the `AddBlazorWebView` extension method on the `ServiceCollection` to wire up all of the Blazor framework-related services. Next we create an instance of the `BlazorWebView` WinForms component; we let it dock to all sides so that the `BlazorWebView` will take up all available space on the form. The `HostPage` is the *index. html* file we have copied over from another Blazor project into the *wwwroot* folder. The `Services` property is the `ServiceCollection` where all Blazor services are registered.

Just like before, we add a `rootcomponent` to the `div` with ID app. In this case, we add the only component our application currently has, the `counter` component. We are free to add as many components as we want; we can copy an entire Blazor application in here with the `MainLayout`, the routing mechanism, and so on.

The final step is adding the `BlazorWebView` to our form's list of controls. Once this is done, we can launch the application and we will see that the Blazor counter component is loaded and visible on a native Windows Forms application. Figure 5-14 shows the running application.

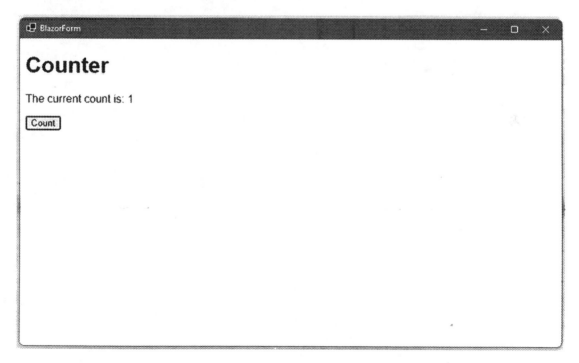

Figure 5-14. *Blazor running inside a WinForms application*

Since this is basically a control running on a form, we are free to mix Blazor components with WinForms controls to create fully hybrid applications.

Wrapping Up

As we have seen, Blazor is Microsoft's answer to popular client-side frameworks like Angular and React. It allows us to build powerful, dynamic, and beautiful web applications using .NET instead of JavaScript. Blazor comes in different flavors, fully client-side, thanks to the power of WebAssembly of client-server, thanks to real-time communication over SignalR.

Besides being a framework for building web applications, Microsoft has been investigating bringing it to different platforms. The result of that can be found in the Prerelease version of the BlazorWebView. With the BlazorWebView, we can share Blazor components from the web to WPF and WinForms and eventually even to mobile applications with MAUI.

CHAPTER 6

MAUI

MAUI, or the Multi-Application User Interface, is the next iteration of Microsoft's Xamarin framework. Xamarin has come a long way since its startup days back in 2011. It has evolved from being a C# wrapper around Java and Objective-C to a world-class cross-platform library, enabling mobile developers to write apps for multiple platforms in the same language, without ever having to switch back to the platform's native language. All of this was, thanks to Mono, an open-source implementation of .NET. Mono's original reason of existence was bringing .NET to the Linux world, enabling Mono developers to build Linux-based desktop applications with C# and Visual Basic. Mono quickly evolved to a platform that brings .NET to a wide range of architectures and operating systems, even into the world of embedded systems. Since Android and iOS are *Nix-based operating systems, it wasn't that far-fetched to get a version of Mono running on these mobile platforms, and thus Xamarin was born.

In 2014 Xamarin released Xamarin.Forms, which adds an extra UI abstraction layer on top of Xamarin. It further abstracts platform differences by enabling developers to write a UI once and run it on different platforms.

Microsoft acquired Xamarin in 2016; they made the framework license free and even gave it a more open open-source license. The Xamarin community has grown large since then. Since the acquisition focus has shifted from more Xamarin Native to Xamarin Forms, pushing XAML as the UI framework of choice. A lot of work was done to improve performance and stability. The tooling greatly increased, bringing us a UI Previewer and telemetry tools.

With MAUI, a new chapter in the life of Xamarin begins. MAUI will aim to shorten the developer loop (develop–build–run) and greatly improve the tooling. MAUI can target Android, iOS, Windows, and MacOS.

© Nico Vermeir 2022
N. Vermeir, *Introducing .NET 6*, https://doi.org/10.1007/978-1-4842-7319-7_6

Project Structure

The most prominent change is the new project structure. A new Xamarin.Forms solution in Visual Studio already contained three projects before any code was written, as shown in Figure 6-1.

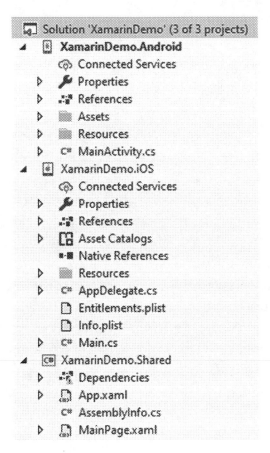

Figure 6-1. *A classic Xamarin Forms project*

A newly created Xamarin.Forms app that can run on Android and iOS consists of three projects: a Xamarin.Android project, a Xamarin.iOS project, and a .NET class library. The Android and iOS project are what we call the "platform heads"; they exist mainly to bootstrap the Xamarin.Forms platform and call into the shared code that lives in the .NET class library, *XamarinDemo.Shared*. The two platform heads are also used whenever an app needs platform-specific implementations; this might be needed if the cross-platform layer doesn't suffice.

Figure 6-2 shows a newly created MAUI application using The Blank MAUI app template in Visual Studio in .NET 6.

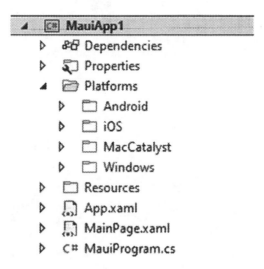

Figure 6-2. *A new .NET 6 MAUI project*

This app supports Android, iOS, Windows, and Mac Catalyst. You'll notice that the multiple platform heads are gone; instead, we get one class library that contains a *Platforms* folder containing a folder for each platform we're supporting with our app. This is mostly done through compiler magic; we still get an APK file for Android and an IPA for iOS, but our code is easier to manage since it's all in one place. Selecting which platform to launch or debug on is built into the new Visual Studio tooling, as shown in *Figure 6-3*.

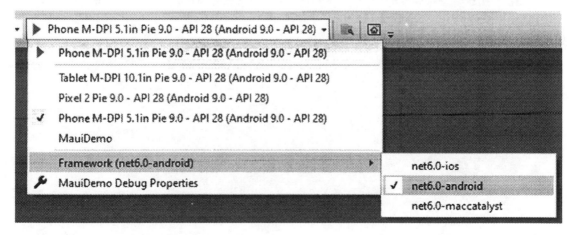

Figure 6-3. *Selecting the debug target*

Figure 6-4 shows the newly created app running on an Android and Windows device.

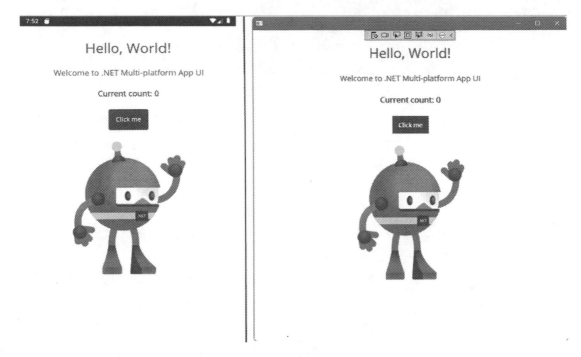

Figure 6-4. *MAUI App running on Android*

Exploring MAUI

The startup of a MAUI project looks quite similar to how ASP.net has been operating ever since .NET Core. It uses a `Microsoft.Extensions.HostBuilder` to bootstrap and launch an app. However, this is where the multiplatform part starts; just like with Xamarin before, we first need to launch the actual application on the operating system that we're targeting; that's what the platform-specific folders are for. Let's take the iOS folder as an example.

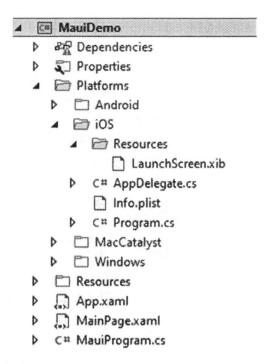

Figure 6-5. *The iOS platform folder*

The contents of this folder should look familiar if you have done Xamarin Forms work before. It looks similar to the contents of the iOS project in a Xamarin.Forms project; it also serves the exact same purpose. Program.cs is the launch class of iOS in this case. It creates a UIApplication instance passing AppDelegate as startup class. These classes are .NET wrappers around the native iOS APIs.

As I've mentioned before, the single project system is mostly compiler tricks, which isn't a bad thing; not having a project for every supported platform greatly simplifies things and makes it easier to maintain an overview once a project grows to a certain size.

A Maui.iOS application starts with Program.cs

Listing 6-1. The starting point of a MAUI iOS application

```
public class Program
{
    // This is the main entry point of the application.
    static void Main(string[] args)
    {
```

```
            UIApplication.Main(args, null, typeof(AppDelegate));
    }
}
```

Nothing exciting going on here, just a basic .NET application starting point. It calls into UIApplication.Main to start the application loop. The parameters passed into this method determine the actual starting point of the iOS application, AppDelegate in this case. Listing 6-2 shows the content of AppDelegate.cs.

Listing 6-2. iOS AppDelegate.cs

```
[Register("AppDelegate")]
public class AppDelegate : MauiUIApplicationDelegate
{
    protected override MauiApp CreateMauiApp() => MauiProgram.
    CreateMauiApp();
}
```

This is where things are starting to really get different from the classic Xamarin way of working. Instead of overriding the FinishedLaunching method and calling into Xamarin.Forms, from there we make sure that AppDelegate inherits from MauiUIApplicationDelegate and calls CreateMauiApp on the MauiProgram class included in the project. The other platforms work in a very similar way. Listing 6-3 shows the corresponding Android file.

Listing 6-3. Android MainApplication.cs

```
[Application]
public class MainApplication : MauiApplication
{
    public MainApplication(IntPtr handle, JniHandleOwnership ownership)
        : base(handle, ownership)
    {
    }

    protected override MauiApp CreateMauiApp() => MauiProgram.
    CreateMauiApp();
}
```

The base class is a different, Android-specific, one; and there is a constructor. That constructor is needed for Android to successfully launch the application. But we do see the same call to MauiProgram.CreateMauiApp.

All our target platforms call MauiProgram.CreateMauiApp() in their startup. This method initializes the cross-platform part of MAUI, while the platform-specific class initializes and bootstraps the application according to the platform. These startup classes can be found in their respective folder in the Platforms folder of your project. For Android, it's called MainApplication, while for iOS and MacOS it's AppDelegate, and for Windows it's App.xaml.cs.

All of these platform-specific classes inherit from a platform-specific Maui base class. This class is where FinishedLaunching moved to. Once the OS has bootstrapped and launched the app, this method fires and initializes the MAUI context. Besides FinishedLaunching, this class also handles all lifecycle events, for example, when the app is activated, moved to the background, terminated, and so on. We'll discuss app lifecycle more a bit further in this chapter.

The Cross-Platform World

Once the operating system has bootstrapped our app, we enter MAUI cross-platform space. MauiProgram.cs creates the MAUI context in a way which should look familiar; it's very similar to the Program.cs we have seen in other frameworks within .NET 6.

Listing 6-4. MauiProgram Startup class

```
public static class MauiProgram
{
    public static MauiApp CreateMauiApp()
    {
        var builder = MauiApp.CreateBuilder();
        builder
            .UseMauiApp<App>()
            .ConfigureFonts(fonts =>
            {
                fonts.AddFont("OpenSans-Regular.ttf",
                "OpenSansRegular");
            });
```

```
            return builder.Build();
    }
}
```

The CreateMauiApp method creates a builder. With that builder, we can set our startup object to the App class; keep in mind that at the point we reach this code, our application is already launched. We are now setting up the cross-platform world. We can use the builder for several other things like configuring external fonts that are packaged with the project, for example. Finally we call the Build method on the builder. From that moment on, control will be passed to the class defined as startup. Listing 6-5 shows the App class.

Listing 6-5. The Application class

```
public partial class App : Application
{
    public App()
    {
        InitializeComponent();

        MainPage = new MainPage();
    }
}
```

This is the part where we finally get into our own code. Everything is set up and bootstrapped, ready to go. InitializeComponent starts building the visual tree; next we instantiate a new instance of MainPage and set that as the current page. The Application base class contains a MainPage property; whatever page is set to that property is the one shown on screen. Things might get a bit confusing here since we are setting a property called MainPage with an instance of a class called MainPage.

Application Lifecycle

Applications go through different stages while running, stages like *starting, stopping, sleeping, and resuming*. These differ depending on the platform your app is running on. A mobile application will go to sleep once it's moved to the background to preserve battery; a WPF application, for example, will keep running even when minimized, choosing efficiency over battery life.

Why is this important to know, and use, as a developer? Consider you're building a mobile app. The app contains a registration form; one of your users is filling out the form and suddenly gets a call before being able to press the save button. A call pushes your app to the background, giving priority to the phone app. If this is a high-end device, the app might keep its data in the background, but the mobile operating system might decide that the app is taking up too many resources in the background and to remove it from memory while still keeping it in the open apps list. That's why, as a developer, you need to hook into the *pausing* event. We can use this event to temporarily store data, like the data already entered in the form, and resume that data when the *resuming* event fires.

Lifecycle events in MAUI are abstracted away from the platform. That means that there is a common API that will work over all platforms, but they have a different implementation under the hood. It also means that the common API is built mostly on top of structures that are available across all platforms. It's possible to break out of the shared layer and go into platform-specific code, should you need more fine-grained control of the lifecycle on a specific platform.

There are a number of lifecycle events available, on different parts of an application. The following *tables* Lifecycle events on application level (*Table 6-1*), Lifecycle events on window level (*Table 6-2*), Lifecycle events on page level (*Table 6-3*), and Lifecycle events on view level (*Table 6-4*) provide a complete list of the available lifecycle events at the time of writing.

Table 6-1. *Lifecycle events on application level*

Lifecycle event	Description
Creating	Fires after the operating system started to create the application in memory
Created	Fires when the application is created in memory, but before anything is rendered on-screen
Resuming	Resuming can fire on two occasions: after the *Created* event or when returning to the app from the background
Resumed	Current window has finished rendering; app is available for use
Pausing	Fires when the application is going into background mode
Paused	Fires when the application has gone into background mode
Stopping	Fires when a user closed the app
Stopped	Fires when the app finished closing

Table 6-2. *Lifecycle events on window level*

Lifecycle event	Description
Creating	Fires after the application has been created, but before the application window is created
Created	Fires after the application's native window has been created. The cross-platform window is available after this event, but nothing is rendering yet
Resuming	A bubble up event from Application.Resuming, giving us access to the *resuming* event from within a window, enabling specific actions per window
Resumed	A bubble up event from Application.Resumed, giving us access to the *resumed* event from within a window, enabling specific actions per window. Also fires whenever a window is being maximized after being minimized on desktop platforms
Pausing	A bubble up event from Application.Pausing, giving us access to the *pausing* event from within a window, enabling specific actions per window

(continued)

Table 6-2. (*continued*)

Lifecycle event	Description
Paused	A bubble up event from Application.Paused, giving us access to the *paused* event from within a window, enabling specific actions per window. Also fires whenever a window is being on desktop platforms
Stopping	Fires when a window is closing
Stopped	Fires when a window is closed

Table 6-3. *Lifecycle events on page level*

Lifecycle event	Description
NavigatingTo	Fires when a page is going to be navigated to and after *NavigatingFrom*
NavigatedTo	Fires when a page has been navigated to through a NavigationPage element
NavigatingFrom	Fires right before the *NavigatingTo* event
NavigatedFrom	Fires after *NavigatingTo*

Table 6-4. *Lifecycle events on view level*

Lifecycle event	Description
AttachingHandler	Fires before a view is created that attaches to the native handler
AttachedHandler	Fires after the native handler has set the view. After this all properties are initialized and ready for use
DetachingHandler	Fires before a view is being detached from a native platform handler
DetachedHandler	Fires after a view has been removed from the native handler
AttachingParent	Fires when a view is about to get connected to a cross-platform visual tree
AttachedParent	Fires when a parent is set on this view
DetachingParent	Fires when a parent is about to be removed from the view
DetachedParent	Fires when a parent is removed from the view

MVVM

Xamarin.Forms brought XAML into the cross-platform mobile world as an abstraction layer on top of the supported platforms their own UI stack. It's an XML-based layout and style engine that transform into platform-native elements at compile time by default. Just like the WPF XAML stack, it supports databinding, templating, resource dictionaries, and so on. This book is not a XAML guide, but MAUI has made some changes in the available design patterns for writing cross-platform apps, so I'll provide a high-level overview.

Model-View-ViewModel (MVVM) was introduced in 2005 by Microsoft architects Ken Cooper and Ted Peters. They developed a pattern that leveraged databinding to decouple data and logic from the view so that the view could be developed separately from the logic and so that the logic could be unit-tested without creating the entire visual tree.

MVVM consists of three layers:

- Model: the domain model

- View: the XAML pages that contain the visual aspects of the application

- ViewModel: the properties and commands that will be used on the view

The most important part is the ViewModel; you can compare it to a controller in MVC, but stateful. A ViewModel for a specific view gathers all the data the view needs, shapes it into bindable properties, and makes sure to react to property changes where needed. A view in MAUI has a `BindingContext` property which needs to contain a reference to the correct ViewModel, as shown in *Listing 6-6*.

Listing 6-6. Setting a BindingContext on a MAUI ContentPage

```
public MainPage()
{
    InitializeComponent();
    BindingContext = new MainViewModel();
}
```

From this moment on, all bindings that do not specify another BindingContext will turn to the MainViewModel class to resolve their bindings when requested.

Databinding in MAUI with XAML is the same as with Xamarin.Forms and quite similar to databinding in WPF (or Silverlight if you want to go way back). Let's look at an example using a ViewModel.

I've created a new project using the default MAUI XAML template. I've added a ViewModels folder and created a MainViewModel inside that folder. Listing 6-7 shows the created MainViewModel.

Listing 6-7. MainViewModel

```
public class MainViewModel
{
    private ICommand _increaseCountCommand;

    public int Count { get; private set; }
    public ICommand IncreaseCountCommand => _increaseCountCommand ??= new
    Command(IncreaseCount);

    private void IncreaseCount()
    {
        Count++;
    }
}
```

Let's start with Count; Count is a basic auto-property with a private set, nothing special there so far. It's a public property which means it's available to bind to. The datatype here is integer, but it can be anything, even complex objects. IncreaseCountCommand is an ICommand which is an abstraction of reacting on user actions. ICommand is an interface from the System.Windows namespace. It's used for exactly this use case in WPF, UWP, and every other XAML-based framework. The Command implementation however lives in the Microsoft.Maui assemblies. This way Microsoft is giving us a way to use familiar concepts, while under the covers, it is a brand new implementation. In this case, we will attach the IncreaseCountCommand to a button tap in a minute. We're using C# 8's null-coalescing assignment feature to assign an ICommand implementation. This means that when the property's getter is called, it will check for null and first assign the value if it is null; if not, it will return the value.

We could also initialize the command using the constructor as shown in Listing 6-8.

Listing 6-8. The same MainViewModel but with command initialization done in the constructor

```
public class MainViewModel
{
    public int Count { get; private set; }
    public ICommand IncreaseCountCommand { get; private set; }

    public MainViewModel()
    {
        IncreaseCountCommand = new Command(IncreaseCount);
    }

    private void IncreaseCount()
    {
        Count++;
    }
}
```

This works just the same, so where's the difference? When binding to an ICommand, the getter is only being called when the command is triggered. Meaning that a page will load, but the IncreaseCountCommand will not be initialized yet as long as the user does not tap the button. On a page with a lot of commands, this shaves of precious time of the viewmodel initialization; we're basically deferring initializing each command until it's needed for the first time.

In MainPage.xaml, we'll transform the basic example from the MAUI template into an MVVM example. We'll start by removing most of the code in MainPage.xaml.cs, as that logic now lives in the MainViewModel.

Listing 6-9. Cleaned up MainPage

```
public partial class MainPage : ContentPage
{
    public MainPage()
    {
        InitializeComponent();
```

```
        BindingContext = new MainViewModel();
    }
}
```

There are some parts we still need of course. Notice that this class is partial; the other part of the partial class is the XAML file itself. The XAML compiler transforms that XAML code into a partial C# class.

Do not remove InitializeComponent; this method call triggers the creation of all elements on page. This should typically be the first call in the constructor of a page. After that, we set the BindingContext; as mentioned before, this will bubble down to all elements on that page unless we specifically assign another BindingContext to an element.

In XAML, we need to change the label and the button to bind to the properties on our ViewModel. Listing 6-10 shows the label.

Listing 6-10. Label with binding

```
<Label
        Text="{Binding Count}"
        Grid.Row="2"
        FontSize="18"
        FontAttributes="Bold"
        x:Name="CounterLabel"
        HorizontalOptions="Center" />
```

Let's zoom into the binding; all other properties speak for themselves. A binding statement is always set between squiggly brackets. We use the Binding keyword to tell MAUI that we want to dynamically bind to a property on the BindingContext. Keep in mind that there is no IntelliSense here because we've set the BindingContext in C# land; the XAML editor does not know this. Since we're compiling our XAML code, we do get compile-time errors on typos. So, by putting Text="{Binding Count}" we're telling MAUI that we want the value of BindingContext.BindingProperty or in this case MainViewModel.Count to be put into the Text property of this label. Listing 6-11 shows the bindings for the Button.

Listing 6-11. Binding a command to a button

```
<Button
    Text="Click me"
    Command="{Binding IncreaseCountCommand}"
    FontAttributes="Bold"
    Grid.Row="3"
    SemanticProperties.Hint="Counts the number of times you click"
    HorizontalOptions="Center" />
```

For the button, we bind to its Command property. When the element's default action (Click or Tap in case of a button) is triggered, the system will try to cast the object bound to Command to an ICommand and trigger its Execute method. Note that it is possible to assign both a click event handler and a command to a button; both will fire if the button is tapped.

Let's try it out! Launch the app and you should see something similar to Figure 6-6 (your version might look different depending on the platform you're targeting).

Hello, World!

Welcome to .NET Multi-platform App UI

0

Click me

Figure 6-6. *Running the MVVM-based app*

Notice the "0" on top of the page? That's our databinding at work; the Count property has a default value of 0, and thanks to databinding, we see that value reflected on page. Click the button and you'll see that... nothing happens? Have we made a mistake? If you put a breakpoint in the IncreaseCount method in the MainViewModel, you'll see that it hits whenever we click the button, and the integer's value does increase, so why doesn't the new value show on the page? The answer is simple: the databinding system does not constantly monitor its BindingContext for changes; this would simply cost too many resources. Instead it trusts us as developers to tell it when a value changes so that it can refresh that property; this is done by using the `InotifyPropertyChanged` interface. We can implement this interface on our MainViewModel as shown in Listing 6-12.

Listing 6-12. Implementing INotifyPropertyChanged

```
Public class MainViewModel : InotifyPropertyChanged
{
    private int _count;
    private Icommand _increaseCountCommand;

    public int Count
    {
        get => _count;
        set
        {
            if (_count == value)
                return;

            _count = value;
            PropertyChanged?.Invoke(this, new PropertyChangedEventArgs
            (nameof(Count)));
        }
    }

    public Icommand IncreaseCountCommand => _increaseCountCommand ??= new
    Command(IncreaseCount);

    private void IncreaseCount()
    {
        Count++;
    }

    public event PropertyChangedEventHandler PropertyChanged;
}
```

INotifyPropertyChanged has one member, an event called PropertyChanged. That event takes the name of the property that just changed as a string parameter. We are using the nameof() method to prevent typing errors in magic strings. The nameof method gets replaced by the actual name of the member we pass in at compile time, so using this has no impact on the runtime performance. The binding framework listens for this event, takes the name of the property that just changed, looks for it in its bindings, and refreshes that specific binding. Triggering that event can happen wherever you need it; often it happens in a property's setter, like in this example. In the setter of Count, we first make sure that there really is a new value, to prevent unnecessary events firing. If the value really did change, we set the new value to the backing field of the property and trigger the event by calling its Invoke method. With this code in place, if we run the app again and tap the button, you will see the UI update whenever the property updates.

Hello, World!

Welcome to .NET Multi-platform App UI

3

Click me

Figure 6-7. *UI is updating*

MVVM Toolkit

MVVM can get a bit tedious to set up, implementing INotifyPropertyChanged everywhere and so on. To make this experience a bit simpler, Microsoft has released an MVVM Toolkit as part of its Windows Community Toolkit. The toolkit can be installed from NuGet.

Listing 6-13. Installing the MVVM Toolkit

```
Add-Package Microsoft.Toolkit.Mvvm
```

The MVVM Toolkit is based on MVVM Light by Laurent Bugnion. There's been quite some renaming and rethinking of what the API surface of the toolkit looks like. Let's look at a simple example: a master-detail app that lists some Apress books.

For the sake of the example, I've created a service that fetches a list of five books. The implementation of the service goes beyond the scope of this example; feel free to have a look in the source code that accompanies this book, but it's mostly hard coded data. The interface is shows in Listing 6-14.

Listing 6-14. The book service used in the example

```
public interface IBookService
{
    Task<BookForList[]> FetchAllBooks();
    Task<BookForDetail> FetchBookDetails();
}
```

We will use this sample service to build a viewmodel-backed page. We will start by creating the page. Add a new class to the ViewModels folder called BooksViewModel. Listing 6-15 shows the viewmodel.

Listing 6-15. BooksViewModel

```
public class BooksViewModel : ObservableObject
{
    private readonly IBookService _bookService;
    private ObservableCollection<BookForList> _books;

    public ObservableCollection<BookForList> Books
    {
        get => _books;
        set => SetProperty(ref _books, value);
    }

    public BooksViewModel(IBookService bookService)
    {
        _bookService = bookService;
        _ = LoadBooks();
    }

    private async Task LoadBooks()
    {
        BookForList[] books = await _bookService.FetchAllBooks();
        Books = new ObservableCollection<BookForList>(books);
    }
}
```

This viewmodel is using the MVVM Toolkit we have just installed. It inherits from `ObservableObject`, which is a base class that already implements `INotifyPropertyChanged` and gives us some helper methods to keep the code in our own viewmodel smaller. An example of this is the `SetProperty` method used in the `Books` property's setter. This method will check if the new value is different from the old one, set the new value, and fire the `PropertyChanged` event, something we did manually in the `MainViewModel`.

Few things to note in this class. We are using an ObservableCollection. This type of collection will fire a CollectionChanged event whenever an item is added or removed from the list. UI elements like a CollectionView in MAUI listen to this event and update their list whenever it fires.

In the constructor of the viewmodel, we see _ = `LoadBooks()`. This underscore is called a discardable in C#. Discardables are throw-away variables that you can assign a value to that you will never use. I am using a discardable here because we are calling an async method from the constructor. We cannot await it so the compiler will complain that we are not awaiting an async operation. By assigning the task to a discardable we clear that compiler warning.

Moving on to the view. Add a new `ContentPage` to the project. Listing 6-16 shows the code-behind.

Listing 6-16. Code-behind for BooksPage

```
public partial class BooksPage : ContentPage
{
    public BooksPage(BooksViewModel viewModel)
    {
        InitializeComponent();
        BindingContext = viewModel;
    }
}
```

The code-behind is quite empty. The most noteworthy thing here is that we are receiving our viewmodel through the constructor and setting it to the `BindingContext`. This will all get wired up through *dependency injection* in a minute.

Listing 6-17 shows the XAML for this page.

Listing 6-17. BooksPage XAML code

```xml
<ContentPage x:Class="MauiDemo.BooksPage"
        xmlns="http://schemas.microsoft.com/dotnet/2021/maui"
        xmlns:x="http://schemas.microsoft.com/winfx/2009/xaml">

    <CollectionView ItemsSource="{Binding Books}">
        <CollectionView.ItemTemplate>
            <DataTemplate>
                <Grid RowDefinitions="30, auto">
                    <Label FontSize="24" Text="{Binding Name}" />
                    <Label Grid.Row="1"
                            Text="{Binding Author}"
                            TextColor="Gray" />
                </Grid>
            </DataTemplate>
        </CollectionView.ItemTemplate>
    </CollectionView>
</ContentPage>
```

We are using a `CollectionView` in this page. In MAUI a `CollectionView` is an element that can show collections of data. By default, this is in a vertical list, but this can be changed to a horizontal list or even a grid layout. More information on the `CollectionView` can be found at `https://docs.microsoft.com/en-us/xamarin/xamarin-forms/user-interface/collectionview/`.

A `CollectionView` needs a template to know what an item in its collection should look like visually. An `ItemTemplate` is a property of type `DataTemplate`. This property contains a XAML snippet that gets inflated for every object in the collection. The bindings in the template have a single collection item as bindingcontext. The template is a grid with two rows; the first row has a height of 30 pixels; this will contain the book's title. The second row has a height of auto, meaning it will calculate its size based on its contents, in this case a label containing the author's name. The first label in the template does not have a property set to place it in a specific grid row, meaning it will default to the first row, or row index 0. The second one is using what is called an attached property to place it in the second row, or row index 1. Attached properties are properties that belong to a parent element but are set on a child.

173

Final piece of the puzzle is wiring everything up using the built-in dependency injection. We do this in *MauiProgram.cs*. Listing 6-18 shows its contents.

Listing 6-18. MauiProgram.cs

```
public static class MauiProgram
{
    public static MauiApp CreateMauiApp()
    {
        var builder = MauiApp.CreateBuilder();
        builder
            .UseMauiApp<App>()
            .ConfigureFonts(fonts =>
            {
                fonts.AddFont("OpenSans-Regular.ttf",
                "OpenSansRegular");
            });
        builder.Services.AddSingleton<BooksPage>();

        builder.Services.AddSingleton<BooksViewModel>();

        builder.Services.AddSingleton<IBookService, BookService>();

        return builder.Build();
    }
}
```

We have seen this class before, but now we have added some services. We are registering the pages, viewmodels, and services as singletons in our dependency injection system. Don't forget to add the `Microsoft.Extensions.DependencyInjection` namespace to get access to the Add* methods.

We are registering pages, viewmodels, and services as singletons, meaning that we will use one instance of each over the lifetime of the app.

The final step is changing App.xaml.cs to make use of dependency injection as well. Listing 6-19 shows the updated class.

Listing 6-19. Updated App.xaml.cs

```
public partial class App : Application
{
    public App(BooksPage page)
    {
        InitializeComponent();

        MainPage = page;
    }
}
```

The change we made here is that we are injecting the page we want to use as startup page in the constructor. That page is set to the MainPage property.

Let's list what will happen in order.

- The platform native application starts.

- MAUI gets bootstrapped.

- Pages, viewmodels, and services are registered.

- BooksPage gets created to inject in App.xaml.cs.

- BooksPage needs a BooksViewModel in its constructor so that is instantiated.

- BooksViewModel needs an IBookService in its constructor; IBookService is known in our DI system as the interface for BookService, so a new BookService is created and injected.

- The page loads and bindings are resolved on the viewmodel.

Figure 6-8 shows the result when running on Windows.

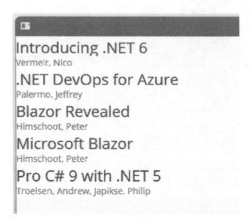

Figure 6-8. *Running MAUI MVVM application*

Wrapping Up

MAUI is the next iteration of Xamarin, Microsoft's native cross-platform framework. As
we have seen in this chapter, Microsoft is doing a lot of work to have a similar way of
working across all of .NET 6. This is clearly visible in the startup class when comparing
`MauiProgram` with `Program` in ASP.NET. Similar startup structure, the same built-in
dependency injection with ServiceCollection, and so on.

Next to unifying the way applications load across .NET, they have also greatly
simplified the project structure when compared with Xamarin Forms. Instead of
three projects in a brand new solution, we now have a single project structure. In that
structure, we have platform-specific folders for all supported platforms, iOS, Android,
MacOS through MacCatalyst, and Windows through WinUI 3.

CHAPTER 7

ASP.NET Core

ASP.NET is the successor of Active Server Pages or ASP. ASP was a classic server-side framework from Microsoft that was released in 1996. The first version of ASP.NET was released in 2002. It was, and still is, built on the .NET Framework CLR, allowing .NET developers to write web applications with .NET.

ASP.NET Core is a complete rewrite of ASP.NET meant to modernize the platform using the latest programming techniques. It greatly increased speed and ease-of-use. As of ASP.NET Core, the framework is open sourced; the source code can be found at `https://github.com/dotnet/aspnetcore`.

For the rest of this chapter, I will be using the term ASP.NET instead of ASP.NET Core. Remember when you read ASP.NET, I mean the latest .NET 6-based version.

Model-View-Controller

Model-View-Controller, or MVC, was first described in SmallTalk back in the 1970s. It did take until the late 1980s for the MVC pattern to be described in an article by which it started to gain adoption across languages. Today MVC is a well-known design pattern that has a default implementation in quite a lot of languages. Besides being well adopted, it also became the base of many other design patterns like Model-View-Presenter and Model-View-ViewModel. ASP.NET comes with its own implementation of the MVC pattern.

Just like with any framework within .NET, ASP.NET also ships with a couple of project types and templates. One of the most used templates is the Model-View-Controller, or MVC, template. The MVC template is built around the Model-View-Controller design pattern. The core strength of the MVC project template in ASP.NET lies in its great tooling, base classes, and convention-based way of working. But before we dive into the template itself, let's look at the design pattern.

© Nico Vermeir 2022
N. Vermeir, *Introducing .NET 6*, https://doi.org/10.1007/978-1-4842-7319-7_7

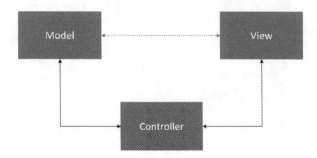

Figure 7-1. *The MVC pattern*

The MVC pattern consists of three building blocks: the view, the controller, and the model. By splitting an application into these blocks, we can separate the concerns of the applications and apply loose coupling. By doing this, we create a code base that is easier to read, easier to maintain, and easier to learn for developers who are new to the team.

- View: the view renders the UI to the user.

- Controller: the controller responds to user input and acts as the glue between the view and the model.

- Model: maintaining state, storing, and retrieving data.

Our view consists of HTML pages since we are developing web applications. HTML is still to this day a very static markup language that cannot understand data and how to shape it, unless modified by JavaScript libraries or when generated by server-side logic. That is where the controller layer comes into play. The controller takes data that was requested by the user, and it takes a form of HTML template that optionally contains some C#-based logic. The controller executes the logic contained in the template using the data as datasource; this is called inflating the template. The result is an HTML page with hard coded data. That snippet is sent back to the client and rendered in the browser.

Now that we know what the Model-View-Controller design pattern is about, let's explore how Microsoft implemented this in ASP.NET.

Figure 7-2 shows the different templates available for ASP.NET:

ASP.NET Core Web App

A project template for creating an ASP.NET Core application with example ASP.NET Razor Pages content.

| C# | Linux | macOS | Windows | Cloud | Service | Web |

ASP.NET Core Empty

An empty project template for creating an ASP.NET Core application. This template does not have any content in it.

| C# | Linux | macOS | Windows | Cloud | Service | Web |

ASP.NET Core Web App (Model-View-Controller)

A project template for creating an ASP.NET Core application with example ASP.NET Core MVC Views and Controllers. This template can also be used for RESTful HTTP services.

| C# | Linux | macOS | Windows | Cloud | Service | Web |

ASP.NET Core Web API

A project template for creating an ASP.NET Core application with an example Controller for a RESTful HTTP service. This template can also be used for ASP.NET Core MVC Views and Controllers.

| C# | Linux | macOS | Windows | Cloud | Service | Web |

***Figure 7-2.** ASP.NET Core templates*

ASP.NET offers different templates for different purposes, and there are many more than the ones we see here. Since we can't talk about all of them, we'll go over the Model-View-Controller, the Web API, and the minimal Web API templates. We'll start with ASP.NET Core Web App (Model-View-Controller). Visual Studio might also show ASP.NET templates without the Core moniker. These are the templates for the traditional .NET framework up to version 4.8; the templates for .NET Core, .NET 5, or .NET 6 are all called ASP.NET Core.

After selecting the ASP.NET Core Web App (Model-View-Controller) template, Visual Studio asks for some extra information. We can select the version of .NET to use, .NET 6 in this case. We can specify an authentication type; the options are None, Microsoft Identity Platform, or Windows. By default, None is selected, but when an option is selected for Authentication Type, the project will be bootstrapped with a login/registration system based on ASP.NET Identity. You can find more information

on that topic on `https://docs.microsoft.com/en-us/aspnet/core/security/`
`authentication/identity?view=aspnetcore-6.0&tabs=visual-studio`. Configure
for HTTPS is selected by default; this will add redirect logic so that all HTTP requests
are automatically redirected to HTTPS. Enable Docker adds a Docker file containing
everything needed to run this application in a Docker container. Both Windows and
Linux Docker containers are supported since .NET 6 also has a Linux runtime: `https://`
`docs.microsoft.com/en-us/dotnet/core/install/linux`.

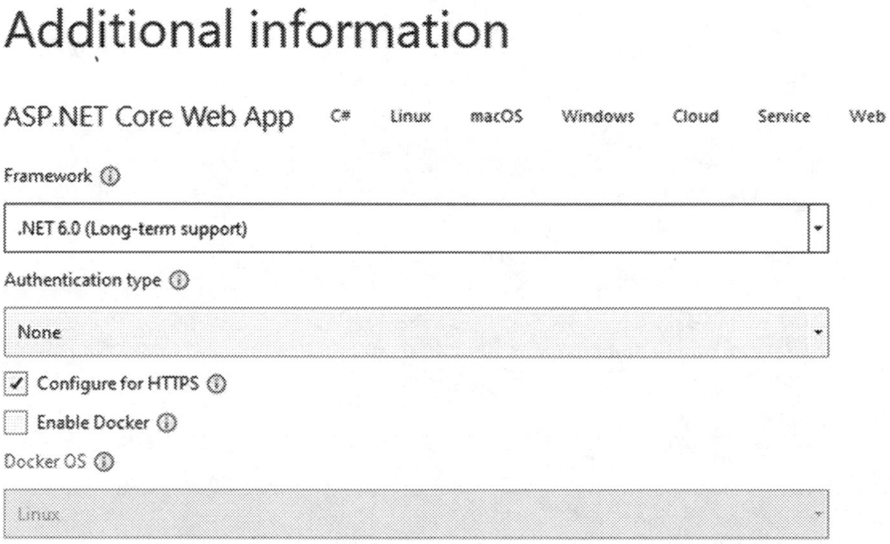

Additional information

ASP.NET Core Web App   C#   Linux   macOS   Windows   Cloud   Service   Web

Framework ⓘ

.NET 6.0 (Long-term support)

Authentication type ⓘ

None

☑ Configure for HTTPS ⓘ
☐ Enable Docker ⓘ
Docker OS ⓘ

Linux

Figure 7-3. *Project wizard*

After creating a project with all default settings, we get the project structure shown in
Figure 7-4.

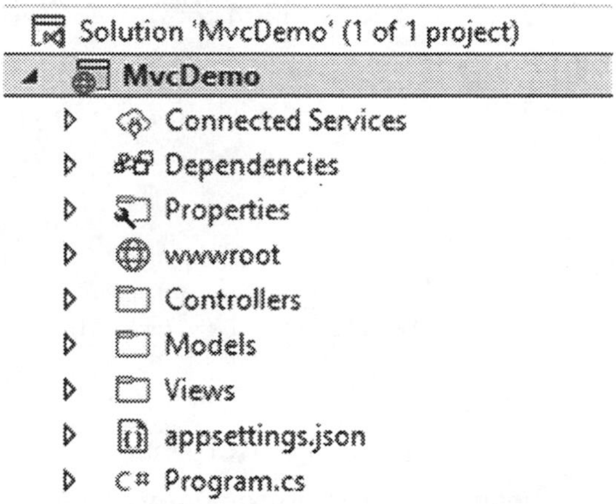

```
Solution 'MvcDemo' (1 of 1 project)
  MvcDemo
    ▷  Connected Services
    ▷  Dependencies
    ▷  Properties
    ▷  wwwroot
    ▷  Controllers
    ▷  Models
    ▷  Views
    ▷  appsettings.json
    ▷  C#  Program.cs
```

Figure 7-4. *MVC project*

The folder structure in the project clearly shows the Model-View-Controller structure. We'll go over the project folder by folder but just like with every .NET 6 project, everything starts with Program.cs.

Program.cs is another top-level class. Just like before, we are using implicit usings and top-level statements, new features in C#10. It combines what used to be two methods in previous versions of ASP.NET, `Configure` and `ConfigureServices`. Not only that, but it also combines Startup.cs and Program.cs, no more trying to remember what goes where. The entire application startup and configuration happens in these less than 30 lines of code.

Listing 7-1. Configuring the WebApplication builder

```
var builder = WebApplication.CreateBuilder(args);

// Add services to the container.
builder.Services.AddControllersWithViews();

var app = builder.Build();
```

The first part of the class is what used to be Program.cs. It configures a `WebApplicationBuilder`. A `WebApplicationBuilder` is a factory for creating a `WebApplication` instance; a `WebApplication` contains the pipeline and routing configuration for the running application. ASP.NET Core comes with a lot of helper methods to get everything up and running fast; one of those is `AddControllersWithViews`. This method registers all MVC controllers and views in the built-in Inversion of Control (IoC) container. Methods like this that help configure the application are usually extension methods on `IServiceCollection` or `IApplicationBuilder`. Listing 7-2 shows the signature of the `AddControllersWithViews` method.

Listing 7-2. AddControllersWithViews method

```
public static IMvcBuilder AddControllersWithViews(this IServiceCollection services)
```

The IServiceCollection is the Inversion of Control mechanism in .NET 6 and lives in the `Microsoft.Extensions.DependencyInjection` namespace.

After the `AddControllersWithViews` call where we can register dependencies ourselves, we will dive into an example soon but for now we keep everything default. The final thing that happens is calling the `Build` method on the `WebApplicationBuilder`; this will create the `WebApplication` instance.

Now that the WebApplication is configured, we are ready to configure the HTTP request pipeline.

ASP.NET Core works with a pipeline. Every request that comes in gets routed through a series of connected middleware systems that we call a pipeline. The middlewares pass the request forward until it reaches the end of the pipeline or gets short-circuited by a middleware. Once it reaches the end, the result is passed back through the pipeline the other way around. Once finished, the request is handled and the result passed back to the user. Examples of these middlewares are authentication, authorization, routing, and so on.

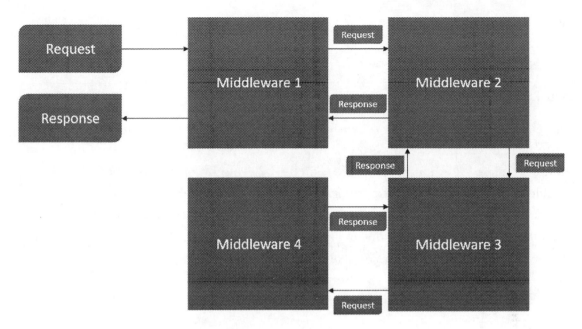

Figure 7-5. *HTTP Request pipeline*

Listing 7-3 shows the default pipeline configuration in an MVC project.

Listing 7-3. Pipeline configuration

```
// Configure the HTTP request pipeline.
if (!app.Environment.IsDevelopment())
{
    app.UseExceptionHandler("/Home/Error");
    // The default HSTS value is 30 days. You may want to change this for
    production scenarios, see https://aka.ms/aspnetcore-hsts.
    app.UseHsts();
}

app.UseHttpsRedirection();
app.UseStaticFiles();

app.UseRouting();

app.UseAuthorization();
```

```
app.MapControllerRoute(
    name: "default",
    pattern: "{controller=Home}/{action=Index}/{id?}");

app.Run();
```

The first configuration is configuring the default exception page, but only when not running in development. This is an example of where we use middleware components in the pipeline. Whether or not we are running in development mode depends on the profile we use for launching the application. In our MVC project is a *Properties* folder containing *a launchsettings.json* file. This file holds the configuration for every profile. By default there are two profiles, one to launch our application using IIS and one for Kestrel. These profiles are reflected in Visual Studio's Debug target selector.

Listing 7-4. Profile configuration

```
"MvcDemo": {
  "commandName": "Project",
  "dotnetRunMessages": true,
  "launchBrowser": true,
  "applicationUrl": "https://localhost:7033;http://localhost:5033",
  "environmentVariables": {
    "ASPNETCORE_ENVIRONMENT": "Development"
  }
}
```

As you can see in Listing 7-4, we can set whatever value we want to the ASPNETCORE_ENVIRONMENT variable. "Development" is by convention the value used when running locally. When running or debugging locally, we usually want to see the stack trace when an unexpected exception occurs, but when running on a deployed environment we want to hide that information from our users, hence the difference in registering error handlers.

After setting the exception handler, we configure HTTP Strict Transport Security, or HSTS when not in development. HSTS is an optional security enhancement. It adds a specific response header to a web application. The browser sending requests to that application will receive the header; from that moment on, all traffic will happen over HTTPS without the possibility to use untrusted or invalid certificates. By using HSTS, we can effectively prevent man-in-the-middle attacks since traffic can no longer be intercepted by using an invalid certificate. The default template only enables HSTS when not running in development; that is because when we want to debug an ASP. NET application, we use a development certificate that HSTS would deem invalid. After configuring environment-specific options, we enable HTTPS redirection by calling `app.UseHttpsRedirection`, meaning that all requests sent to HTTP will automatically redirect to HTTPS. UseStaticFiles enables the web server to serve files without trying to interpret them, not calling this method means that the web server will interpret everything and won't be able to serve static files. UseRouting enables the routing system, more about that in the next section. UseAuthorization allows us to secure specific pieces of the application by hiding it behind a login system; we have mentioned ASP.NET Identity in the beginning of the chapter. More information can be found here `https:// docs.microsoft.com/en-us/aspnet/core/security/authentication/identity?view =aspnetcore-6.0&tabs=visual-studio`. MapControllerRoute sets the default route; we can add more routes here if needed. And finally we run the application to execute the request. The pipeline is now configured, and every request that comes in will be piped through the pipeline before being executed. Keep in mind that the order we configure the middleware components is exactly the order they will be executed in whenever a request passes through the pipeline.

Routing

As mentioned before, ASP.NET MVC works by convention; this is particularly visible in the routing system. Routing is not done on a file bases as it is in default HTML; instead, it is done by the concept of controllers and actions. Listing 7-3 showed us a default routing path; Listing 7-5 repeats that path.

Listing 7-5. Mapping a route

```
app.MapControllerRoute(
    name: "default",
    pattern: "{controller=Home}/{action=Index}/{id?}");
```

This is the default routing set bij ASP.NET, but we are always free to change it when needed. For now let's keep it at default. Let's take `https://localhost:5001/Employees/ Detail/5` as an example. When routing this URL into our ASP.NET MVC application, it will break it apart and try to map it onto a controller route. The route called "default" is the one it will usually try, unless we specify a specific one. The pattern in the route breaks into three parts, controller/action/optional id. If we look at the URL, passed the base address, we also notice three parts, Employees/Detail/5. The route will map Employees as a controller, meaning it will search for an EmployeesController class. It will do this because, by convention, a controller ends in "Controller." The second part is the action, in our case Detail. The system will look for a public function called Detail that returns an IActionResult and lives in the EmployeesController. Finally, because we pass in an id, the Detail method also needs to accept a parameter. Figure 7-6 shows the code for our Detail method and that the parameter of the method gets filled in through the routing system. We are getting an integer into our parameter; note that this is not a nullable int even though it looks like one in the routing template. Marking it with a question mark in the routing template just means that it is optional; the methods receiving the parameter do not need to match the optional or nullable notation; as long as the datatype matches, we should be fine.

```
public class Employees : Controller
{
    0 references
    public IActionResult Detail(int id)    id = 5
    {                                    id    5
        return View();    ≤8.599ms elapsed
    }
}
```

Figure 7-6. *Parameter passed from url to variable*

From here, the matching view is found and inflated and passed back to the user in the form of HTML.

Views

The views in an MVC scenario are the actual pages that a user gets to see on his monitor. In ASP.NET, views are built using an HTML-like syntax called Razor. Figure 7-7 shows the views in a default ASP.NET MVC template.

Figure 7-7. *Views in ASP.NET MVC*

Another one of ASP.NET MVC's conventions dictates that for every controller, there is
a folder containing its views. By default, we get a HomeController, so we also get a Home
folder containing the views. Views are files with the *.cshtml, or *.vbhtml extensions,
depending on the language we are using to write the application in. The Shared folder
contains components that are reused across multiple views. Those shared components
are usually prefixed with an underscore.

Razor works with master layouts; the default one is in the Shared folder and is
called _Layout.cshtml. In the _Layout.cshtml file, we can declare our root html element,
include the necessary CSS and JS files, and set up the navigation and structure of our
application. In .NET 6, the ASP.NET team has also added scoped CSS files, meaning that
the _Layout.cshtml file looks like it has a sort of code-behind file in the tree structure
visible in the Solution Explorer in Visual Studio. This is a partial CSS file where the styles
defined are only applied to the content of the file they are attached to. Adding a scoped
CSS file to a cshtml file is as simple as creating a new CSS file with the same name as the
cshtml file. Somewhere in the layout file you can find the snippet shown in Listing 7-6.

Listing 7-6. Rendering the body of the application

```
<div class="container">
    <main role="main" class="pb-3">
        @RenderBody()
    </main>
</div>
```

Razor might look like generic HTML but we can add .NET code to it by prefixing a one line statement with an @ or an entire code block with @{ //code here }. The @RenderBody method is the place where your Razor views will be rendered inside of the template. Putting some labels around the RenderBody method shows exactly what I mean.

Listing 7-7. Labels around RenderBody

```
<main role="main" class="pb-3">
    <h2>My Components</h2>
    @RenderBody()
    <h2>/My Components</h2>
</main>
```

MvcDemo   Home   Privacy

My Components

Welcome

Learn about building Web apps with ASP.NET Core.

/My Components

Figure 7-8. *Rendering components in the template*

As you can tell from the placement of the h2 elements, it really is only the actual content that comes from the different views. The general styling and layout of the application is done from the main layout file. Listing 7-8 shows the default Index.cshtml view. This is the Index.cshtml file in the Home folder.

Listing 7-8. Home/Index view

```
@{
    ViewData["Title"] = "Home Page";
}

<div class="text-center">
    <h1 class="display-4">Welcome</h1>
    <p>Learn about <a href="https://docs.microsoft.com/aspnet/
    core">building Web apps with ASP.NET Core</a>.</p>
</div>
```

The default home component does little more than welcome the user to the application and link to the ASP.NET documentation. But, it does start with a code block setting a value in the ViewData. ViewData is a specific sort of typed dictionary that can transfer data for a specific model type from the controller to the view, but not the other way around. It lives for the duration for the request; for any next requests, new ViewData instances are created. In this example, we are setting the KeyValue pair with key "Title" to what we want to be the title of this page. We do want that value to be reflected in the main layout, in the Title tag. All of this ViewData code then gets executed when a controller method is creating an HTML response to a request. Remember that ASP.NET MVC always creates the entire page as a response, and while creating the static HTML for a page, the system has time to evaluate all the ViewData logic.

Listing 7-9. Rendering the title through ViewData in _Layout.cshtml

```
<head>
    <meta charset="utf-8" />
    <meta name="viewport" content="width=device-width, initial-scale=1.0" />
    <title>@ViewData["Title"] - MvcDemo</title>
    <link rel="stylesheet" href="~/lib/bootstrap/dist/css/bootstrap.
    min.css" />
    <link rel="stylesheet" href="~/css/site.css" asp-append-version="true" />
</head>
```

The rest of Index.cshtml is basic HTML code; we'll go through some more exciting views in a minute.

Controllers

Controllers are the glue in an MVC application; they are the connector between the data and the view. As we have seen, the routing system brings us from a url straight into a controller method. In general, that method will load data from somewhere, optionally using any parameters passed into the method; it will inflate a view, execute all .NET code in that Razor view so that we end up with static generated HTML code, and send that back to the user. ASP.NET is a client-server framework; all .NET-based logic is executed on a server, and only the result, in the shape of HTML, is sent back to the client. This is simply because browsers do not understand .NET by default. Silverlight fixed this by installing an add-in in browsers so they could run compiled .NET code, but the add-in

189

system is not ideal in today's world of mobile browsers and devices. The next best thing is running the code on the server and sending only the result back. In short, it is very important to realize that everything in ASP.NET MVC runs on the server; only the result of a request, which is generated HTML code based on Razor files, is sent back to the client.

Let's go through the flow of creating a new controller, method, and view to clear up how MVC and its built-in tooling work. We'll build a controller for the Apress book collection.

First we start with the model. Listing 7-10 shows the Book class.

Listing 7-10. The Book class

```
public class Book
{
    public Book(int id, string title, string description, string author)
    {
        Id = id;
        Title = title;
        Description = description;
        Author = author;
    }

    public int Id { get; set; }
    public string Title { get; set; }
    public string Description { get; set; }
    public string Author { get; set; }
}
```

We're keeping things pretty basic for sake of the example. I've created a dummy BookCatalogService that returns a hardcoded list of books. We won't go into the code for that specific service, but if you are interested you can find it on the book's GitHub repository. For now it is just important to know that the service is registered in ASP.NET's DI container by calling `builder.Services.AddSingleton<IBookCatalogService, BookCatalogService>()` in Program.cs. Now that we have our data source and DI setup, it's time to add the controller. A controller is a class that inherits from Controller. Keep in mind that we are registering the service as singleton so that we can abuse it as an in-memory datastore.

Be very careful with this in real applications; singleton means not only that you will get the same instance every time but that same instance is also shared across all your users.

Listing 7-11. The BookController

```
public class BookController : Controller
{
    private readonly IBookCatalogService _bookCatalogService;

    public BookController(IBookCatalogService bookCatalogService)
    {
        _bookCatalogService = bookCatalogService;
    }

    public async Task<IActionResult> Index()
    {
        Book[] books = await _bookCatalogService.FetchBookCatalog();
        return View(books);
    }
}
```

Listing 7-11 shows the implementation of the BookController. The constructor takes the dummy BookCatalogService as a parameter. The parameter will be filled in by ASP. NET's ServiceCollection. The Index method fetches an array of books from the service and passes that array into a method called View.

The method called Index will be called by ASP.NET MVC's routing system when we navigate to https://<url>:<port>/book. In case you are wondering why we don't have to specify Index in the url, that is because Index is set as the default action when no action is provided.

Listing 7-12. Setting the route defaults in Program.cs

```
app.MapControllerRoute(
    name: "default",
    pattern: "{controller=Home}/{action=Index}/{id?}");
```

The `View` method that is called in the `Index` method comes from the `Controller` base class. It is used to select the correct view, depending on the name of the controller and the action method, and inflate it.

Now that we have a controller, it is time to add a view. Visual Studio provides tooling to easily add views. Adding a view can be done through right-clicking the call to `View` and selecting *Add View*.

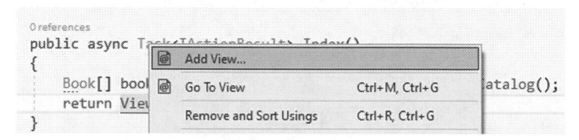

Figure 7-9. *Adding a view through tooling*

Second step is selecting what type of view we want to generate, an empty Razor View or a scaffolded one. Scaffolding in ASP.NET is done by the *Microsoft.VisualStudio. Web.CodeGeneration.Design* NuGet package. The first time you launch a scaffolding command in Visual Studio this package will get added to the project. With scaffolding, we can easily generate entire parts of the application, from controller to view, including all the actions and even database operations. We will select the *Razor View* template. A dialog pops up where we can specify what model class we want to generate a view for, what it should be called, and what template to use. The name for the view is prefilled with the same name of the method we were just working on; the template is basically a list of basic create–read–update–delete or CRUD screens that we can take as a base for our view. Figure 7-10 shows the settings that we used for this example.

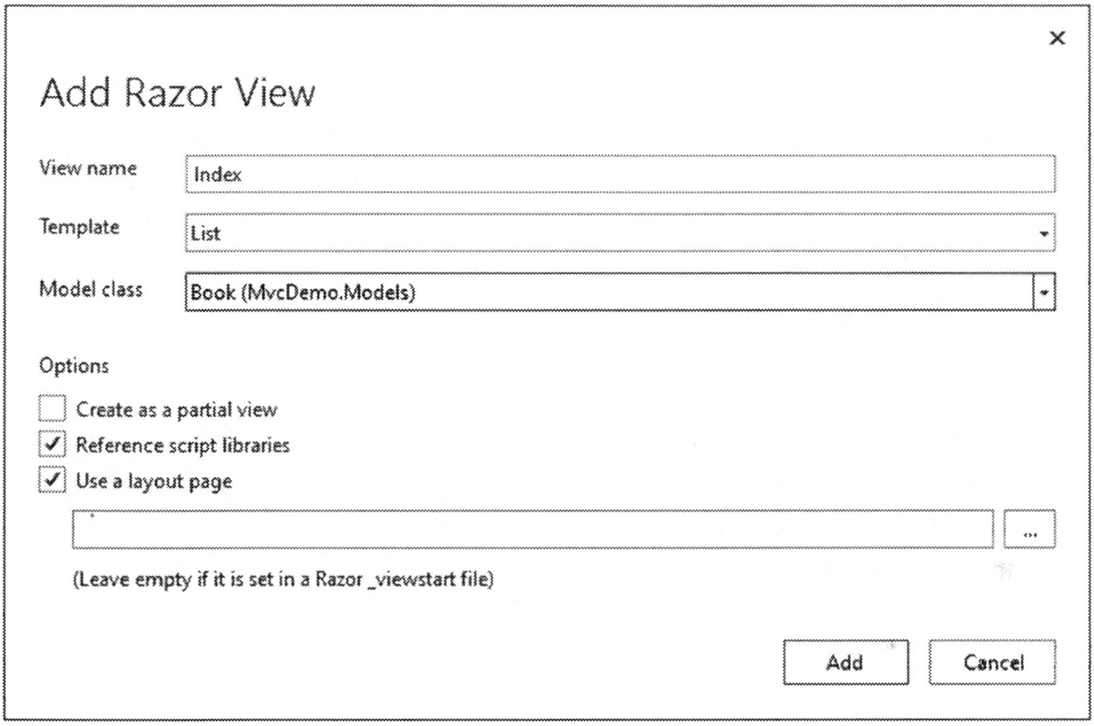

Add Razor View   ✕

View name | Index |

Template | List   ▾ |

Model class | Book (MvcDemo.Models)   ▾ |

Options

☐ Create as a partial view
☑ Reference script libraries
☑ Use a layout page

| | ... |

(Leave empty if it is set in a Razor _viewstart file)

                                      Add   Cancel

Figure 7-10. *Scaffolding a view using a template*

When scaffolding is done, you will notice a new folder in the Views folder called Book, containing an Index.cshtml file.

Listing 7-13. Model declaration and ASP tags

```
@model IEnumerable<MvcDemo.Models.Book>

@{
    ViewData["Title"] = "Index";
}

<h1>Index</h1>

<p>
    <a asp-action="Create">Create New</a>
</p>
```

Listing 7-13 shows the top of the generated page. A Razor view can specify a model class, in this case an `IEnumerable` of Book. I would advise to switch from IEnumerable to a more specific interface as soon as possible, since having it as an IEnumerable has no added value whatsoever. In this case we can go with an `ICollection<Book>` if we wanted to. With this model attribute set, we get access to a property called `Model`, which is of the type we just specified using the `model` attribute. The anchor tag contains an asp-action attribute. It is not the default HTML anchor tag; in this case, it is an ASP.NET tag helper, an extension of existing HTML tags. The asp-action attribute takes the name of a controller action and transforms that into a correct url using the routing system in ASP.NET MVC.

The generated view is meant to be a list of books. In the Razor view template, this is an HTML table. But tables are static, just like HTML is. Using Razor we can, on the server, generate all static HTML and send it back to the client. Listing 7-14 shows how it is done for a table. As I just mentioned, we get a `Model` property that is an `IEnumerable<Book>`; we can loop over that `IEnumerable` and generate a table row for every book in the collection.

Listing 7-14. Generating a table in Razor

```
@foreach (var item in Model) {
        <tr>
            <td>
                @Html.DisplayFor(modelItem => item.Id)
            </td>
            <td>
                @Html.DisplayFor(modelItem => item.Title)
            </td>
            <td>
                @Html.DisplayFor(modelItem => item.Description)
            </td>
            <td>
                @Html.DisplayFor(modelItem => item.Author)
            </td>
            <td>
                @Html.ActionLink("Edit", "Edit", new { /* id=item.
                PrimaryKey */ }) |
```

```
            @Html.ActionLink("Details", "Details", new { /* id=item.
            PrimaryKey */ }) |
            @Html.ActionLink("Delete", "Delete", new { /* id=item.
            PrimaryKey */ })
        </td>
    </tr>
}
```

For the book information, we use the Html.DisplayFor tag helper. This helper generates HTML content based on the model property we specify using a lambda. The generated HTML from DisplayFor is based on a default template that could be overwritten if needed, but that goes beyond the scope of this book. The Razor template also specifies action links to edit or delete the book or to load the details of a specific book. Those links are generated using Html.ActionLink, which is quite similar to the ASP.NET anchor TagHelper we just saw. An action link takes in a label that it will show on the actual page, a controller action, and an optional controller name for when the action we want to execute is in another controller than the one this view is linked to and some optional parameters like, for example, the id of the entity we want to delete. In the generated view code, the id is not set in the route values as the system can't decide for us what the unique identifier is. There is commented code in the *Details* and *Delete* links that we can use to set our id.

Let's have a look at the result of the generated page.

Index

Create New

Id	Title	Description	Author	
1	.NET DevOps for Azure	A Developer's Guide to DevOps Architecture the Right Way	Palermo, Jeffrey	Edit | Details | Delete
2	Pro .NET Memory Management	For Better Code, Performance, and Scalability	Kokosa, Konrad	Edit | Details | Delete
3	Design Patterns in C#	A Hands-on Guide with Real-world Examples	Sarcar, Vaskaran	Edit | Details | Delete
4	Beginning Azure Functions	Building Scalable and Serverless Apps	Sawhney, Rahul	Edit | Details | Delete
5	Azure and Xamarin Forms	Cross Platform Mobile Development	Fustino, Russell	Edit | Details | Delete

Figure 7-11. *The generated list view*

The generated Razor view uses the default CSS from the ASP.NET MVC template and looks rather nice. We get a good looking table, nicely listing our books and showing the generated actions. Do note that the scaffolding does not include any logic to hide primary keys or IDs from the user. So always adjust the scaffolded code to hide that information. In our case the first column in the table is the book IDs, that is, internal information that should not be leaked on screen.

Listing data on screen is quite easy; we only need to pull data from the datastore, shape it according to what we need on screen, and display it. There is a bit more work involved if we want to edit or create data. For example, let's create the logic to add extra books to the list.

We'll start by adding two methods to the BookController. We need two methods this time, one to prepare a book instance to ready the fields on the create form and one to actually receive the entered data and store it in our data store.

Listing 7-15. Creating a new Book

```
[HttpGet]
public IActionResult Create()
{
    return View(new Book());
}

[HttpPost]
public async Task<IActionResult> Create(Book book)
{
    await _bookCatalogService.AddBook(book);
    return RedirectToAction("Index");
}
```

Both methods have the same name, but they have different purposes. The Create method without parameters is the one that will be called to open the form in the application. It is decorated with an HttpGet attribute, telling the MVC pipeline that this method can only be reached with a GET request. GET is the default for controller actions in MVC; however, I like to explicitly decorate the method in this case to avoid confusion. The second Create method is decorated with the HttpPost attribute so that it will only be reached via a POST method that will receive the data entered on the form. Since our form is in the shape of a book, data-wise, the ASP.NET MVC pipeline can safely bind the received value to a Book instance. If we inspect the request, we can see that the only thing that is going over the wire is basic HTML form data.

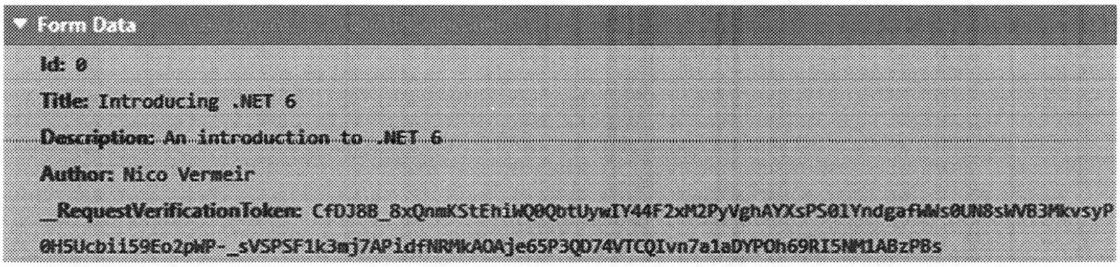

▼ Form Data
Id: 0
Title: Introducing .NET 6
Description: An introduction to .NET 6
Author: Nico Vermeir
_RequestVerificationToken: CfDJ8B_8xQnmKStEhiWQ0QbtUywIY44F2xM2PyVghAYXsPS01YndgafWWs0UN8sWVB3MkvsyP
0H5Ucbii59Eo2pWP-_sVSPSF1k3mj7APidfNRMkAOAje65P3QD74VTCQIvn7a1aDYPOh69RI5NM1ABzPBs

***Figure 7-12.** Inspecting a create request*

As you can see, the data going over the wire is in the shape of a book, but there is no notice of it being a book. The `_RequestVerificationToken` is an extra security token added by ASP.NET to verify that the received data on the server was not manipulated by a man-in-the-middle attack.

If we inspect the `POST Create` method, we can see that the parameter is filled in with an instance of `Book`, containing all the values we just entered on the form.

Create(Book book)
book = {Book}
book
{MvcDemo.Models.Book}
Book(book);
x");
Author
View
"Nico Vermeir"
Description
View
"An introduction to .NET 6"
Id
0
Title
View
"Introducing .NET 6"

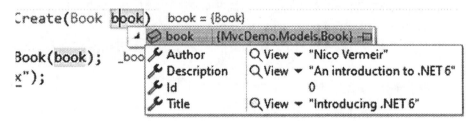

***Figure 7-13.** Parsed data in the controller method*

In a real application, we of course need to do data validation before storing the data in the datastore. For the sake of the demo, we can assume that this validation happens in the service. Once the book is added in the datastore, we redirect from the `Create` action to the `Index` action so that we end up on the list of books, including our freshly created book.

Once again, we can let ASP.NET generate a view for us. This time we are selecting the *Create* template. I have already removed the entry for ID since we are not allowing our users to choose their own primary keys.

Listing 7-16. Generated Create form

```
<form asp-action="Create">
    <div asp-validation-summary="ModelOnly" class="text-danger"></div>
    <div class="form-group">
        <label asp-for="Title" class="control-label"></label>
        <input asp-for="Title" class="form-control" />
        <span asp-validation-for="Title" class="text-danger"></span>
    </div>
    <div class="form-group">
        <label asp-for="Description" class="control-label"></label>
        <input asp-for="Description" class="form-control" />
        <span asp-validation-for="Description" class="text-danger"></span>
    </div>
    <div class="form-group">
        <label asp-for="Author" class="control-label"></label>
        <input asp-for="Author" class="form-control" />
        <span asp-validation-for="Author" class="text-danger"></span>
    </div>
    <div class="form-group">
        <input type="submit" value="Create" class="btn btn-primary" />
    </div>
</form>
```

A form is a basic HTML form containing an action where the data in the form can be posted to. We are once again using ASP.NET taghelpers to generate the correct url based on controller and action names. For every property we want our users to fill in, three elements are generated, one that serves as the label. By default, the property name is shown as label but this can be overwritten. The second element is the actual input field; ASP.NET's source generation will try to pick the correct input field based on the datatype. For a string we'll get a text field, Boolean will give us a checkbox and so on. The third element is a placeholder for when client-side validation fails. Figure 7-14 shows the form with failed validations.

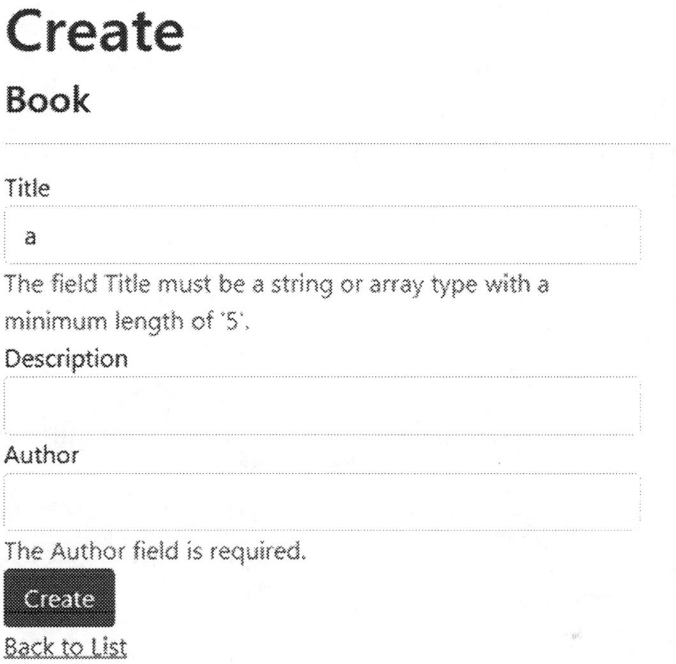

Create

Book

Title

```
a
```

The field Title must be a string or array type with a
minimum length of '5'.

Description

Author

The Author field is required.

Create

Back to List

Figure 7-14. *Failed validations*

So, where are these validations coming from? There are some basic validations based on datatype such as fields being required if they are not nullable. However, in this case, I have added validation rules directly on the Book class using data annotations from the System.ComponentModel.DataAnnotations namespace. Listing 7-17 shows these data annotations, together with a way to make the validation error message a bit more user-friendly instead of bombarding our users with terms like *string* and *array*.

Listing 7-17. Book class with validation rules

```
public class Book
{
    public Book(int id, string title, string description, string author)
    {
        Id = id;
        Title = title;
        Description = description;
        Author = author;
    }
```

```
    public int Id { get; set; }

    [MinLength(5, ErrorMessage = "The title needs to have at least 5
    characters")]
    public string Title { get; set; }

    public string? Description { get; set; }

    [Required]
    public string Author { get; set; }
}
```

Using data annotations, we can specify required fields, minimum and maximum length, and much more.

The rest of the operations that can be generated by ASP.NET work in a very similar way so we won't go into any more detail here. Instead, let's have a look at another member of the ASP.NET family.

Web API

ASP.NET WebAPI is Microsoft's version of a REST-based service. API is an industry term that stands for Application Programming Interface. In short, an API provides endpoints that, instead of HTML, return just a set of data. The collection of endpoints that provide data we call a contract. WebAPI is a RESTful API, meaning that it conforms to a set of guidelines. The term guidelines is very important here. REST is not set in stone, the rules of a REST service are not enforced in any way, and it is up to the developer to comply to the guidelines according to their skills and needs. ASP.NET WebAPI provides us with a set of helper methods and classes to guide us through the guidelines of REST to help us provide an API that complies to the guidelines as much as possible.

Before .NET 6, WebAPI was largely based on the MVC principle. We had models and controllers, but no view. Instead of inflating an HTML template and returning HTML, the controllers took the data, serialized them into JSON, and returned that. It gave us a very familiar way to build RESTful services. Meanwhile, the world of APIs evolved, and setting up a quick and easy API to consume some data became very easy in technologies like NodeJS but was often found bloated and involved in ASP.NET WebAPI. To counter this, the .NET team introduced minimal APIs in .NET 6. Figure 7-15 shows both a default WebAPI project next to a minimal API project to show the difference in project structure.

```
▲  📰 MinimalApiDemo
   ▷  ☁ Connected Services
   ▷  ⚙ Dependencies
   ▷  🗔 Properties
   ▷  🗍 appsettings.json
   ▷  C# Program.cs
▲  📰 WebApiDemo
   ▷  ☁ Connected Services
   ▷  ⚙ Dependencies
   ▷  🗔 Properties
   ▲  📁 Controllers
      ▷   C# WeatherForecastController.cs
   ▷  🗍 appsettings.json
   ▷  C# Program.cs
   ▷  C# WeatherForecast.cs
```

Figure 7-15. *Minimal API vs. WebApi*

As you can tell, the minimal APIs are, well, more minimal. The entire API, which consists of one demo call in the default template, is set in Program.cs. Before we dig deeper into minimal APIs, let's start with the traditional WebAPI project.

Controller-Based APIs

The type of project that you end up with depends on a specific checkbox during project creation. The project type we need is *ASP.NET Core Web API*. Once selected, we get a popup similar to the one we got when creating an ASP.NET MVC application.

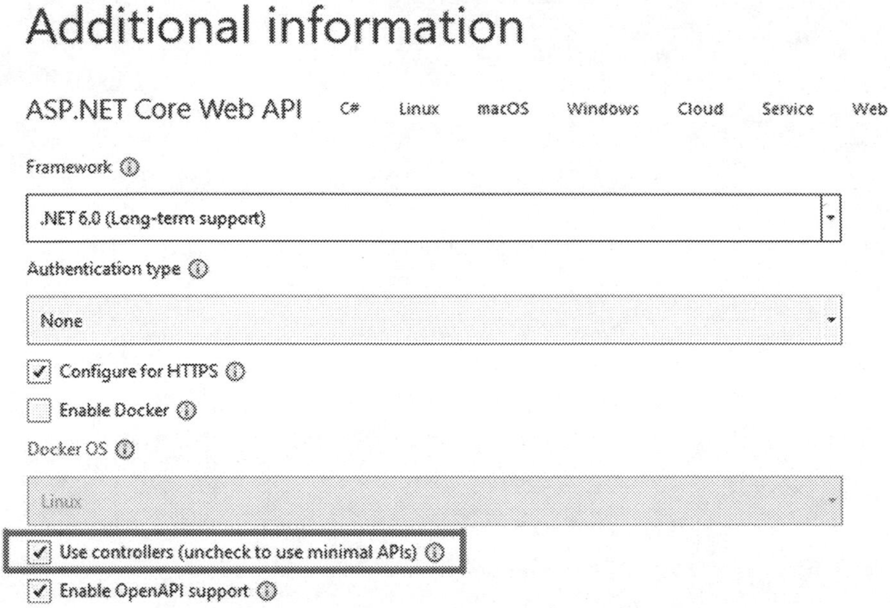

Additional information

ASP.NET Core Web API   C#   Linux   macOS   Windows   Cloud   Service   Web

Framework ⓘ

| .NET 6.0 (Long-term support) | ▾ |

Authentication type ⓘ

| None | ▾ |

☑ Configure for HTTPS ⓘ

☐ Enable Docker ⓘ

Docker OS ⓘ

| Linux | ▾ |

☑ Use controllers (uncheck to use minimal APIs) ⓘ

☑ Enable OpenAPI support ⓘ

Figure 7-16. *Creating a new WebAPI project*

Figure 7-16 shows the checkbox that will determine whether or not we end up with a minimal API project. By checking that we want to use controllers, we end up with an MVC-like template, except for the views. Listing 7-18 shows a snippet from the demo controller that is part of the template.

Listing 7-18. API controller

```
[ApiController]
[Route("[controller]")]
public class WeatherForecastController : ControllerBase
{
    [HttpGet(Name = "GetWeatherForecast")]
    public IEnumerable<WeatherForecast> Get()
    {
        return Enumerable.Range(1, 5).Select(index => new WeatherForecast
            {
                Date = DateTime.Now.AddDays(index),
                TemperatureC = Random.Shared.Next(-20, 55),
```

```
            Summary = Summaries[Random.Shared.Next(Summaries.Length)]
        })
        .ToArray();
}
```

Our REST controller inherits from `ControllerBase`; an MVC controller inherits from `Controller`, which in turn inherits from `ControllerBase`. So both flavors of ASP.NET are using the same base classes. The difference is that the Controller class from MVC inflates the HTML templates, something we do not need in WebAPI, so there is no need for an extra layer in between.

REST controllers are decorated with the ApiController attribute. This attribute enables a couple of things:

- Controllers need to explicitly define their routes; classic routing by convention like in ASP.NET MVC does not work here. Some conventions, like ending a controller name with *Controller*, are still valid.

- The framework will automatically validate incoming data and request and generate HTTP 400 responses where needed. We talk more about HTTP responses a bit further in this chapter.

- Incoming data can be bound to parameters in the action methods.

The third bullet is one of the things that make WebAPI easy to use. The framework can automatically parse incoming request data to parameters. Let's clarify with an example. We will take the book example we used in the MVC part of this chapter and build a REST service for the books. I have copied the BookCatalogService and Book model to a WebAPI project. The Program.cs looks very similar to the Program.cs from MVC with a few important differences.

Listing 7-19. Program.cs in a WebAPI controller-based project

```
builder.Services.AddControllers();
builder.Services.AddEndpointsApiExplorer();
builder.Services.AddSwaggerGen();
builder.Services.AddSingleton<IBookCatalogService, BookCatalogService>();

var app = builder.Build();
```

```
// Configure the HTTP request pipeline.
if (app.Environment.IsDevelopment())
{
    app.UseSwagger();
    app.UseSwaggerUI();
}
```

Listing 7-19 shows a snippet from Program.cs. The differences with MVC are AddEndpointsApiExplorer, AddSwaggerGen, UseSwagger, and UseSwaggerUI. All of these are used to configure Swagger in the project. Swagger is a third-party tool that works according to the OpenAPI Specification, or OAS. Let's take a step back for a moment to clarify some things.

The OpenAPI Initiative (OAI) is an initiative run by a consortium of industry expert. Their aim is to describe a standardized way of how APIs should be structured. The OAI is part of the Linux Foundation, meaning it is run out in the open and completely vendor neutral. Their website is found at https://www.openapis.org/; the OAS itself is at https://spec.openapis.org/oas/latest.html

The OAS describes what the response of an API should look like, what datatypes can be used, how error messages should be structured, and so on.

Since we have an official, albeit optional, specification for our APIs, we can start building and using tools that leverage the structure the OAS described. Swagger is one of those tools; in fact, it was the people behind Swagger who drafted the first version of a Swagger Specification and donated that specification to the OAI who continued to build their version with the Swagger Specification as a solid basis. Later versions of Swagger stepped away from their Swagger Specification and started leveraging the OAS.

So, where is the power in this specification? Why is it useful? Circling back to our WebAPI about books, we have successfully set up and configured Swagger. If we run the application, Swagger will go through our controllers and actions and create a JSON file that describes our entire API surface according to the OAS. Listing 7-20 shows the JSON for our books API.

Listing 7-20. OAS compatible JSON

```
{
  "openapi": "3.1.0",
  "info": {
    "title": "WebApiDemo",
```

```json
    "version": "1.0"
  },
  "paths": {
    "/api/Book": {
      "get": {
        "tags": [
          "Book"
        ],
        "responses": {
          "200": {
            "description": "Success"
          }
        }
      }
    }
  },
  "components": {}
}
```

The JSON starts with declaring what version of OAS it is using. It shows information about our API and its title and version, and it lists the paths or endpoints. Here we can see that we have a /api/book endpoint that is a GET operation and it can return an HTTP 200; this information is generated from our new book controller, added in the next paragraph. The more we work on our API, the more information will show in this JSON.

Listing 7-21. BookController

```csharp
[ApiController]
[Route("api/[controller]")]
public class BookController : ControllerBase
{
    private readonly IBookCatalogService _bookCatalogService;

    public BookController(IBookCatalogService bookCatalogService)
    {
        _bookCatalogService = bookCatalogService;
    }
```

```
[HttpGet]
public async Task<IActionResult> Index()
{
    Book[] books = await _bookCatalogService.FetchBookCatalog();
    return Ok(books);
}
}
```

Listing 7-21 shows our BookController. Notice the specified route on the controller. That route is the path described in the JSON. The GET request maps to the Index method in this controller by convention; if we have multiple methods decorated with the HttpGet attribute, the system will map to the correct one based on the parameters. The Index method fetches an array of books and calls the Ok method, passing in the array of books. The Ok method is one of many helper methods in WebAPI. It creates a response object containing the data and sets the HTTP response to HTTP 200 – OK. By using those methods, we can make sure that we are respecting the OAS.

A quick sidenote about HTTP status codes. I have mentioned HTTP status codes a few times now. Those status codes are used by browsers and application to check what the result of an HTTP request is. The full list of HTTP status codes can be found at https://www.iana.org/assignments/http-status-codes/http-status-codes.xhtml or https://developer.mozilla.org/en-US/docs/Web/HTTP/Status for a more readable list (do check out HTTP 418). In short, the status codes can be grouped into five groups.

- HTTP 100-199: informational

- HTTP 200-299: successful (OK, Created, …)

- HTTP 300-399: redirection

- HTTP 400-499: client error (not found, bad request, …)

- HTTP 500-599: server error

The most famous status code is no doubt HTTP 404 – Not Found. The 500 range usually means that there was an unexpected error on the backend that should be handled by the developers.

Let's get some more information in our generated JSON API description. We can decorate the Index method with an attribute detailing what we can expect as an HTTP status code and what the return type will be.

Listing 7-22. Expanding openAPI information with attributes

```
[HttpGet]
[ProducesResponseType(typeof(Book[]), (int)HttpStatusCode.OK)]
public async Task<IActionResult> Index()
{
    Book[] books = await _bookCatalogService.FetchBookCatalog();
    return Ok(books);
}
```

Looking at the JSON now, we can find some extra information; Listing 7-23 shows a snippet.

Listing 7-23. Extended JSON information

```
"/api/Book": {
      "get": {
        "tags": [
          "Book"
        ],
        "responses": {
          "200": {
            "description": "Success",
            "content": {
              "text/plain": {
                "schema": {
                  "type": "array",
                  "items": {
                    "$ref": "#/components/schemas/Book"
                  }
                }
              },
```

```
          "application/json": {
            "schema": {
              "type": "array",
              "items": {
                "$ref": "#/components/schemas/Book"
              }
            }
          }
```

Notice the $ref that refers to a book? Our JSON schema knows what a book is now and describes it.

Listing 7-24. Model in JSON

```
"components": {
    "schemas": {
      "Book": {
        "required": [
          "author",
          "title"
        ],
        "type": "object",
        "properties": {
          "id": {
            "type": "integer",
            "format": "int32"
          },
          "title": {
            "minLength": 5,
            "type": "string"
          },
          "description": {
            "type": "string",
            "nullable": true
          },
```

```
      "author": {
        "type": "string"
      }
    },
    "additionalProperties": false
  }
 }
}
```

This JSON can be imported in different tools to, for example, generate client implementations that consume this API. There are even tools that do this as part of the build pipeline process. A tool included in .NET 6 is Swagger UI. Swagger UI takes the JSON and generates a visual test client for testing the API endpoints. Enabling Swagger UI in ASP.NET Core 6 is done in Program.cs by calling app.UseSwaggerUI() after app.UseSwagger().

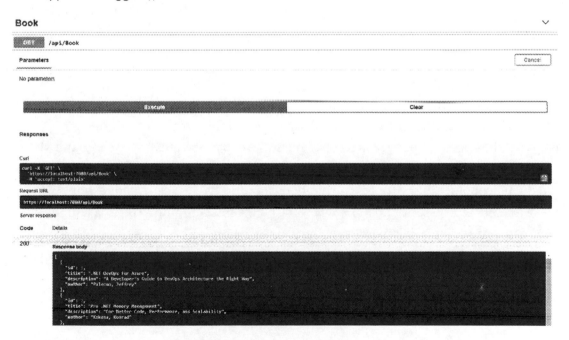

Figure 7-17. *Testing a REST call with Swagger UI*

Using Swagger UI can really speed up the dev cycle; it gives a nice overview of all endpoints, allows entering parameters, and shows the status code and errors.

Let's look at another example. Listing 7-25 shows the controller method for fetching a book detail.

Listing 7-25. Fetching a book detail

```
[HttpGet]
[Route("{id}")]
[ProducesResponseType(typeof(Book), (int)HttpStatusCode.OK)]
[ProducesResponseType((int)HttpStatusCode.NotFound)]
public async Task<IActionResult> Details(int id)
{
    Book? book = await _bookCatalogService.FetchBookById(id);

    if (book == null)
    {
        return NotFound(id);
    }

    return Ok(book);
}
```

We once again have a GET method; there is a route attribute on the Details method. This route will combine with the route set on the controller to get, for example, https://<hostname>:<port>/api/book/5. The 5 will be inserted as value into the id parameter of the method; it is very important to have same name for the parameter and the placeholder in the route. The method can produce two expected response types, an HTTP 200 – OK or an HTTP 404 – NOT FOUND. According to the logic in the BookCatalogService, when passing in the id, we get either a book instance or NULL back. We create the correct HTTP response using the NotFound or Ok helper methods. Swagger UI picks these changes up quite nicely, based on the two ProducesResponseType attributes we have added.

```
  GET    /api/Book/{id}
```

Parameters

Name	Description
id * required integer($int32) (path)	5

```
                              Execute
```

Responses

Curl

```
curl -X 'GET' \
  'https://localhost:7080/api/Book/5' \
  -H 'accept: text/plain'
```

Request URL

```
https://localhost:7080/api/Book/5
```

Server response

Code	Details
200	Response body

```
{
  "id": 5,
  "title": "Azure and Xamarin Forms",
  "description": "Cross Platform Mobile Development",
  "author": "Fustino, Russell"
}
```

Figure 7-18. *Parameters in Swagger UI*

As a final example, let's see what a POST request looks like. Listing 7-26 shows the controller action for adding a book to the collection.

211

Listing 7-26. Adding a book

```
[HttpPost]
[ProducesResponseType(typeof(Book), (int)HttpStatusCode.Created)]
[ProducesResponseType((int)HttpStatusCode.BadRequest)]
public async Task<IActionResult> Create([FromBody] Book book)
{
    await _bookCatalogService.AddBook(book);
    return Created($"/{book.Id}", book);
}
```

A couple of new things here. Instead of a GET request, we are now doing a POST, which is the typical verb to create a new record. The HTTP status code to return is HTTP 201 – Created, which is generated by calling the Created method. The Created method needs an endpoint where the details of the newly created book can be requested and it sends the created book back as the response body, according to the OpenAPI Specification. The parameter of the method is decorated with the FromBody attribute. The attribute ApiController on controller level enables these attributes. The FromBody attribute parses the form data in the request body to the type of the parameter. Figure 7-19 shows the resulting entry in Swagger UI.

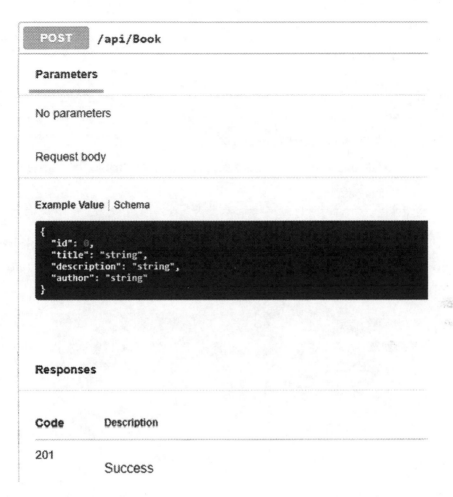

Figure 7-19. *POST request in Swagger UI*

Notice the color? POSTs are green, GETs are blue, DELETE will be red, and so on. Every HTTP verb is color coded in Swagger UI. Table 7-1 shows the complete list of HTTP verbs.

Table 7-1. *List of HTTP verbs*

Verb	Description
GET	Fetch data
POST	Create new data
PUT	Update data by sending back a complete, updated object
PATCH	Update data by sending back a patch document with only the updated properties
DELETE	Delete data

If we fill in some values in Swagger UI, set a breakpoint in the Create action on the controller; hit the Execute button and you will see that the breakpoint is hit and the parameter is nicely filled in with the values we entered in Swagger.

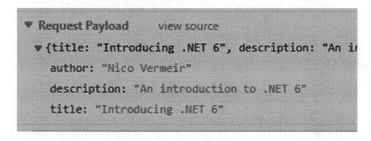

Figure 7-20. *HTTP Request captured by the browser*

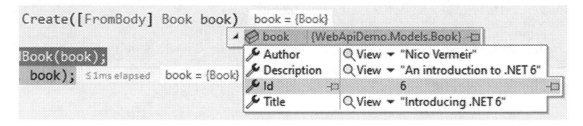

Figure 7-21. *ID generated and parameter parsed from HTTP form data*

Minimal APIs

As mentioned in the introduction of this chapter, minimal APIs are Microsoft's answer to fast REST API development as can be found in frameworks like NodeJS, where you can put the entire API surface in one file. Looking at minimal APIs, we effectively have one file containing everything. From application setup to the actual endpoints, and even better: Swagger and Swagger UI know how to interpret this new style of .NET REST APIs.

I have implemented the same book API in minimal API; a quick count of lines of code shows the following result:

- Controller-based API: 78 lines of code

- Minimal API: 57 lines of code

Lines of code are the bootstrap logic in `Program.cs` and the book endpoints, so not counting any models or services. That is 25% less code. But less code is not always better. Listing 7-27 shows the first part of `Program.cs` that sets up the application.

Listing 7-27. Bootstrapping a minimal API project

```
var builder = WebApplication.CreateBuilder(args);

// Add services to the container.
// Learn more about configuring Swagger/OpenAPI at https://aka.ms/
aspnetcore/swashbuckle
builder.Services.AddEndpointsApiExplorer();
builder.Services.AddSwaggerGen();
builder.Services.AddSingleton<IBookCatalogService, BookCatalogService>();

var app = builder.Build();

// Configure the HTTP request pipeline.
if (app.Environment.IsDevelopment())
{
    app.UseSwagger();
    app.UseSwaggerUI();
}

app.UseHttpsRedirection();
```

Almost identical to controller-based APIs, except for the builder.Services. AddControllers call, we have no controllers in a minimal API, so no need to add them to the ServiceCollection.

The next part of Program.cs is the endpoints; after defining the endpoints, there is a small line of code that says app.Run(). These few characters make the API launch and be useful. Do not remove this call or nothing will work.

Listing 7-28 shows the action to fetch an array of books.

Listing 7-28. Creating a GET request in a minimal API

```
app.MapGet("/api/book", async ([FromServices] IBookCatalogService
bookCatalogService) =>
{
    Book[] books = await bookCatalogService.FetchBookCatalog();
    return Results.Ok(books);
})
.WithName("GetBooks")
.Produces<Book[]>();
```

Creating API endpoints is done on the WebApplication object that is also used for configuring the application as seen in Listing 7-27. WebApplication has different Map methods depending on the type of HTTP verb you want to create an endpoint for. In this example, we are creating a GET request. The first parameter of the method is the path on which the endpoint is reachable. The second parameter is the delegate that is called whenever the endpoint is called. This delegate can be placed in a separate method, but I personally prefer the anonymous method style. In a minimal API, we can't do constructor injection since we don't have a constructor. Instead, we can use the FromServices attribute to decorate a parameter in the delegate. The ServiceCollection will inject the instance right there. In controller-based APIs, we could use helper methods like Ok and NotFound from the controller base class. We don't have a base class in a minimal API, but we can use the static class Results that exposes the same methods. Finally we have some configuration methods; these are mostly used for generating the OpenAPI JSON and for Swagger UI. WithName sets a name for this endpoint. Produces sets the possible HTTP status codes and the type of data we can expect. In this example, we are not explicitly setting a status code; HTTP 200 will be used as default.

Listing 7-29. Parameters in a minimal API endpoint

```
app.MapGet("/api/book/{id}", async ([FromServices] IBookCatalogService
bookCatalogService, int id) =>
{
    Book? book = await bookCatalogService.FetchBookById(id);

    if (book == null)
    {
        return Results.NotFound(id);
    }

    return Results.Ok(book);
})
.WithName("GetBookById")
.Produces<Book>()
.Produces((int)HttpStatusCode.NotFound);
```

The API call for fetching book details looks very similar. The major difference is that we are expecting a parameter, the book ID, to be passed in. Passing parameters is done by setting a placeholder between curly braces in the route and creating a method parameter in the delegate with the same name as the placeholder. The framework will take care of mapping the passed in parameter to the .NET parameter, very similar to the way routing works as we have seen in ASP.NET MVC. This example also shows defining two possible results. The method can either produce a book with HTTP 200 – OK or it can produce an empty result with HTTP 404 – Not Found.

Listing 7-30. Posting data to a minimal API

```
app.MapPost("/api/book", async ([FromServices] IBookCatalogService
bookCatalogService, [FromBody] Book book) =>
{
    await bookCatalogService.AddBook(book);
    return Results.Created($"/api/book/{book.Id}", book);
})
.WithName("AddBook")
.Produces<Book>((int)HttpStatusCode.Created);
```

Creating a POST endpoint is very similar; we just use the `MapPost` method instead of `MapGet`. Using the `FromBody` attribute, we can get the posted HTTP form data as a .NET object passed into the delegate. The return type is HTTP 201 – Created.

If you like this style of API programming but you don't want a large `Program.cs` once all your endpoints are defined, you can use extension methods to split your endpoint definitions in separate files.

Listing 7-31. Extension methods for defining book endpoints

```
public static class BookEndpoints
{
    public static void MapBookEndpoints(this WebApplication app)
    {
        app.MapGet("/api/book", async ([FromServices] IBookCatalogService
        bookCatalogService) =>
            {
                Book[] books = await bookCatalogService.FetchBookCatalog();
                return Results.Ok(books);
            })
            .WithName("GetBooks")
            .Produces<Book[]>();

    }
}
```

I have only added one endpoint in Listing 7-31 for brevity. The full method with the three endpoints can be found on the book's GitHub page. With this extension method in place, we can shorten `Program.cs` by calling `app.MapBookEndpoints` instead of defining all endpoints there.

Wrapping Up

ASP.NET has been a popular choice for building enterprise web applications or services for years, and the framework keeps evolving. MVC is easy to use and familiar for those coming from other languages since it largely depends on the Model-View-Controller pattern. WebAPI uses the same design pattern to provide easy to build and use RESTful APIs. In .NET 6, we got minimal APIs, which is a brand-new member of the ASP.NET family. With minimal APIs, we can start building APIs faster than ever before, but we do give up a bit of structure. It is a trade-off. Controller-based APIs are built using a very well-known design pattern, but for smaller APIs, it is easy to get lost in the large amount of files in a project. With minimal APIs, there is a minimal amount of files or code required, but structure might get lost quickly. So choose wisely and use extension methods to group your endpoints together.

CHAPTER 8

Microsoft Azure

Over the past couple of years, cloud computing has grown to gigantic proportions, and it is not hard to see why. Companies can potentially save tons of money by not buying and maintaining their own server hardware; instead, they can opt for a pay-per-use model that can scale from one server to hundreds and back to one in mere minutes. Cloud providers like Microsoft make it very easy to get your software up and running on a cloud service and at the same time give you power tools to fully configure a cloud-based network that can even be an extension to your on-premise network.

Microsoft Azure, or just Azure for short, is Microsoft's public cloud platform. Everyone with a credit card can create an account and start creating and publishing cloud services. The entire breadth of Azure is too big to describe in one chapter of a book, so I have selected much used services where .NET 6 can be important.

Configuring Azure services can be done in multiple ways. When starting with Azure, you will most likely first encounter the Azure portal `https://portal.azure.com`. A second popular approach is through the CLI. The Azure SDK ships with its own command line tools; these tools can be used to automate Azure actions, for example, to include them in a CI/CD pipeline. Visual Studio also ships with some Azure integrations, for example, to publish web applications to Azure. These integrations are very useful for a quick start but are quite limited in the end. The examples in this chapter are all done through the Azure portal. Keep in mind that the Azure portal is a web application that evolves very fast, so by the time you read this, things might look slightly different but the concepts will remain the same.

In this chapter, we'll walk through some of the Azure services. To follow along, you will need an Azure account; costs may be involved depending on the services and tiers selected. Free Azure trials are available at `https://azure.microsoft.com/en-us/free`.

© Nico Vermeir 2022
N. Vermeir, *Introducing .NET 6*, https://doi.org/10.1007/978-1-4842-7319-7_8

Web Apps

Azure Web Apps are easiest described as your basic web hosting that you can get from thousands of providers all over the world. The difference being that since this is a cloud service this can scale to huge scales. By default, web apps support applications in:

- .NET

- .NET Classic

- Java

- Ruby

- NodeJS

- PHP

- Python

Let's start building our first web app. As mentioned before, there are several ways to create Azure resources, but for now we will use the portal. The portal greets you with a list of recent resources and a list of resource types that are commonly created.

Creating an App Service

To be able to follow along with this demo, you will need to have an ASP.NET Core 6 project checked into a GitHub repository.

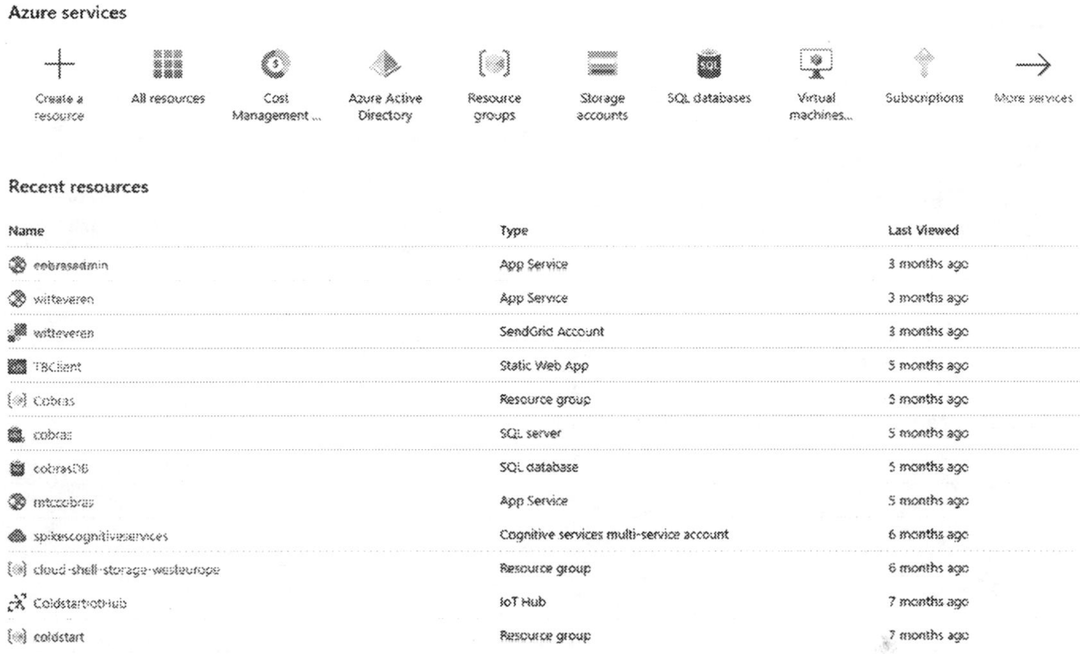

Azure services

Create a resource	All resources	Cost Management ...	Azure Active Directory	Resource groups	Storage accounts	SQL databases	Virtual machines...	Subscriptions	More services

Recent resources

Name	Type	Last Viewed
cobrasadmin	App Service	3 months ago
witteveren	App Service	3 months ago
witteveren	SendGrid Account	3 months ago
TBClient	Static Web App	5 months ago
Cobras	Resource group	5 months ago
cobras	SQL server	5 months ago
cobrasDB	SQL database	5 months ago
mtcobras	App Service	5 months ago
spikescognitiveservices	Cognitive services multi-service account	6 months ago
cloud-shell-storage-westeurope	Resource group	6 months ago
ColdstartIotHub	IoT Hub	7 months ago
coldstart	Resource group	7 months ago

Figure 8-1. *Azure portal start page*

There is a button with a big + icon to create a new resource. This will once again bring up a page with some quick options for resource types but also a search to search through the extensive catalog of Azure services. It is important to know that not every service in the Azure services catalog is a Microsoft product. There are tons of third-party services in there as well. Some examples are MariaDB, SendGrid, several Linux distros for virtual machines, and many more. For this example, we need a web app. After we find it in the catalog and click *Create,* we enter into a setup wizard.

Make sure to select Web App, not Static Web App. Those are for the next section.

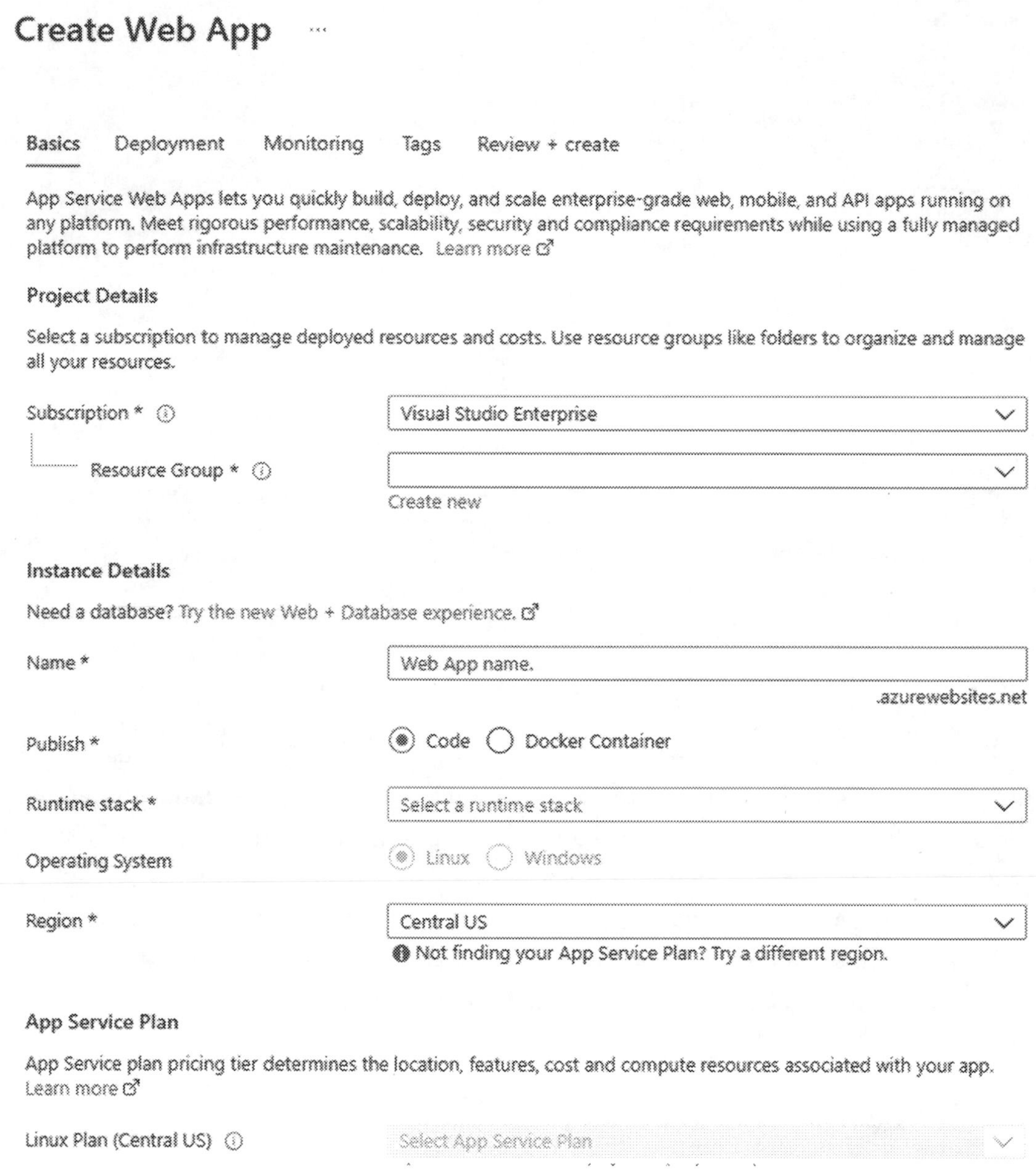

Create Web App   ···

Basics   Deployment   Monitoring   Tags   Review + create

App Service Web Apps lets you quickly build, deploy, and scale enterprise-grade web, mobile, and API apps running on any platform. Meet rigorous performance, scalability, security and compliance requirements while using a fully managed platform to perform infrastructure maintenance. Learn more ⧉

Project Details

Select a subscription to manage deployed resources and costs. Use resource groups like folders to organize and manage all your resources.

Subscription * ⓘ | Visual Studio Enterprise   ⌄ |

└──── Resource Group * ⓘ | ⌄ |
                                                  Create new

Instance Details

Need a database? Try the new Web + Database experience. ⧉

Name * | Web App name. |
                                                                                    .azurewebsites.net

Publish *   ● Code   ○ Docker Container

Runtime stack * | Select a runtime stack   ⌄ |

Operating System   ◉ Linux   ○ Windows

Region * | Central US   ⌄ |
                                                 ❶ Not finding your App Service Plan? Try a different region.

App Service Plan

App Service plan pricing tier determines the location, features, cost and compute resources associated with your app. Learn more ⧉

Linux Plan (Central US) ⓘ | Select App Service Plan   ⌄ |

Figure 8-2. *Web App creation wizard*

First we need to select a subscription. Being an Azure user means you have a subscription. Azure has a lot of free services, but depending on how much flexibility, scale, or redundancy you need, you will quickly get into paid territory. To track what you use, Microsoft requires you to have a subscription. You can have several subscription tied to the same email address. As a Visual Studio customer, you get monthly Azure credits that you can spend. The amount depends on the type of Visual Studio license you have.

A Resource Group is a functional group that you can place your services in. Resource Groups are mostly meant for customers to order their services. Azure resources in the same resource group share the same lifecycle, permissions, and policies. Click *Create New* and give your resource group a name.

Next step is configuring the resource itself. Most important is how you want to call this. This name needs to be unique across all Azure customers since the name will be used as a url. As an Azure Web App user, you get a free domain in the form of https://<your web app name>.azurewebsites.net. This makes your web application easily reachable across the Internet, and you can make use of the SSL certificate for *.azurewebsites.net free of charge. It is of course possible to attach your own domain name to a web app instance, but that also means that you are responsible for the SSL certificate.

After selecting a name, we can choose if we want to deploy our project as code or as a Docker container. Azure supports multiple ways of deploying containerized applications; this is one of the more basic versions. When deploying as a container, Azure assumes that the container contains a web application that exposes ports 80 (http) or 443 (https). Deploying as code means that we publish our generated binaries onto the file system and the web server interprets and serves the response, just like in a shared hosting with any hosting provider. For now, we will stick to deploy as code and we will get into Docker later on in this chapter.

The runtime stack is where we define the technology that we used for building our application. As mentioned in the start of this chapter, we have quite a lot of options. Since this book is about .NET 6, we will select .NET 6 (LTS) as runtime stack. Depending on the option you select in the runtime stack dropdown, the option for selecting an operating system might light up. That is because not all runtime stack options support both Linux and Windows, for example, classic ASP.NET 4.x can only run on Windows hosts. Ever since .NET Core, .NET became cross-platform so we can run on Linux as well. There are several differences between running an app service on Linux or Windows; most of them have to do with pricing. Running a Windows service is more expensive than running a Linux service. Figure 8-3 shows the difference using the Azure pricing calculator.

App Service

REGION:	OPERATING SYSTEM:	TIER:
West US	Windows	Basic

Basic

INSTANCE:

B1: 1 Cores(s), 1.75 GB RAM, 10 GB Storage, $0.075

1	×	730	Hours		=	$54.75
Instances						

App Service

REGION:	OPERATING SYSTEM:	TIER:
West US	Linux	Basic

Basic

INSTANCE:

B1: 1 Cores(s), 1.75 GB RAM, 10 GB Storage, $0.018

1	×	730	Hours		=	$13.14
Instances						

Figure 8-3. *Price difference Linux – Windows*

The pricing shown in Figure 8-3 is monthly cost calculated for a basic instance estimating 730 hours of usage. Looking at the pricing in the calculator, Windows is four times as expensive as Linux. However, Linux does not have a free tier in web app while Windows does. So there is more to it than just selecting the cheapest option. Make sure that you know very well what the different options are.

The next option is the region. Azure has datacenters across the world, but a region is not just one datacenter. A region is a collection of datacenters that are relatively close to each other. When you deploy a service to a region, you know that your application is running in one or more of the datacenters in that region but you do not know which one. The reason for this is redundancy; should one datacenter loose connection, one of the others in the same region can take over. There are several assurances of where data is stored and how data is transferred. These were put in place to comply to privacy regulations like GDPR in Europe. The list of regions is constantly extending as Azure is growing. At the time of writing, Azure has 33 regions. Do note that not every region supports every resource type. Newer resource types are usually available in US regions first and are gradually rolled out across the entire Azure network.

Final option to set is the App Service Plan. App Service Plans are another grouping method, but while resource groups go about lifecycle, permissions, and policies, App Service Plans are about location, features, cost, and resources. A service plan is tied to a region, so if you want all of your services in the same service plan, they also need to be in the same region. The SKU is the computing power you want this service to have. More power comes with a higher cost.

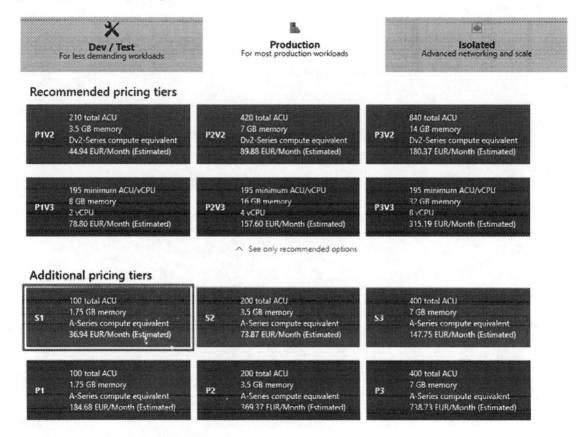

Figure 8-4. *Selecting an SKU*

The selection screen groups the available SKUs according to workloads and immediately shows estimated monthly cost. The selected SKU can be adjusted later on, for example, when your application usage is on the rise. If you switch to the *Dev/Test* tab at the top, you can select the Free tier; this will be sufficient for the demo and will keep you from spending Azure credits. After selecting the right SKU for your project, we can advance to step 2 of the wizard: Deployment.

Azure App Services can integrate with GitHub Actions to automatically set up a CI/CD pipeline. With CI/CD, we can automatically build and deploy our application. Connect the Azure portal to the GitHub account that has access to the GitHub repository we mentioned in the beginning of this section. Once connected, you can select the right organization, repository, and branch.

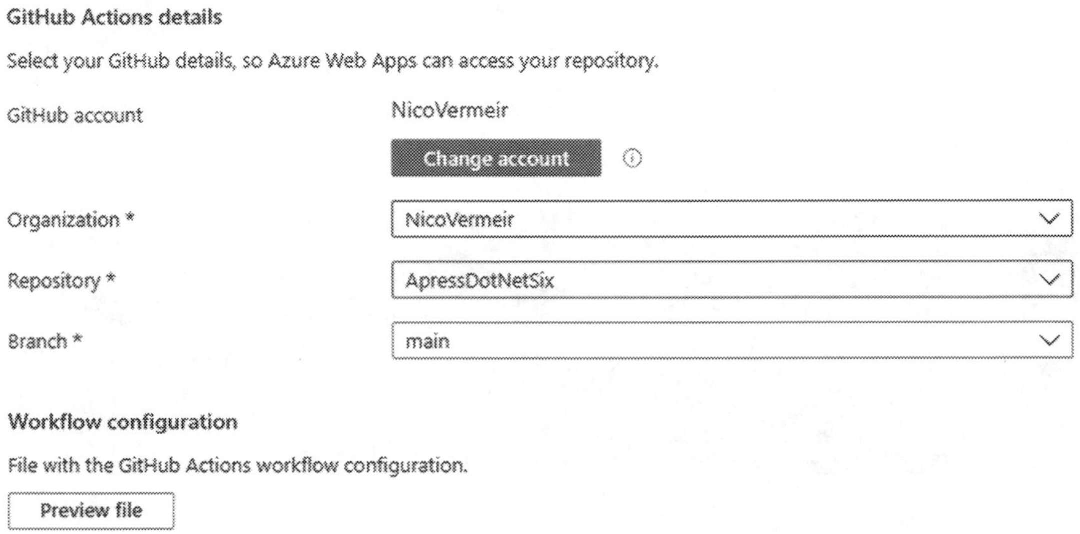

GitHub Actions details

Select your GitHub details, so Azure Web Apps can access your repository.

GitHub account   NicoVermeir

[Change account] ⓘ

Organization *   [NicoVermeir   ⌄]

Repository *   [ApressDotNetSix   ⌄]

Branch *   [main   ⌄]

Workflow configuration

File with the GitHub Actions workflow configuration.

[Preview file]

Figure 8-5. *Automatically configure CI/CD from Azure*

Setting this up will generate a YAML file that is added to the code repository for a GitHub action. That action can automatically build and deploy your application to the newly created Azure Web App. A preview of the YAML file can be seen here in the Azure portal before it is added to your repository on GitHub. For more information on setting up the connection between Azure and GitHub Action, go checkout the documentation `https://docs.microsoft.com/en-us/azure/app-service/deploy-github-actions?tabs=applevel`.

The next step in setting up an Azure App Service instance is Monitoring.

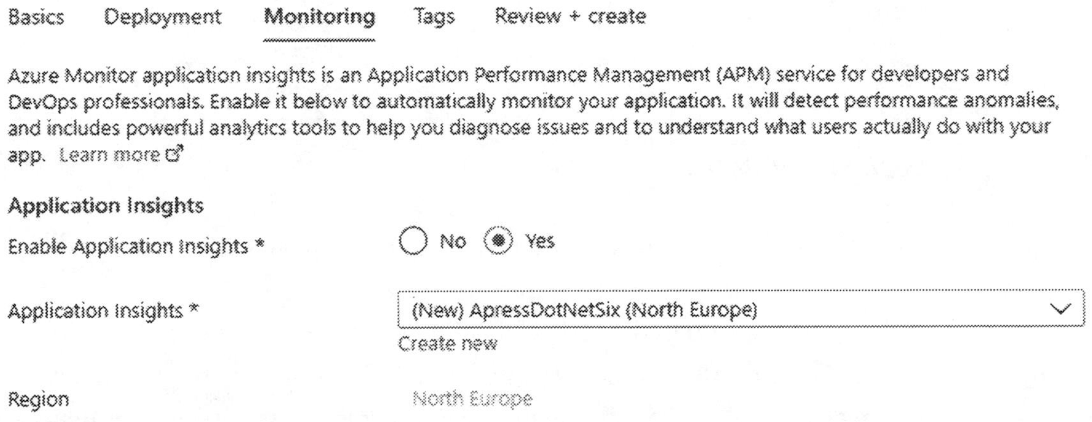

Basics   Deployment   **Monitoring**   Tags   Review + create

Azure Monitor application insights is an Application Performance Management (APM) service for developers and DevOps professionals. Enable it below to automatically monitor your application. It will detect performance anomalies, and includes powerful analytics tools to help you diagnose issues and to understand what users actually do with your app. Learn more ☐

Application Insights

Enable Application Insights *   ◯ No ⦿ Yes

Application Insights * | (New) ApressDotNetSix (North Europe)   ⌄ |
                                        Create new

Region   North Europe

Figure 8-6. *Configuring monitoring*

Application Insights is another Azure service that provides extensive logging and monitoring capabilities. Enabling it here will provide error and crash logging; for further logging, you will need to add the Application Insights SDK to your project.

The final step in the wizard allows for tagging your resources. With these tags, you can create categories for your services to allow for easier filtering when searching through your Azure services.

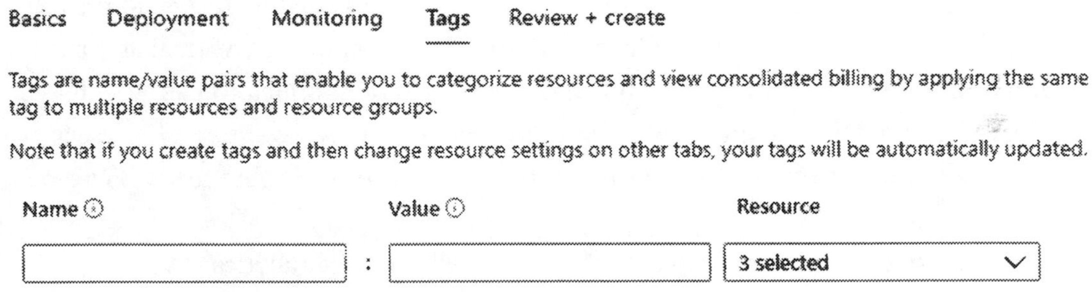

Basics   Deployment   Monitoring   **Tags**   Review + create

Tags are name/value pairs that enable you to categorize resources and view consolidated billing by applying the same tag to multiple resources and resource groups.

Note that if you create tags and then change resource settings on other tabs, your tags will be automatically updated.

Name ⓘ	Value ⓘ	Resource
	:	3 selected ⌄

Figure 8-7. *Tagging the resources*

Right before the Azure resource is created, you will get a final overview of all the selected options. If everything looks okay, we can click Create and Azure will work its magic.

Deployment is in progress

Deployment name: Microsoft.Web-WebApp-Portal-808677fa-913b   Start time: 11/10/2021, 2:15:53 PM
Subscription: Visual Studio Enterprise   Correlation ID: f4fd66a2-a398-41e4-89c5-57e8216efbd2
Resource group: ApressBookDemo

Figure 8-8. *Deployment status*

Azure will keep you informed about the deployment status. You are free to leave this
page and come back later; deployment will continue just fine.

For this demo, I have checked in the ASP.NET MVC demo project from the previous
chapter. I have selected the GitHub repository and branch that point to this project. Now
that Azure is creating the resource, it will also deploy our project. After a few minutes, we
get the result shown in Figure 8-9.

Figure 8-9. *Deployment complete*

To summarize, the following things just happened. Azure created an App Service
instance to host our .NET 6 web application. Azure also generated a YAML file for a
GitHub Build/Deploy pipeline. GitHub Actions compiled our application and deployed
it to the newly generated Azure App Service. From now on, whenever new changes are
committed to the main branch of the GitHub repository, the GitHub Action will compile
and deploy a new version.

On the portal side of things, we get a dashboard with some analytics, if we kept
Application Insights enabled.

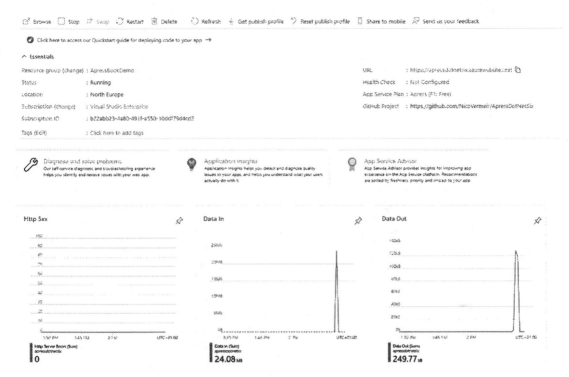

Figure 8-10. *Dashboard on the Azure portal*

From here we can stop, start, or restart our application server, look into our application logs, change the configuration, change service plans, and so on.

We can also download a publish profile that we can import in Visual Studio to deploy directly from the IDE to the cloud. The publish profile is a configuration file that we can import in Visual Studio from the Deploy option that we will use in a minute. In the Deploy wizard, we can either create a new publish profile or import a downloaded one.

To summarize, we have created an Azure App Service instance to host our .NET 6-based web application. We deploy this code directly from GitHub using its built-in CI/CD pipeline (more about CI/CD in the architecture chapter). Deploying directly from GitHub is optional; we can deploy directly from Visual Studio using publishing profiles or connect to Azure using the Visual Studio right-click on a project ➤ publish tooling. In the publish wizard, we select publish to Azure and an Azure App Service.

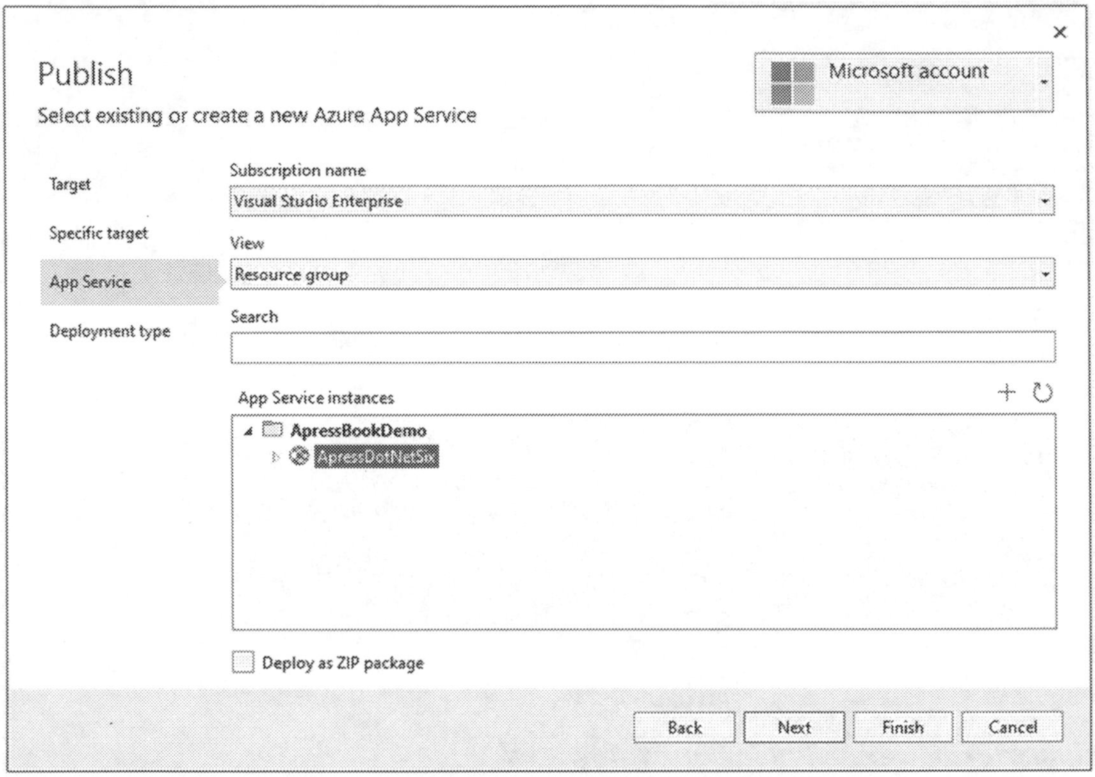

Figure 8-11. *Deploying to Azure from Visual Studio*

When publishing from within Visual Studio, we can login with our Microsoft account that has an Azure subscription attached to it. After authenticating, we can publish directly to an existing resource or create a new one. The publish wizard allows for filtering on resource type to easily find the existing resource you want to publish to. Finishing this wizard will generate a publish profile in the form of a pubxml file. This publishing profile serves the same purpose as the one you can download from the Azure portal, but it is in a different format. The publishing profile from the portal contains three nodes for three different publishing methods, zip deploy, web deploy, and FTP upload. Listings 8-1 and 8-2 compare both publishing profiles. I have removed two of the three publishing methods from the publishing profile from the portal for brevity.

Listing 8-1. Publishing profile from Azure portal

```
<?xml version="1.0" encoding="UTF-8"?>
<publishData>
    <publishProfile
            profileName="ApressDotNetSix - Web Deploy"
            publishMethod="MSDeploy"
            publishUrl="apressdotnetsix.scm.azurewebsites.net:443"
            msdeploySite="ApressDotNetSix"
            userName="$ApressDotNetSix"
            userPWD="***"
            destinationAppUrl="http://apressdotnetsix.azurewebsites.net"
            SQLServerDBConnectionString=""
            mySQLDBConnectionString=""
            hostingProviderForumLink=""
            controlPanelLink="http://windows.azure.com"
            webSystem="WebSites">
        <databases />
    </publishProfile>
</publishData>
```

Listing 8-2. Publishing profile from Visual Studio

```
<Project ToolsVersion="4.0" xmlns="http://schemas.microsoft.com/developer/
msbuild/2003">
  <PropertyGroup>
    <WebPublishMethod>MSDeploy</WebPublishMethod>
    <ResourceId>/subscriptions/**/ApressDotNetSix</ResourceId>
    <ResourceGroup>ApressBookDemo</ResourceGroup>
    <PublishProvider>AzureWebSite</PublishProvider>
    <LastUsedBuildConfiguration>Release</LastUsedBuildConfiguration>
    <LastUsedPlatform>Any CPU</LastUsedPlatform>
    <SiteUrlToLaunchAfterPublish>http://apressdotnetsix.azurewebsites.net
    </SiteUrlToLaunchAfterPublish>
    <LaunchSiteAfterPublish>True</LaunchSiteAfterPublish>
    <ExcludeApp_Data>False</ExcludeApp_Data>
    <ProjectGuid>cab9ed7b-f056-4849-98aa-db947b3cd09e</ProjectGuid>
```

```
    <MSDeployServiceURL>apressdotnetsix.scm.azurewebsites.net:443
    </MSDeployServiceURL>
    <DeployIisAppPath>ApressDotNetSix</DeployIisAppPath>
    <RemoteSitePhysicalPath />
    <SkipExtraFilesOnServer>True</SkipExtraFilesOnServer>
    <MSDeployPublishMethod>WMSVC</MSDeployPublishMethod>
    <EnableMSDeployBackup>True</EnableMSDeployBackup>
    <EnableMsDeployAppOffline>True</EnableMsDeployAppOffline>
    <UserName>$ApressDotNetSix</UserName>
    <_SavePWD>True</_SavePWD>
    <_DestinationType>AzureWebSite</_DestinationType>
  </PropertyGroup>
</Project>
```

Very different files that serve the same function. The reason these are different is that the publishing profile from the Azure portal is catered especially to cloud deployments, while the version from Visual Studio is more generic and can do deploys to other endpoints like the Windows filesystem, Docker, or any IIS server, for example.

Azure Web Apps or App Service is a great resource for publishing web-based applications. But there might be a better option if your application is pure HTML, CSS, and JavaScript based.

Static Web Apps

Static apps are becoming more and more the norm on frontend web development. Frameworks like Angular, Vue, React, and Blazor all generate client-side logic, relying heavily on RESTful APIs for the heavy lifting and data access. Since everything is executed client-side, we need a way to get the application on the client. In case of JavaScript-based frameworks like Angular, React, and Vue, those are all HTML, CSS, and JavaScript files, something a browser on the client can work with. In case of Blazor, this will be HTML, CSS, JavaScript, and DLL files, something browsers that support WebAssembly can work with. For more information on Blazor, see the Blazor chapter in this book. To get those files onto the client, we need a webserver that serves those files. This is where static web apps on Azure can help. Static web apps are a cloud service that serves files. Static apps can distribute the assets globally so that your application is in the Azure region closest to your customers for minimal delay.

Setting up a static web app is very similar to setting up a default web app. The first step in the creation of wizard should look familiar with a few specific fields.

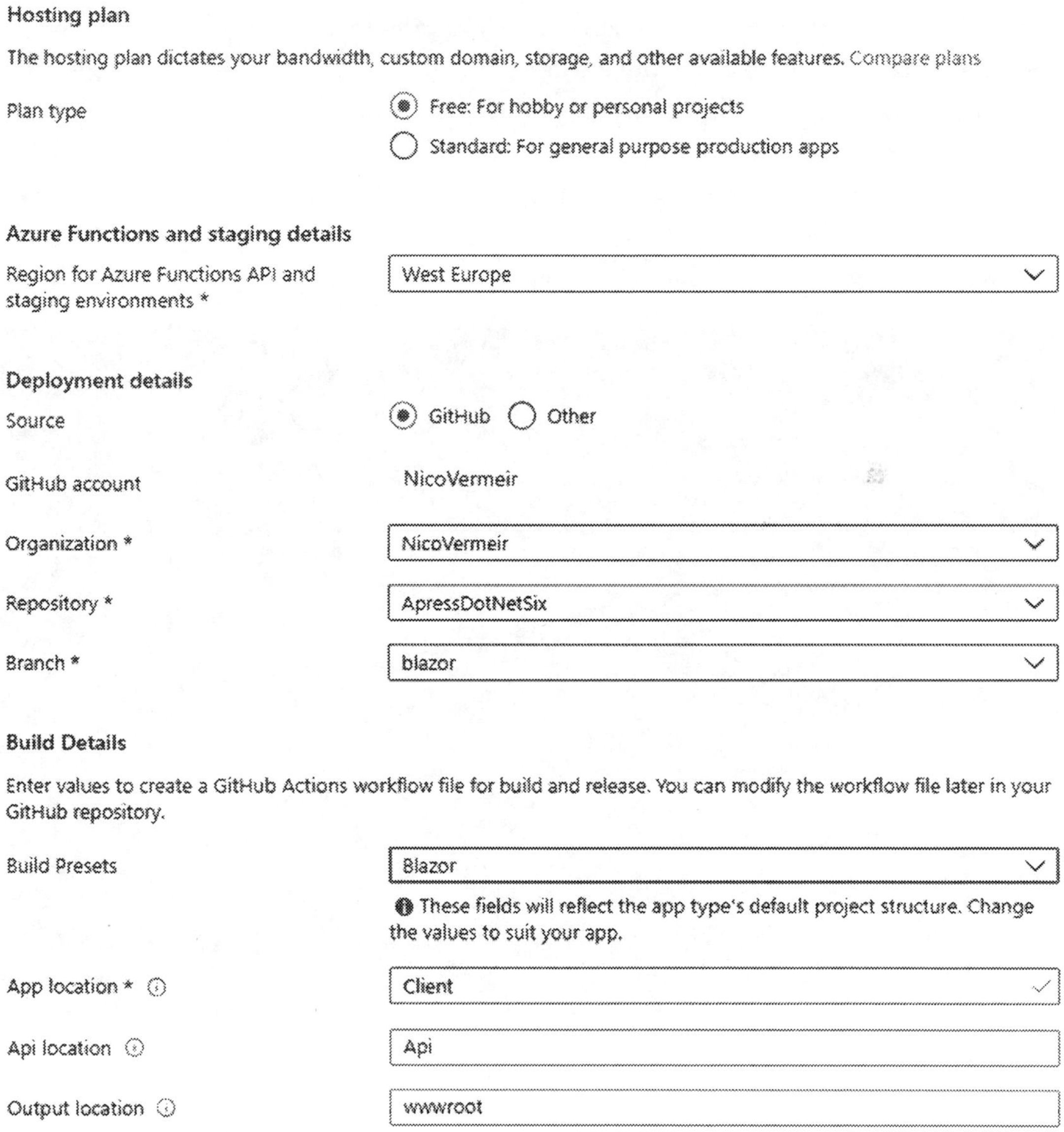

Hosting plan

The hosting plan dictates your bandwidth, custom domain, storage, and other available features. Compare plans

Plan type
- ⦿ Free: For hobby or personal projects
- ◯ Standard: For general purpose production apps

Azure Functions and staging details

Region for Azure Functions API and staging environments *

West Europe	⌄

Deployment details

Source   ⦿ GitHub ◯ Other

GitHub account   NicoVermeir

Organization *	NicoVermeir	⌄

Repository *	ApressDotNetSix	⌄

Branch *	blazor	⌄

Build Details

Enter values to create a GitHub Actions workflow file for build and release. You can modify the workflow file later in your GitHub repository.

Build Presets	Blazor	⌄

ℹ These fields will reflect the app type's default project structure. Change the values to suit your app.

App location * ⓘ	Client	✓

Api location ⓘ	Api	

Output location ⓘ	wwwroot	

Figure 8-12. *Creating a static web app*

First static web app-specific field is the hosting plan. Static web apps provide a free version for personal projects and a standard plan for professional projects.

Second part is the deployment details. Unlike Azure Web Apps, there is no support for publishing profiles in static apps. Static apps work solely with CI/CD integration, meaning that we need to link our Azure resource to a source repository. The wizard in the portal has a very good GitHub integration as you can see in Figure 8-12. There is support for any source repository, but it will need to be configured from the build server itself instead of here on the Azure portal. For this demo, I have created a default Blazor WebAssembly project.

After creating the resource, a new YAML file will be pushed to the source repository and a GitHub Action will trigger, building and deploying the Blazor application. When checking GitHub Actions, we should see Figure 8-13.

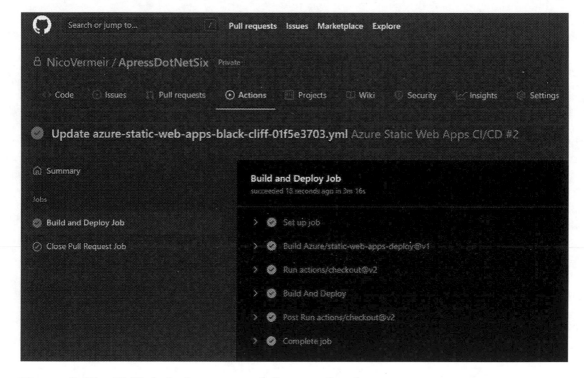

Figure 8-13. *GitHub Action successfully completed*

After successfully compiling and zipping the Blazor output, the zip file is uploaded to Azure. Once uploaded, the static web app service will unzip everything; while that is happening, our GitHub Action will poll the service for completion. Static web apps don't allow us to choose our own hostname like Azure Web Apps did; instead, it generates a unique url that we can find on the portal. We did have to enter an application name when creating the static web app resource, but that is purely an administrative name used for our purposes. Of course, we can still buy a custom domain and hook that up.

Once everything is finished, we can go to the generated domain name.

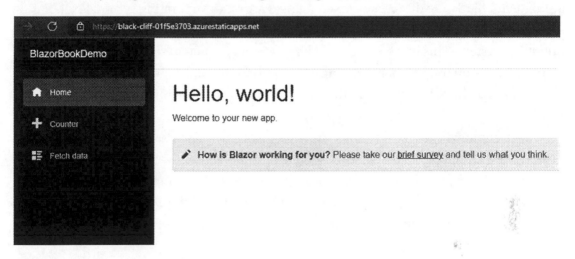

Figure 8-14. *Blazor app running on Azure static web apps*

We have successfully configured a Blazor app on static web apps. There is nothing happening server-side besides serving of files, client download everything and executes everything locally. The Blazor app shown here as a demo is compiled by GitHub using .NET 6 on an Ubuntu build host. Other supported frameworks include Angular, Vue, React, or static site generators like Gatsby. For a full up-to-date list of supported frameworks, see `https://docs.microsoft.com/en-us/azure/static-web-apps/front-end-frameworks`.

Web App for Containers

Web apps support a second hosting model as we have seen in the deployment wizard. Besides just deploying code, we can deploy our application as a Docker container. The ins-and-outs of Docker are way beyond the scope of this book, but just to get everyone on the same page, here is a quick primer of what Docker is.

Docker

Docker is a set of tools build upon the *containerd* runtime to create containerized applications. Containers are basically an evolution of virtual machines. Virtual machines emulate full hardware devices where containers are on the operating system level. A container bundles software, libraries, and configuration for running on a specific operating system. This means that a container is a fully isolated, self-configured unit of work that runs on top of the underlying operating system of the Docker host. This means that containers have less overhead than virtual machines, allowing more containers to run on one physical device than virtual machines.

Using containerized applications simplifies a lot of things. Moving from one cloud host to another, let's say from Amazon AWS to Microsoft Azure, can be very easy since no configuration changes to the application are needed. Updating an application is as simple as restarting the container and so on. The majority of the work is in setting up an application for containerization. To get an application in a Docker container up and running, we need:

- A Docker file describing entry points, ports, and configuration.

- Docker image, a containerized application, ready to startup and being used.

- A Docker registry, this is like a package repository (NuGet, NPM, etc.) but for containers. It contains the container images we want to deploy.

- A Docker runtime.

- Docker runner, a system that pulls an image from a Docker registry and deploys it to a Docker runtime.

The Docker registry is needed as this is where Docker runners pull their images from. Let's try to dockerize our MVC demo application.

First thing we need is to install Docker Desktop on our system. The installer can be downloaded from their website `https://hub.docker.com/editions/community/docker-ce-desktop-windows`. The installer will guide you through the process of installing WSL2 and making sure the right updates are installed, after which Docker and Docker Desktop will be installed. Docker Desktop is the Windows version of Docker. It provides a UI to configure Docker and a CLI. Most importantly, it connects the Docker engine to Visual Studio for debugging.

After Docker Desktop is installed, we can open our solution, right-click the project we want to containerize, and select Add > Docker Support. Note that you can already generate the file without installing Docker first, but you won't be able to run your containerized application.

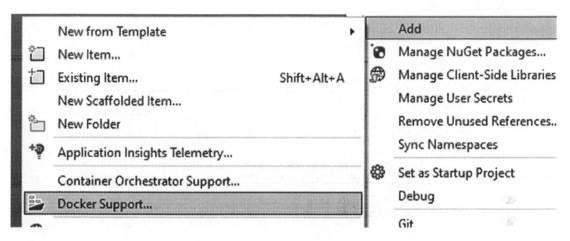

Figure 8-15. *Adding Docker support to an application*

Selecting this will ask if we want a Linux- or Windows-based container. Select Linux and continue. Visual Studio will generate a Docker file. This file contains all the instructions needed to build and run our .NET 6-based application in a container.

After adding the Docker file, Visual Studio will show Docker as a new debug target. If Docker is selected as debug target, Visual Studio will take the Dockerfile into account and follow its instructions to build the application whenever we launch the Build command. When we launch the app in debug, a container will spin up in Docker Desktop and a debugger will attach to that container. The first time you do this you might see some command line windows pop up. These are the Docker tooling downloading the correct images for this type of project.

```
C:\Windows\System32\cmd.exe
If you want to cancel the download, please close this window
6.0: Pulling from dotnet/aspnet
7d63c13d9b9b: Downloading [==========================>          ]  17.35MB/31.36MB
c560354b7c0a: Download complete
3f9174812a0d: Downloading [==============================>      ]  19.99MB/31.6MB
3d1acc595444: Download complete
94796297cf33: Download complete
```

Figure 8-16. *Downloading Docker images for ASP.NET*

Visual Studio provides us with a container pane showing us all running containers and their environment configuration.

Figure 8-17. *Running containers in Visual Studio*

To be able to use this container for deployment, we first need to upload it to a container repository. Docker has a public repository where we can upload containers called Docker Hub, but Azure also has a service that allows us to create private container registries. This service is called the Azure Container Registry, or ACR.

An ACR instance can be created through the portal, similar to web apps.

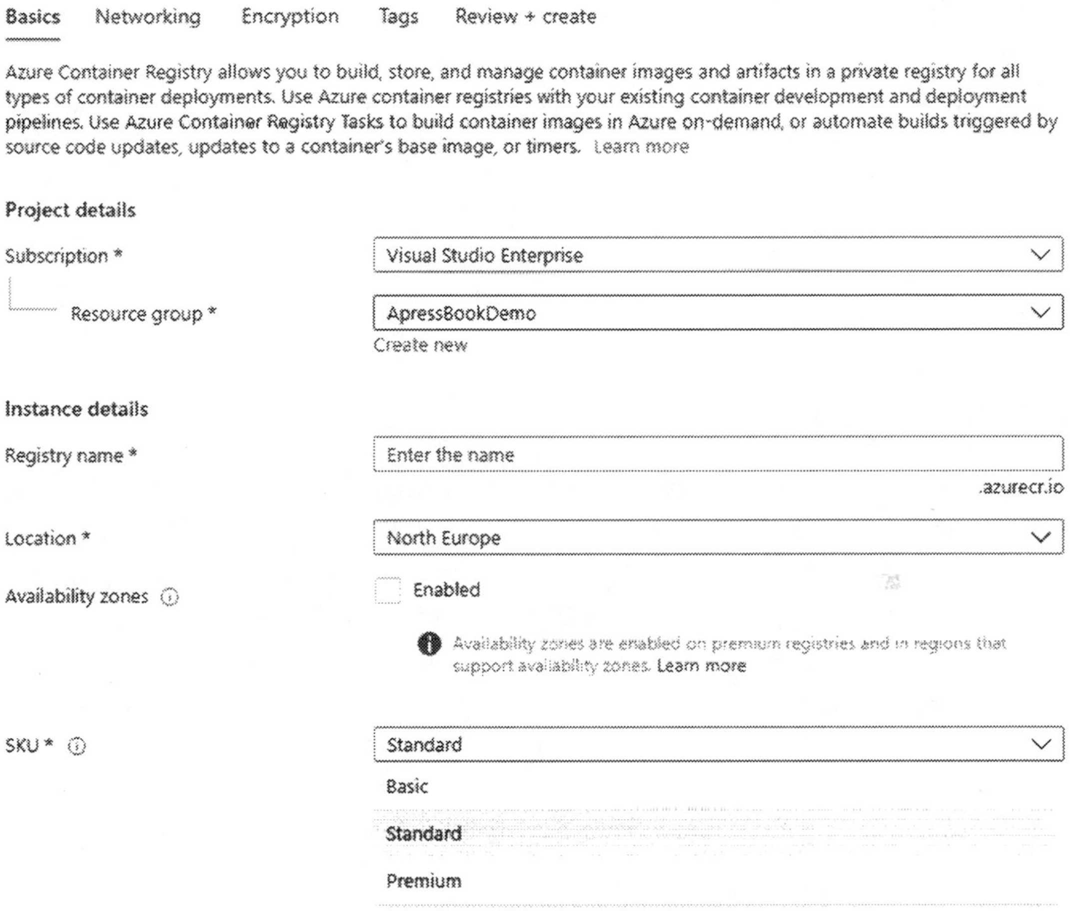

Basics   Networking   Encryption   Tags   Review + create

Azure Container Registry allows you to build, store, and manage container images and artifacts in a private registry for all types of container deployments. Use Azure container registries with your existing container development and deployment pipelines. Use Azure Container Registry Tasks to build container images in Azure on-demand, or automate builds triggered by source code updates, updates to a container's base image, or timers. Learn more

Project details

Subscription *   Visual Studio Enterprise   ∨

       Resource group *   ApressBookDemo   ∨
                          Create new

Instance details

Registry name *   Enter the name
                                                                    .azurecr.io

Location *   North Europe   ∨

Availability zones ⓘ ☐ Enabled

                          ❶ Availability zones are enabled on premium registries and in regions that
                             support availability zones. Learn more

SKU * ⓘ   Standard   ∨

                          Basic

                          Standard

                          Premium

Figure 8-18. *Creating an ACR instance*

Creating an ACR instance is quite easy; the most important thing is the name. We need the <hostname>.azurecr.io domain in our commands to upload our containers to the correct registry.

The next step would be to use the Docker CLI to buildour container; unfortunately, if we try to do this with the Dockerfile that was generated by Visual Studio, we get an error.

```
> docker build . -t dotnetsix.azurecr.io/mvcdemo
[+] Building 7.1s (13/17)
 => [internal] load build definition from Dockerfile                                    0.0s
 => => transferring dockerfile: 32B                                                     0.0s
 => [internal] load .dockerignore                                                       0.0s
 => => transferring context: 2B                                                         0.0s
 => [internal] load metadata for mcr.microsoft.com/dotnet/sdk:6.0                       0.3s
 => [internal] load metadata for mcr.microsoft.com/dotnet/aspnet:6.0                    0.0s
 => [internal] load build context                                                       1.2s
 => => transferring context: 61.97MB                                                    1.2s
 => [build 1/7] FROM mcr.microsoft.com/dotnet/sdk:6.0@sha256:33adb6c49f4b0017832eb4ab11649a3f822b9aafd24dE8980fbc 0.0s
 => [base 1/2] FROM mcr.microsoft.com/dotnet/aspnet:6.0                                 0.0s
 => CACHED [build 2/7] WORKDIR /src                                                     0.0s
 => CACHED [build 3/7] COPY [MvcDemo/MvcDemo.csproj, MvcDemo/]                          0.0s
 => CACHED [build 4/7] RUN dotnet restore "MvcDemo/MvcDemo.csproj"                      0.0s
 => [build 5/7] COPY .                                                                  0.5s
 => [build 6/7] WORKDIR /src/MvcDemo                                                    0.1s
 => ERROR [build 7/7] RUN dotnet build "MvcDemo.csproj" -c Release -o /app/build        4.0s
```

Figure 8-19. *Error on Docker build*

The reason is that this Dockerfile is used by the Visual Studio tooling to enable debugging and integrations. The Docker tooling internally uses different relative paths, assuming that the Docker file is on solution level, but Visual Studio places it on project level. The fastest solution is to copy the Docker file and duplicate it on solution level. In this way, both the Visual Studio tooling and Docker CLI tooling will work.

Once that is done, we are ready to build our container. Make sure your command line is in the solution directory, not the project directory.

Listing 8-3. Docker build command

```
docker build . -t dotnetsix.azurecr.io/mvcdemo
```

The *Docker build* command takes a path, which we define relatively by ". "; it will look for a Docker file and build according to the info in that file. The *tag*, or *t*, command is what you want to tag the container image as. A *tag* is in the form of *repositoryname:tag*.

```
> docker build . -t dotnetsix.azurecr.io/mvcdemo
[+] Building 3.7s (6/17)
=> [build 1/7] FROM mcr.microsoft.com/dotnet/sdk:6.0@sha256:33adb6c49f400817632eb4ab11649a3f422b9aafd24d88988fbc    2.6s
=> => sha256:60837c4accedebb52a579c04e4d18a7e7adc846b22cccb6b9a80447e6a3c55c8 10.49MB / 25.36MB                    2.6s
=> => sha256:7f6afd8e56633014f71f5b33d350dafe7d9b718a634b753dbb8cdd82d4c2be0a 8.39MB / 13.31MB                     2.6s
=> => sha256:766a0e1ec57e6842df2efbefb7cd4a7a5a5abcdd6413e6381d9c3d42d5d32a64 8.39MB / 136.57MB                    2.6s
```

Figure 8-20. *Building the container*

We now have successfully created our container image; it is fully ready to be uploaded to our Azure Container Registry. However, since the ACR instance is private, we need to authenticate to Azure and ACR first. Make sure to have the Azure CLI installed for authenticating with the cloud platform. The CLI can be found at `https://docs.microsoft.com/en-us/cli/azure/install-azure-cli`.

Once the Azure CLI is installed, we can authenticate against Azure with a simple command.

Listing 8-4. Authenticating with Azure

`az login`

This command will open a browser window to authenticate you with the correct Azure account. Once authenticated, a token will be set that can be accessed by the CLI. The next step is authenticating against the ACR instance.

Listing 8-5. Authenticating against ACR

`az acr login --name dotnetsix.azurecr.io`

If everything is set up correctly, we will get a *Login Succeeded* message. With this, authentication is set and we can push our container image to the registry.

Listing 8-6. Pushing container images to the ACR

`docker push dotnetsix.azurecr.io/mvcdemo`

We are not explicitly setting a tag so our image will automatically be tagged with *:latest*.

After upload we can inspect our image on the Azure portal in the ACR instance by going to Repositories, selecting the repository and the correcting tag.

Figure 8-21. *Container image on ACR*

The final step is creating a new Azure Web Apps instance and selecting Docker instead of code. The second step of the wizard will be the Docker setup.

Basics	**Docker**	Monitoring	Tags	Review + create

Pull container images from Azure Container Registry, Docker Hub or a private Docker repository. App Service will deploy the containerized app with your preferred dependencies to production in seconds.

Options	Single Container ⌄
Image Source	Azure Container Registry ⌄

Azure container registry options

Registry *	dotnetsix ⌄
Image *	mvcdemo ⌄
Tag *	latest ⌄
Startup Command ⓘ	

Figure 8-22. *Setting up an Azure Web App using ACR*

The wizard can connect to our ACR instance and read the list of images and tags. Azure will create a new instance, pull in the image from ACR, and create a container. Note that browsing to a Docker-based web app might take time; the container needs to be generated and spun up on first browse.

I have shown you the manual steps involved in building and deploying a Docker-based application. A next step would be to automate this entire process in your CI/CD pipeline.

Azure Functions

The final part in our discovery of Microsoft Azure brings us to serverless computing. Serverless computing means you have a piece of code running in the cloud without needing to worry about maintenance of the server, updating the operating system, scaling, containers, all of those classic overhead units of work are not needed in serverless systems. Obviously we still use servers to run our code in the cloud, but the fact that we can just build something and deploy it and it just works is where the term serverless computing comes from.

Serverless computing on Azure is done through a service called Azure Functions. Think back to RESTful APIs for a second. Remember how we created controllers with GET and POST requests? Imagine that you isolate one of those requests, the GET requests that load the list of books, for example. Now imagine that you can take that one request and deploy it to the cloud without any ASP.NET overhead, just the bare request, nothing else. That is what an Azure Function is. There is going to be a small overhead to define how the function is called as we will see, but it is much smaller than the overhead of setting up the entire ASP.NET environment.

Azure Functions are called by a trigger. Triggers are like events. These triggers can originate from different places; there are HTTP triggers that are called by doing an HTTP request to the function endpoint, very similar to a REST call. There are also numerous triggers that originate from other Azure resources, like a blob trigger that fires whenever a blob is added to a Blob Storage Container or a service bus queue trigger that fires whenever a message is received by a service bus.

Azure Functions can be written in different languages such as JavaScript and C# and different IDEs such as Visual Studio Code and Visual Studio 2022. Since this book is about .NET 6, we will focus on writing Functions with C# in Visual Studio 2022. When we select Azure Functions as a project type in Visual Studio 2022, the wizard lists the available triggers for us.

Queue trigger

A C# function that will be run whenever a message is added to a specified Azure Queue Storage

 Http trigger

A C# function that will be run whenever it receives an HTTP request

 Http trigger with OpenAPI

A C# function that will be run whenever it receives an HTTP request and is preconfigured to generate and render OpenAPI document

 Blob trigger

A C# function that will be run whenever a blob is added to a specified container.

 Timer trigger

A C# function that will be run on a specified schedule

 Durable Functions Orchestration

A C# Orchestration function that invokes activity functions in a sequence.

 SendGrid

A function that sends a confirmation e-mail when a new item is added to a particular queue.

 Event Hub trigger

A C# function that will be run whenever an event hub receives a new event

 Service Bus Queue trigger

A C# function that will be run whenever a message is added to a specified Service Bus queue

 Service Bus Topic trigger

A C# function that will be run whenever a message is added to the specified Service Bus topic

 Event Grid trigger

Figure 8-23. *Function triggers in Visual Studio*

There are two modes for Azure Functions. By default an Azure Function runs in-process with the Functions runtime, meaning that the class library containing our Function code is executed on the same runtime as the Functions process is running on.

This means that our code is tightly coupled to the runtime version of Azure Functions itself. This is fine for now since the Azure Functions runtime is currently running on .NET 6, but back when .NET 5 was released, this really was a problem. That is when support for out of process functions was added. That way the function itself can run in its own process, with its own self-contained runtime. For .NET 6 we can choose between *.NET 6*, which is in-process, or *.NET 6 (isolated)* which is out of process.

```
▲  InProcFunction
   ▷  Connected Services
   ▷  Dependencies
   ▷  Properties
      .gitignore
   ▷  C#  Function1.cs
      host.json
      local.settings.json
▲  OutProcFunction
   ▷  Connected Services
   ▷  Dependencies
   ▷  Properties
      .gitignore
   ▷  C#  Function1.cs
      host.json
      local.settings.json
   ▷  C#  Program.cs
```

Figure 8-24. *In-proc vs. out-proc projects*

There are a few differences in template availability between both modes, and there is a small difference in template as well; the out-of-process version needs a Program.cs to serve as a starting point for the function. For now we will continue with the in-process function. To get Azure Functions support in Visual Studio, you will need to add the Azure workload using the Visual Studio Installer.

For this demo, I have selected a function with HttpTrigger and OpenAPI support. When running the generated project, we get a result very similar to an ASP.NET WebAPI, a Swagger UI with an endpoint we can call.

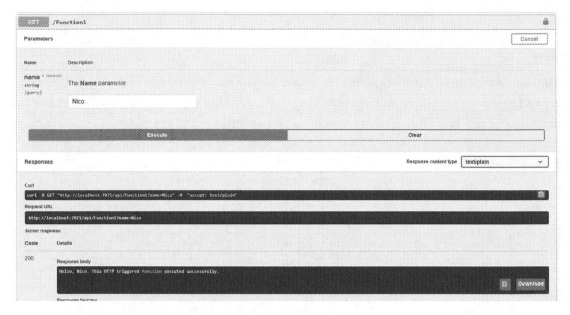

Figure 8-25. *Swagger UI for Azure Functions*

This function is running locally using the Azure Functions tools; since we have an HTTP trigger, it behaves exactly like a REST API. Let's dive into the function code. Listing 8-7 shows the code for this function.

Listing 8-7. A default Azure Function

```
[FunctionName("Function1")]
[OpenApiOperation(operationId: "Run", tags: new[] { "name" })]
[OpenApiSecurity("function_key", SecuritySchemeType.ApiKey, Name = "code",
In = OpenApiSecurityLocationType.Query)]
[OpenApiParameter(name: "name", In = ParameterLocation.Query, Required =
true, Type = typeof(string), Description = "The **Name** parameter")]
[OpenApiResponseWithBody(statusCode: HttpStatusCode.OK, contentType: "text/
plain", bodyType: typeof(string), Description = "The OK response")]
public async Task<IActionResult> Run(
    [HttpTrigger(AuthorizationLevel.Function, "get", "post", Route = null)]
    HttpRequest req)
{
    string name = req.Query["name"];
```

```
string requestBody = await new StreamReader(req.Body).ReadToEndAsync();
dynamic data = JsonConvert.DeserializeObject(requestBody);
name = name ?? data?.name;

string responseMessage = $"Hello, {name}. This HTTP triggered function
executed successfully.";

return new OkObjectResult(responseMessage);
}
```

We start with a couple of attributes. The first one gives the function its name. The name is used in Swagger UI and the Azure Portal. The other attributes are all used to describe the function according to the OpenAPI spec so that Swagger UI can generate a great experience; we have looked at Swagger and OAS in detail in the previous chapter. The HttpTrigger attribute configures the trigger for this function. It registers the function as an HTTP endpoint with specific verbs, in this case GET and POST, in the Azure Functions runtime. The HttpRequest comes in through the req parameter; from this request, we can fetch the request body, deserialize it, and use the request parameters to build the response. We will go a bit deeper with a more clear example.

For this example, we will port the book service we have created in the ASP.NET WebAPI chapter over to Azure Functions. In the WebAPI version, we use dependency injection to inject the IBookService into our controller or minimal API. We need to add some extra configuration to our Azure Function since an in-process function does not have a startup class by default. To add a startup object to an Azure Function, we first need to add the *Microsoft.Azure.Functions.Extensions* NuGet package to the project. Once that is added, we can create a startup object to configure Dependency Injection in our Function.

Listing 8-8. Custom startup object in an Azure Function

```
[assembly: FunctionsStartup(typeof(FunctionsDemo.Startup))]
namespace FunctionsDemo;

public class Startup : FunctionsStartup
{
```

```
public override void Configure(IFunctionsHostBuilder builder)
{
    builder.Services.AddSingleton<IBookCatalogService,
    BookCatalogService>();

}
}
```

The class name itself is not important; it is important that the class inherits from FunctionsStartup and that the namespace is decorated with an assembly-level FunctionsStartup attribute. We need to override the Configure method from the FunctionsStartup base class. The IFunctionsHostBuilder object that is passed in serves the same function as the WebApplicationBuilder from ASP.NET. We use the builder to register our service as a singleton, and that is all we need to do here. Listing 8-9 shows the class declaration, constructor, and a field to hold our injected service for our Azure Function that we will write.

Listing 8-9. BookFunctions class

```
public class BookFunctions
{
    private readonly IBookCatalogService _bookCatalogService;

    public BookFunctions(IBookCatalogService bookCatalogService)
    {
        _bookCatalogService = bookCatalogService;
    }
}
```

In our functions class, we can now inject the IBookCatalogService, just like we did in previous chapters. Listing 8-10 is the actual Function that we add to the class we just defined.

Listing 8-10. Fetching a list of books through an Azure Function

```
[FunctionName("FetchBooks")]
[OpenApiOperation(operationId: "FetchAll", tags: new[] { "Books" })]
[OpenApiResponseWithBody(statusCode: HttpStatusCode.OK, contentType:
"application/json", bodyType: typeof(Book[]), Description = "A list of books")]
```

```
public async Task<IActionResult> Run([HttpTrigger("get", Route = "books")]
HttpRequest req)
{
    Book[] books = await _bookCatalogService.FetchBookCatalog();

    return new OkObjectResult(books);
}
```

The first function will fetch a list of all books, hence the function name "FetchBooks."
The *OpenApiOperation* specifies the name of this operation and what group it belongs to.
This grouping of operations can be clearly seen in Swagger UI. *OpenApiResponseWithBody*
specifies the response type, HTTP status code, and content type. The method parameter
specifies that we have an HTTP Trigger using a GET verb.

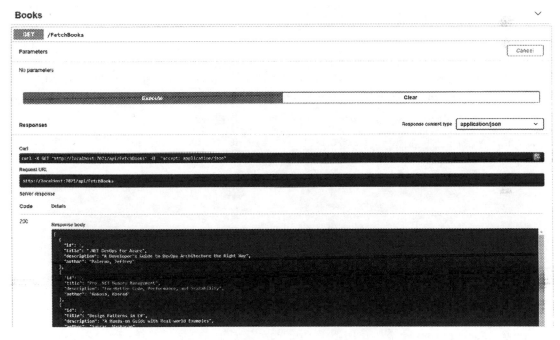

Figure 8-26. *Fetching books in Swagger UI*

Listing 8-11. Fetching a specific book by ID

```
[FunctionName("FetchBookByID")]
[OpenApiOperation(operationId: "FetchBookByID", tags: new[] { "Books" })]
[OpenApiParameter("id", Description = "The ID of a specific book",
Type = typeof(int))]
[OpenApiResponseWithBody(statusCode: HttpStatusCode.OK, contentType:
"application/json", bodyType: typeof(Book), Description =
"A specific book")]
public async Task<IActionResult> FetchBookById([HttpTrigger("get",
Route = "books/{id:int}")] HttpRequest req, int id)
{
    Book book = await _bookCatalogService.FetchBookById(id);

    return new OkObjectResult(book);
}
```

The second operation is fetching a book by ID. We specify an OpenApiParameter via an attribute to light up the input field in Swagger UI. The route specifies {id:int} as a parameter; this way we can add an extra id parameter to the method. Using that parameter, we can fetch the correct result from our datastore and pass it back to the requester.

```
[FunctionName("FetchBookByID")]
[OpenApiOperation(operationId: "FetchBookByID", tags: new[] { "Books" })]
[OpenApiParameter("id", Description = "The ID of a specific book", Type = typeof(int))]
[OpenApiResponseWithBody(statusCode: HttpStatusCode.OK, contentType: "application/json", bodyType: typeof(Book), Description = "A
0 references
public async Task<IActionResult> FetchBookById([HttpTrigger("get", Route = "books/{id:int}")] HttpRequest req, int id)  req = {Micro
{                                                                                            id    3
    Book book = await _bookCatalogService.FetchBookById(id);  book = {Book}

    return new OkObjectResult(book);  book = {Book}
}
```

Figure 8-27. *Parameter filled in through routing*

The final operation we are going to implement is a POST request to create a new book.

Listing 8-12. HTTP Trigger with POST

```
[FunctionName("AddBook")]
[OpenApiOperation(operationId: "AddBook", tags: new[] { "Books" })]
[OpenApiRequestBody("application/json", typeof(Book), Required = true)]
[OpenApiResponseWithBody(statusCode: HttpStatusCode.Created, contentType:
"application/json", bodyType: typeof(Book), Description = "A newly
added book")]
public async Task<IActionResult> AddBook([HttpTrigger("post", Route =
"books")] HttpRequest req)
{
    var book = await JsonSerializer.DeserializeAsync<Book>(req.Body);
    await _bookCatalogService.AddBook(book);

    return new CreatedResult($"/books/{book.Id}", book);
}
```

The major difference with the *GET* requests is that we specify the trigger to be of type *POST* and that we need to fetch the request body from the `HttpRequest` object. The Body property is a stream; fortunately, the `JsonSerializer` in `System.Text.Json` can accept a stream and deserialize it to any type.

Deploying Azure Functions

Finally we need to get these Functions in the cloud. We can do this straight from Visual Studio 2022 by right-clicking the project and selecting *Publish*. In the first step of the wizard, we specify that we want to publish to Azure. In the second step, we can choose if we want to create an Azure Function running on Windows or Linux or in a container.

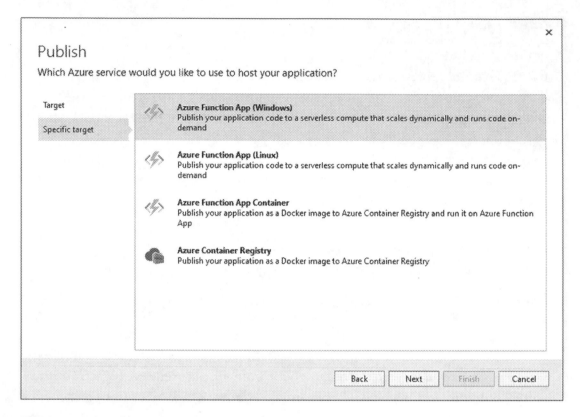

Figure 8-28. *Choosing a Function type*

For this demo, we will choose a Windows-based Function, but other options work just as well. In the next step of the wizard, we can click the + sign to start creating a new Function. The Function Name we choose here needs to be unique across Azure. The Plan Type has three options, *Consumption, Premium,* and *Dedicated (App Service)*. What you choose here has an impact on scaling, resources per instance, and support for advanced functionality such as virtual network connectivity. More information on the different plan types is found at https://docs.microsoft.com/en-us/azure/azure-functions/functions-scale. Azure Functions also require a Storage account because they rely on storage for managing Triggers and logging.

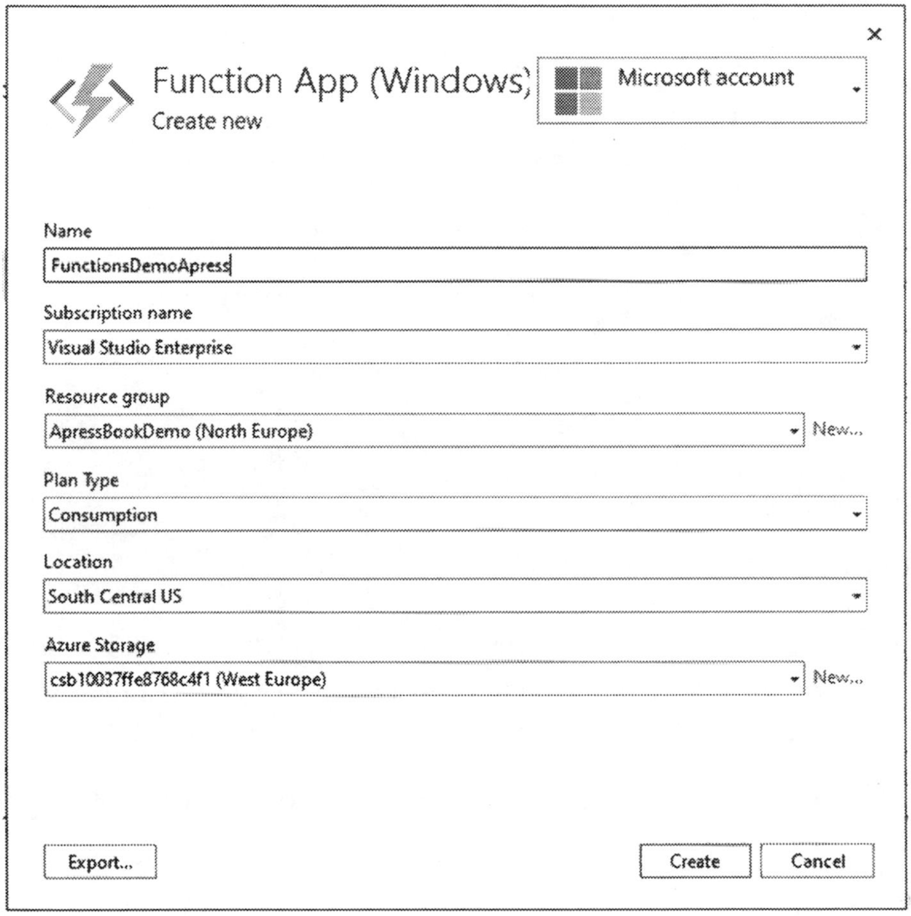

Figure 8-29. *Creating a new Function*

After the function is created, we can go to the API Management step. This is an option to integrate Functions into an API management resource, but that goes beyond the scope of this book, so we can safely skip this step by selecting the *Skip this step* option that will enable the *Create* button. Once all steps are done, we can hit the Publish button and Visual Studio will work its magic creating Azure resources and pushing our Function to it.

Looking at the Azure Portal, we can find our newly created Azure Functions resource, with the three Functions that we defined in code.

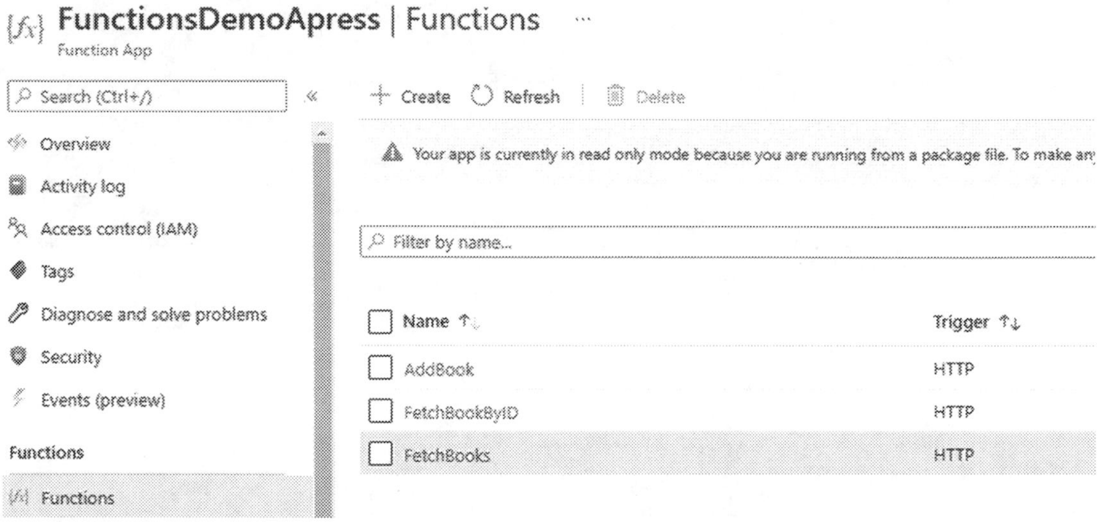

{fx} **FunctionsDemoApress** | Functions   ...
Function App

🔍 Search (Ctrl+/)   «   ＋ Create ○ Refresh | 🗑 Delete

✧ Overview   ⚠ Your app is currently in read only mode because you are running from a package file. To make any

🗄 Activity log

🍋 Access control (IAM)   🔍 Filter by name...

🏷 Tags

🖉 Diagnose and solve problems

🛡 Security   ☐ Name ↑↓   Trigger ↑↓

⚡ Events (preview)   ☐ AddBook   HTTP

Functions   ☐ FetchBookByID   HTTP

⌘ Functions   ☐ FetchBooks   HTTP

Figure 8-30. *Functions on the portal*

Opening the details of a function gives us the option to copy the url. The url is more than the route we defined in code; it needs to include a code for security reasons.

Get Function Url

| default (function key)   ∨ | https://functionsdemoapress.azurewebsites.net/api/books?code=nIZEZ1D4l |

▓ OK ▓

Figure 8-31. *Function url with function key*

Executing a GET request to this URL using Postman gives the result in Figure 8-32.

Figure 8-32. *Calling a Function from Postman*

Wrapping Up

Microsoft Azure is a powerful, globally distributed, versatile platform. The vast majority of available resources is large enough to fill multiple books on its own, so we have only scratched the surface here. I do hope that it has triggered you enough to go explore further and dive into the wonderous world of cloud-native applications and hybrid applications. With .NET being a first-class citizen in the Microsoft world, and .NET 6 being an important major release, it comes as no surprise that Azure was day 1 ready for .NET 6. Multiple services have supported it even back when .NET 6 was in preview. All of this is made complete with great Azure integration in Visual Studio 2022, allowing us to create resources and publish new code to them without leaving the IDE.

CHAPTER 9

Application Architecture

Together with .NET 6 came tooling to help developers build better architectures. Projects like Dapr and example project like eShop On Containers help tremendously with building well-designed and well-architected platforms.

So where can .NET 6 help in building great architectures? There are a few concepts in .NET that help simplify some things; but not to worry, .NET is not pushing you into any direction. We still have full flexibility to architect our applications however we see fit. What we do have is numerous syntax concepts that help keep our code small and readable.

Record Types

The quickest win is Data Transfer Objects, or DTOs. DTOs are a representation of an entity that will be passed over the wire over a data transfer protocol such as HTTP. DTOs are important because they prevent leaking nonpublic, internal information about entities to foreign systems. In most cases, they are a basic class containing auto-properties that map in a straightforward way onto the entity that they represent. Listing 9-1 shows an example of an entity.

Listing 9-1. The entity

```
public class Event : Entity, IAggregateRoot
{
    private readonly List<Attendee.Attendee> _attendees;

    public string Title { get; private set; }
    public DateTime StartDate { get; private set; }
    public DateTime EndDate { get; private set; }
    public decimal Price { get; private set; }
```

© Nico Vermeir 2022
N. Vermeir, *Introducing .NET 6*, https://doi.org/10.1007/978-1-4842-7319-7_9

```
    public int? AddressId { get; private set; }
    public Address Address { get; private set; }

    public virtual IReadOnlyCollection<Attendee.Attendee> Attendees =>
    _attendees;

    public Event(string title, DateTime startDate, DateTime endDate,
    decimal price)
    {
        _attendees = new List<Attendee.Attendee>();

        Title = title;
        StartDate = startDate;
        EndDate = endDate;
        Price = price;
    }

    public void SetAddress(Address address)
    {
        AddressId = address.Id;
        Address = address;
    }
}
```

This is a very basic example of an entity from an application build using the Domain-Driven-Design principles. It inherits from Entity, which has an Id property to give us a uniquely identifiable property, and it is an IAggregateRoot, which means that this object can be stored and retrieved on its own. Entities who are not an IAggregateRoot are not meant to exist by themselves; they depend on other objects to be a member of.

Let's say we need to fetch a list of events to show in our frontend; not using DTOs would mean that we could possibly fetch hundreds of events with all Attendee and Address details, while maybe all we want to do is show a list of upcoming events. To simply, list all events that would be too much data. Instead, we use a DTO to simplify the object that goes over the wire according to the use case we need.

Listing 9-2 shows an example what a DTO could look like for when we want a list of events.

Listing 9-2. DTO for listing events

```
public class EventForList
{
    public int Id { get; set; }

    public string Title { get; set; }

    public DateTime StartDate { get; set; }

    public DateTime EndDate { get; set; }
}
```

Way less data to send over the wire, and just enough. When needing to fetch the details for an Event, we of course need another DTO containing all the info an event detail page might need. You may realize that this can become tedious quite fast, writing DTO after DTO, mapping them to the entity, and so on. A neat compiler trick that came with .NET 5 can help speed this process up; that trick is called records. Listing 9-3 shows the DTO from Listing 9-2 again but written as a record.

Listing 9-3. DTO as a record

```
public record ActivityForListRecord (int Id, string Title, DateTime
StartDate, DateTime EndDate);
```

That is one line of code to replace all the auto-properties. A record is a shorthand for writing a class, but there is more to it. Equality, for example, in a normal class, two variables of the same reference type are equal when they point to the same reference. With a record, they are equal when they have the same value. In this case, a class that only contains properties. Another difference is that a record is immutable. The complete documentation on records can be found here https://docs.microsoft.com/en-us/dotnet/csharp/language-reference/builtin-types/record.

The values between the brackets are not parameters; they are properties, hence the Pascal Casing. As for the output, records are nothing more than a clever compiler trick, a pinch of syntactic sugar. Listing 9-4 compares the intermediate language definition of the EventForList class with the EventForList record. I have renamed them EventForListClass and EventForListRecord for convenience.

Listing 9-4. IL output for a record and a class

```
.class public auto ansi beforefieldinit ActivityForListRecord
    extends [System.Runtime]System.Object
```

```
.class public auto ansi beforefieldinit ActivityForListClass
    extends [System.Runtime]System.Object
```

As you can see, the outputs are identical, meaning records are known to the C# compiler but not to the runtime.

New to the C# language since C# 10 is value-type records. Up until now, records could only be reference types, classes. C# 10 introduces record structs which are value-type records. Listing 9-5 shows the earlier record example as a value type; notice the *struct* keyword.

Listing 9-5. Value-type records

```
public record struct ActivityForListRecord (int Id, string Title, DateTime
StartDate, DateTime EndDate);
```

Let's have a look at the IL again. Listing 9-6 shows the generated IL code.

Listing 9-6. IL output for a record struct and a class

```
.class public sequential ansi sealed beforefieldinit ActivityForListRecord
extends [System.Runtime]System.ValueType
```

```
.class public auto ansi beforefieldinit ActivityForListClass
    extends [System.Runtime]System.Object
```

Struct records follow the same rules as normal structs. Structs are often used because they are cheaper and memory-wise because they are value-typed. This often results in better performance. They do have limitations when compared to classes, for example, structs don't allow inheritance. A major difference between records and record structs is that record structs are not immutable by default; they can be if we mark them as readonly.

Monolith Architecture

Monolith applications are applications that contain everything in one or two services. Usually a frontend and a backend. Before Microservices, which we will talk about next, monoliths were very common. Figure 9-1 describes what a monolith architecture looks like.

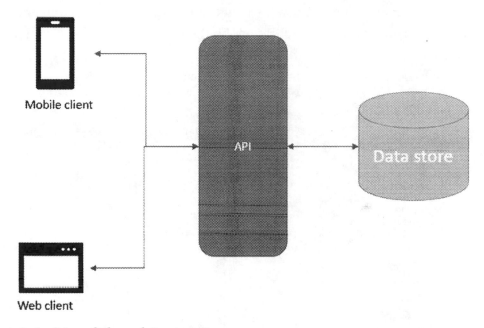

Figure 9-1. *Monolith architecture*

In this example, we have a web client and a mobile client; both speak to the same API that in turn is connected to a data store. Depending on the size of the application, this API can potentially be huge. Let's say there is one part of the API that is seeing intense usage and is slowing the entire API down. To solve this, we would need to scale the entire API or move it to a server with more power. Even worse, the entire system can go down because of a bottleneck in one place.

Another disadvantage of monolith services is maintainability. One big service containing all business logic is hard to maintain or even to keep an overview of what is where in the source code.

However, not everything is bad about monolith architecture. Depending on the size and complexity of your application, this might still be the right choice for you as microservices create extra layers of complexity besides the advantages they bring.

Microservices

Microservice architecture is a variation on service-oriented architecture. Creating a Microservices-based application means that the backend is split up into different loosely coupled services. Each service has its own responsibility and has no knowledge of the other services. Communication between services usually happens over a message bus. To prevent applications having to implement multiple endpoints, we can implement a gateway per application or type of application should we need to. That gateway knows the endpoints of the Microservices the application needs. Figure 9-2 shows a high-level architecture schema for a Microservices-based application.

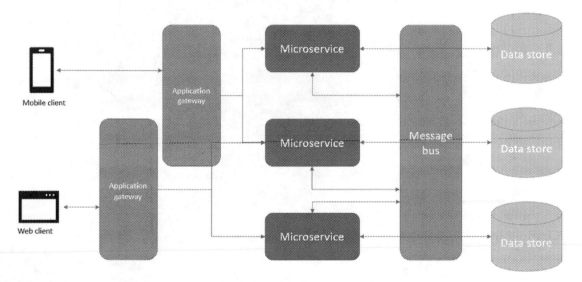

Figure 9-2. *Microservices architecture*

There is a lot to like about a Microservices-oriented architecture. The split responsibilities mean that we can scale the parts where scaling is needed instead of just pumping more memory into the virtual server. We can create gateways per client so that only the absolute necessary parts of the backend platform are exposed and so on. It also brings with it added complexity and cost; since each service is basically its own application, we need a lot of application servers; all of those servers need to be maintained. Even if we went with a container orchestration system like Kubernetes, we get extra overhead, and exactly this is the danger of overengineering or over-architecting an application. Microservices are a great architecture pattern, but they are not the silver bullet for all applications; depending on your use case, a monolith application might be just fine.

Microservices work great in a Domain-Driven-Design (DDD) or Clean Architecture (CA) scenario. The scope of a microservice can, in most cases, map to a bounded context. Domain-Driven-Design and Clean Architecture are widely popular design patterns for enterprise applications. They both give the domain model responsibility for changes and nicely decouple read and write requests. Both are really great patterns to add to your arsenal as a developer.

A bounded context is a functional block of your application that can be isolated. For example, the orders of a webshop can contain products, customers, purchases, and so on. That isolated block of orders functionality can be a bounded context. However, just like with Microservices, DDD and CA have their place in larger applications. Don't overengineer; use the right tool for the job instead of using a sledgehammer to drive a nail in a wooden board.

If you are interested in learning more about Clean Architecture or Domain-Driven-Design, I can advise you to take a look at the e-book of eshop on containers or the *Practical Event-Driven Microservices Architecture* book available from Apress.

Container Orchestration

We have talked about containers, specifically Docker-based containers, in the ASP.NET chapter. Containers and Microservices are a great match, if there is an orchestrator. A container orchestrator is a tool that manages a set of different container images and how they relate to each other. Can they communicate? Over what port? Which containers get exposed outside of the cluster? And so on. The most common orchestrators are Kubernetes and Docker Compose.

Kubernetes

Kubernetes, or k8s for short (`https://kubernetes.io`), is a container orchestrator. It can automatically deploy and scale your containerized applications. A set of containers deployed on a Kubernetes instance is called a cluster. To explore the capabilities of Kubernetes, I can advise you to install Minikube via `https://minikube.sigs.k8s.io/`. Minikube is a local Kubernetes cluster installation that you can use for development. It is available for Windows, Linux, and Mac OS. The installer and install instructions can be downloaded at `https://minikube.sigs.k8s.io/docs/start/`.

```
nico@Noctis:/mnt/c/Users/nico_$ minikube start
🎉  minikube v1.20.0 on Ubuntu 20.04 (amd64)
✨  Using the docker driver based on existing profile
🏄  Starting control plane node minikube in cluster minikube
🔄  Pulling base image ...
🎮  Updating the running docker "minikube" container ...
🐳  Preparing Kubernetes v1.20.2 on Docker 20.10.6 ...
🔎  Verifying Kubernetes components...
    ▪ Using image kubernetesui/dashboard:v2.1.0
    ▪ Using image kubernetesui/metrics-scraper:v1.0.4
    ▪ Using image gcr.io/k8s-minikube/storage-provisioner:v5
🌟  Enabled addons: storage-provisioner, default-storageclass, dashboard
🏄  Done! kubectl is now configured to use "minikube" cluster and "default" namespace by default
```

Figure 9-3. *Running Minikube on WSL2*

Once Minikube is installed, we can use the Kubernetes CLI through the *kubectl* command.

```
nico@Noctis:/mnt/c/Users/nico_$ kubectl version
Client Version: version.Info{Major:"1", Minor:"21", GitVersion:"v1.21.5", GitCommit:"aea7bbadd2fc0cd689de94a54e5b7b75886
9d691", GitTreeState:"clean", BuildDate:"2021-09-15T21:10:45Z", GoVersion:"go1.16.8", Compiler:"gc", Platform:"linux/amd
64"}
Server Version: version.Info{Major:"1", Minor:"20", GitVersion:"v1.20.2", GitCommit:"faecb196815e248d3ecfb03c680a4507229
c2a56", GitTreeState:"clean", BuildDate:"2021-01-13T13:20:00Z", GoVersion:"go1.15.5", Compiler:"gc", Platform:"linux/amd
64"}
```

Figure 9-4. *Kubernetes CLI*

Time for some terminology. Kubernetes is a cluster consisting of Nodes. Nodes are actual machines, virtual or physical servers, that have Kubernetes installed and are added to the cluster. Running kubectl gets nodes list the available nodes in the cluster; a local installation of Minikube is a cluster with one node.

```
nico@Noctis:/mnt/c/Users/nico_$ kubectl get nodes
NAME       STATUS    ROLES                 AGE    VERSION
minikube   Ready     control-plane,master  197d   v1.20.2
```

Figure 9-5. *Nodes in a Minikube cluster*

One of the nodes is the control plane: the node that controls the cluster. Communication to and from the control plane happens over the Kubernetes API.

A deployed container on a node is called a Pod. For this example, we will create a Pod from one of the services in eShop On Containers. eShop On Containers is an open source reference architecture by Microsoft; it can be found at `https://github.com/dotnet-architecture/eShopOnContainers`. The reason we are using this as an example is because the eShop is a container-ready Microservices architecture. It fits quite right with the topic we are dealing with at the moment.

Time to create a Pod. Listing 9-7 shows the command to create a deployment on our local Kubernetes cluster.

Listing 9-7. Creating a new deployment to Kubernetes

```
kubectl create deployment apresseshop --image=eshop/catalog.api
```

The deployment, and the pod, gets created. The image will start pulling in the background and the container will spin up when ready. To check the status of the nodes, we can use `kubectl get pods`.

```
> kubectl get pods
NAME                          READY   STATUS    RESTARTS   AGE
apresseshop-68f55f8d58-glr79   1/1    Running   1          4m58s
```

Figure 9-6. *1 Pod running on local cluster*

Of course, this is a very basic example and complete overkill of what Kubernetes is intended for. As a more elaborate example, I have deployed the entire eShop On Container example on my local cluster.

```
> kubectl get pods
NAME                                          READY   STATUS            RESTARTS   AGE
eshop-apigwms-7b8fd7b8b7-7qt47                1/1     Running           0          2m42s
eshop-apigwws-86548bfd5f-5924x                0/1     ContainerCreating 0          2m41s
eshop-basket-api-75798bc897-qm6gl             0/1     Running           0          3m4s
eshop-basket-data-566f8cd988-gjqvw            1/1     Running           0          3m6s
eshop-catalog-api-75fd55845f-gxq9q            0/1     Running           0          3m3s
eshop-identity-api-b556c6787-ztkkk            0/1     Running           0          3m1s
eshop-keystore-data-f78cfc774-qc6gd           1/1     Running           0          3m7s
eshop-mobileshoppingagg-b44795855-6sksh       0/1     ContainerCreating 0          3m
eshop-nosql-data-fddb866ff-zc7zq              1/1     Running           0          3m10s
eshop-ordering-api-6f89f5fc7c-c8vh2           0/1     ContainerCreating 0          2m58s
eshop-ordering-backgroundtasks-7f57fb95b4-5mg66 0/1   ContainerCreating 0          2m57s
eshop-ordering-signalrhub-5b5dc6854d-rtwcc    0/1     ContainerCreating 0          2m55s
eshop-payment-api-695f9d5866-4vbgt            0/1     ContainerCreating 0          2m53s
eshop-rabbitmq-679457db7-k64rm                1/1     Running           0          3m9s
eshop-sql-data-66b6658c6c-mjc9x               1/1     Running           0          3m11s
eshop-webhooks-api-5c7db8964-zs9v2            0/1     ContainerCreating 0          2m45s
eshop-webhooks-web-78b65f4847-q567q           0/1     ContainerCreating 0          2m44s
eshop-webmvc-59c94588cf-mxwv6                 0/1     ContainerCreating 0          2m52s
eshop-webshoppingagg-75bdb755cc-5xbfj         0/1     ContainerCreating 0          2m50s
eshop-webspa-5df7f8d448-xrqn2                 0/1     ContainerCreating 0          2m48s
eshop-webstatus-7bdf569cf6-rdvxl              0/1     ContainerCreating 0          2m47s
```

Figure 9-7. *Deploying a larger Kubernetes cluster*

I didn't have to manually create each container that would defeat the purpose of a container orchestrator. Instead, the project contains yaml files that Kubernetes can use to deploy and configure a set of services.

Listing 9-8. An example Kubernetes file

```
apiVersion: apps/v1
kind: Deployment
metadata:
  name: catalog
  labels:
    app: catalogApi
spec:
  replicas: 1
  selector:
    matchLabels:
      app: catalog
  template:
    metadata:
      labels:
        app: catalog
    spec:
      containers:
        - name: catalog
          imagePullPolicy: IfNotPresent
          image: eshop/catalog.api
```

Listing 9-8 shows an example of a Kubernetes file that spins up a pod of the catalog API.

Docker Compose

Docker Compose is a popular alternative to Kubernetes. It is more designed to work on a single node, while Kubernetes really shines in big enterprise, multi-server environments. This also means that the learning curve for Docker Compose is much smaller. Using Docker Compose is simple: make sure your applications have their own Docker file, create a *docker-compose.yml,* and run the *up* command on the Docker Compose CLI.

We should already have Docker installed since we have installed Docker Desktop in the previous chapter. Docker is packaged together with Docker Desktop on Windows. On Linux it can be installed through Python's package manager PIP or by downloading the binary from GitHub. Detailed instructions can be found in the Docker Compose documentation `https://docs.docker.com/compose/install/`. Listing 9-9 shows a simple example of a Docker Compose file using two of the eshop images.

Listing 9-9. Example of Docker Compose file

```
version: "3"
services:
  catalogapi:
    container_name: catalogApi
    image: eshop/catalog.api
    restart: unless-stopped

  webmvc:
    container_name: webmvc
    image: eshop/webmvc
    restart: unless-stopped
```

To run this, we execute `docker-compose up` in a command line window.

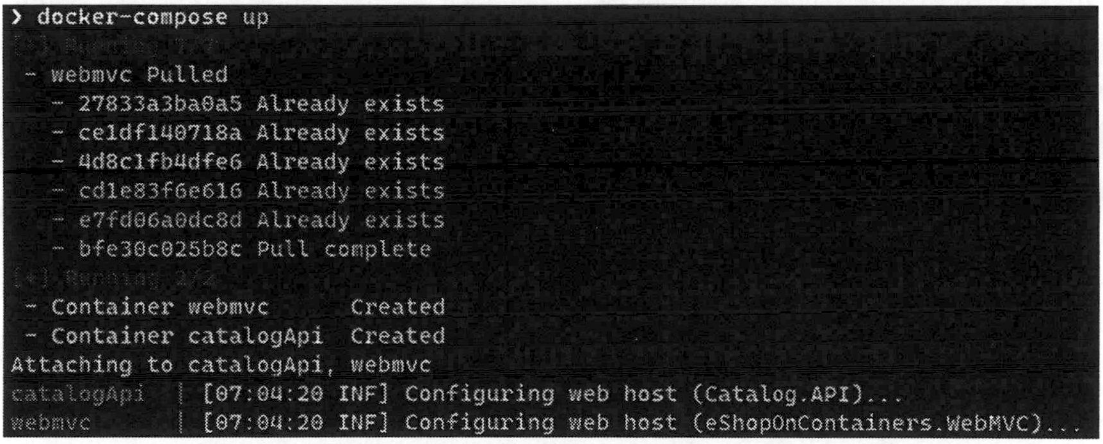

```
> docker-compose up

- webmvc Pulled
  - 27833a3ba0a5 Already exists
  - ce1df140718a Already exists
  - 4d8c1fb4dfe6 Already exists
  - cd1e83f6e616 Already exists
  - e7fd06a0dc8d Already exists
  - bfe30c025b8c Pull complete

- Container webmvc      Created
- Container catalogApi  Created
Attaching to catalogApi, webmvc
catalogApi | [07:04:20 INF] Configuring web host (Catalog.API)...
webmvc     | [07:04:20 INF] Configuring web host (eShopOnContainers.WebMVC)...
```

Figure 9-8. *Running two containers in Docker Compose*

From this point on, the CLI will start printing the debug output from the different running containers. If you want to run your containers in the background, you can use the *-d* flag.

Listing 9-10. Running Docker Compose in the background

```
docker-compose up -d
```

The Docker Compose file can be further expanded by adding volumes for persistent storage or network capabilities; all the information on how to do that can be found at the official Docker Compose documentation.

Dapr

The Distributed Application Runtime (Dapr) provides APIs that simplify microservice connectivity. The complete documentation for Dapr is found at `https://docs.dapr.io/`. It is a Microsoft-owned open-source project that can help simplify the management of large distributed systems. Consider it a "Microservices toolkit." Dapr provides capabilities such as service-to-service communication, state management, publish/subscribe messaging pattern, observables, secrets, and so on. All these capabilities are abstracted away by Dapr's building blocks. Dapr by itself is large enough to fill an entire book; what I want to do here is give you an idea of what Dapr is about so you can determine for yourself if you can use it in your project.

Installing Dapr

First step is installing the Dapr CLI. Dapr provides scripts that download the binaries and updates path variables. The easiest way is to execute the script in Listing 9-11. Other ways to install can be found on `https://docs.dapr.io/getting-started/install-dapr-cli/`.

Listing 9-11. Installing Dapr CLI

```
powershell -Command "iwr -useb https://raw.githubusercontent.com/dapr/cli/master/install/install.ps1 | iex"
```

Once the CLI is installed, we need to initialize our Dapr environment by calling dapr init on the command line. Make sure to have Docker installed before Dapr, as Dapr relies on containers to get its components up and running locally.

```
> dapr init
Making the jump to hyperspace...
Installing runtime version 1.5.0
Downloading binaries and setting up components...
Downloaded binaries and completed components set up.
daprd binary has been installed to C:\Users\nico_\.dapr\bin.
dapr_placement container is running.
dapr_redis container is running.
dapr_zipkin container is running.
Use 'docker ps' to check running containers.
Success! Dapr is up and running. To get started, go here: https://aka.ms/dapr-getting-started
```

Figure 9-9. *Setting up Dapr*

Once initialized, we can find some new containers running in our local Docker setup.

```
> docker ps
CONTAINER ID    IMAGE                   COMMAND
a95e55111af9    daprio/dapr:1.5.0       "./placement"
62559c973bbc    openzipkin/zipkin       "start-zipkin"
fb96a7fc631f    redis                   "docker-entrypoint.s…"
17d1df98f65f    a3f21ec4bd11            "/entrypoint.sh /ngi…"
```

Figure 9-10. *Dapr containers running on Docker*

Now we have everything set up, we can get to work. Dapr works according to the sidecar pattern. Meaning that we don't have to include all components and code in our own application; we only need to make Dapr API calls that go to the sidecar that is attached to our application. That sidecar abstracts all logic away from us.

The sidecar pattern is a design pattern where components of an application are deployed into separate processes or containers. This provides isolation and encapsulation.

Dapr State Management

Let's use the Dapr state management component as an example. State management in Dapr is done by default through Redis Cache. Dapr abstracts the logic of setting up Redis and calling its APIs away from us. We only need to call Dapr APIs to get state management up and running.

For this example, I have created a blank Console application using .NET 6.

Listing 9-12. Calling Dapr state management

```
using Dapr.Client;

const string storeName = "daprstate";
const string key = "counter";

var daprClient = new DaprClientBuilder().Build();
var counter = await daprClient.GetStateAsync<int>(storeName, key);

while (true)
{
    Console.WriteLine($"Counter state: {counter++}");

    await daprClient.SaveStateAsync(storeName, key, counter);
    await Task.Delay(1000);
}
```

We need to add the Dapr.Client NuGet package to the project and make sure Dapr is up and running. Once everything is set up correctly, we can start Dapr and run our .NET 6 application inside the Dapr environment with the Redis sidecar. Listing 9-13 shows the command that we can use to launch our application.

Listing 9-13. Launching the application using Dapr CLI

```
dapr run --app-id DaprCounter dotnet run
```

The output will be the counter increasing. If we stop and relaunch the application, you will notice that the counter did not start from zero again; it saved its state in Redis across restarts.

Figure 9-11.   *The Dapr sidecar model*

This was just one very simple example of Dapr. The major advantage is that Dapr takes a bunch of components and principles and bundles them into one developer model. We only need to develop against the Dapr API; everything else is handled by the runtime.

Wrapping Up

.NET has always been a framework that promotes good, clean architectures, and it continues that trend with .NET 6. Open-source reference projects like eShop On Containers help guide developers and application architects in finding the best architecture for their projects. Frameworks like Dapr can help ease the struggles of managing all the different building blocks in distributed applications. But as always, there is no one-size-fits-all. Look at the project you want to build from a higher, abstracter place, and choose the right architecture for the job. Not everything is suited for a complex DDD setup; don't overengineer but keep things simple.

CHAPTER 10

.NET Compiler Platform

A part of the strength and flexibility of .NET comes from its compiler platform. Most people have known it under its project name Roslyn. With the compiler platform, developers can analyze their code, enforce coding guidelines, and more. Besides Roslyn, Microsoft has also introduced source generators. Source generators leverage Roslyn to generate code at compile time and include that generated code into the compilation.

Roslyn

Developers rely heavily on their tools to help their development. Just look at what Visual Studio does to help you write better code, or look at the rich ecosystem of Visual Studio extensions. IDE features like IntelliSense and Find All References need an understanding of the current code base; this is typically information that a compiler can provide. Compilers used to be black boxes that took your source code and transformed it into, in our case, intermediate language. With Roslyn, Microsoft aimed to open up the compiler platform and provide it with an API set for everyone to use to write code enhancing tools.

With Roslyn, we can write analyzers and code fixes. Analyzers look at your code and notify you when you write a piece of code that is not according to what the analyzer knows. .NET even ships with a default set of Analyzers; just open a new .NET 6 project and use solution explorer to have a look at Dependencies ➤ Analyzers, as shown in Figure 10-1.

© Nico Vermeir 2022
N. Vermeir, *Introducing .NET 6*, https://doi.org/10.1007/978-1-4842-7319-7_10

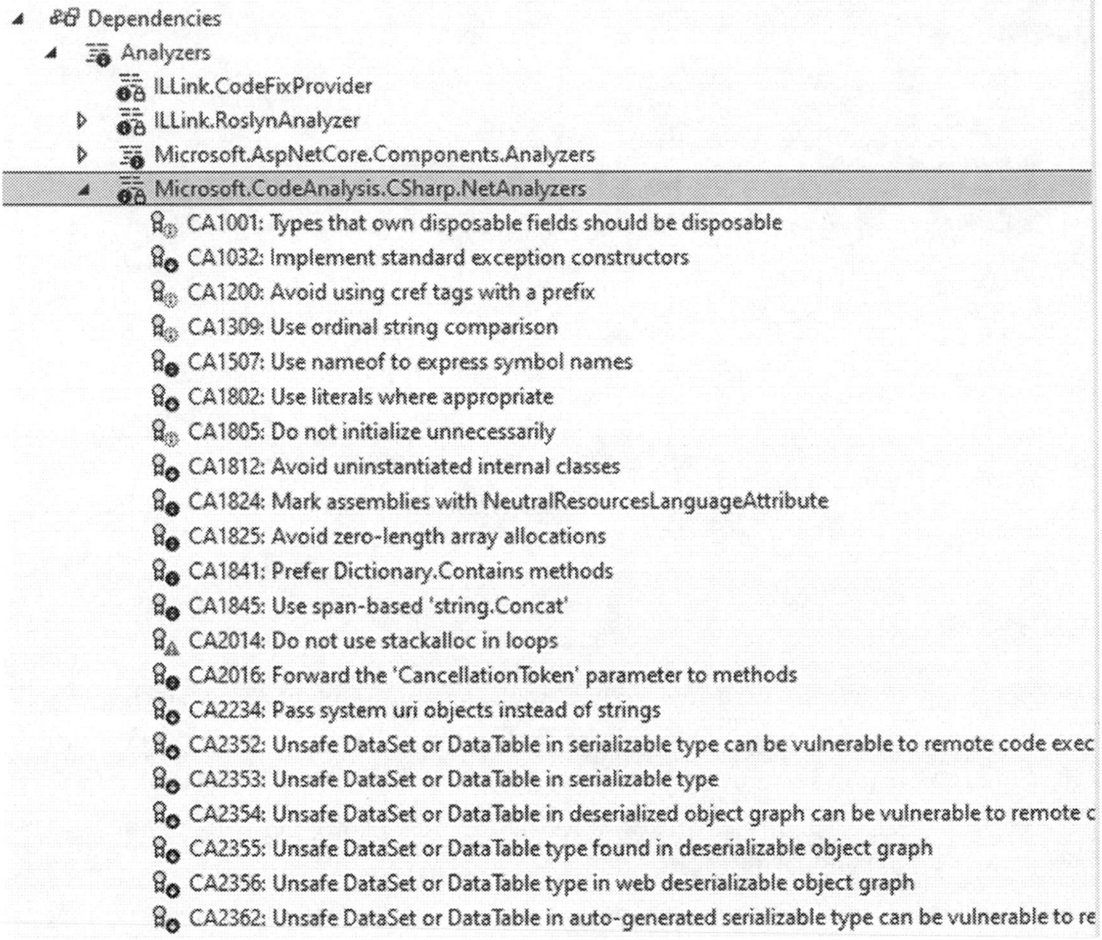

▲ 🔗 Dependencies
   ▲ 📇 Analyzers
       📇 ILLink.CodeFixProvider
    ▷ 📇 ILLink.RoslynAnalyzer
    ▷ 📇 Microsoft.AspNetCore.Components.Analyzers
    ▲ 📇 Microsoft.CodeAnalysis.CSharp.NetAnalyzers
         ⚙ CA1001: Types that own disposable fields should be disposable
         ⚙ CA1032: Implement standard exception constructors
         ⚙ CA1200: Avoid using cref tags with a prefix
         ⚙ CA1309: Use ordinal string comparison
         ⚙ CA1507: Use nameof to express symbol names
         ⚙ CA1802: Use literals where appropriate
         ⚙ CA1805: Do not initialize unnecessarily
         ⚙ CA1812: Avoid uninstantiated internal classes
         ⚙ CA1824: Mark assemblies with NeutralResourcesLanguageAttribute
         ⚙ CA1825: Avoid zero-length array allocations
         ⚙ CA1841: Prefer Dictionary.Contains methods
         ⚙ CA1845: Use span-based 'string.Concat'
         ⚙ CA2014: Do not use stackalloc in loops
         ⚙ CA2016: Forward the 'CancellationToken' parameter to methods
         ⚙ CA2234: Pass system uri objects instead of strings
         ⚙ CA2352: Unsafe DataSet or DataTable in serializable type can be vulnerable to remote code exec
         ⚙ CA2353: Unsafe DataSet or DataTable in serializable type
         ⚙ CA2354: Unsafe DataSet or DataTable in deserialized object graph can be vulnerable to remote c
         ⚙ CA2355: Unsafe DataSet or DataTable type found in deserializable object graph
         ⚙ CA2356: Unsafe DataSet or DataTable type in web deserializable object graph
         ⚙ CA2362: Unsafe DataSet or DataTable in auto-generated serializable type can be vulnerable to re

Figure 10-1. *Built-in analyzers*

As you can see, Roslyn can provide numerous checks for best practices. The different icons point to the different severity levels of the checks. Some are warnings; others are errors and will cause builds to fail. Code fixes on the other hand provide proposals to the developer on how to refactor the code to fix an analyzer warning. A code fix can, for example, turn a For Each block into a simple LINQ statement by the push of a button. Figure 10-2 shows an example of this.

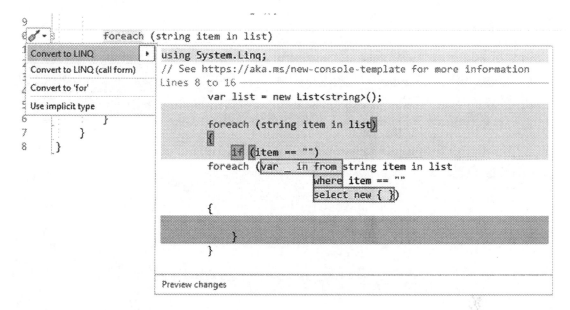

Figure 10-2. *Using an analyzer to convert a For Each to LINQ*

Roslyn ships with an SDK. That SDK provides us with all the tools we need to hook into the compiler pipeline. From the SDK we get compiler APIs, diagnostic APIs, scripting APIs, and workspace APIs.

Compiler API

The Compiler API contains the actual language-specific code compiler; in case of C#, this would be *csc.exe*. The API itself contains object models for each phase in the compiler pipeline. Figure 10-3 shows a diagram of the compiler pipeline.

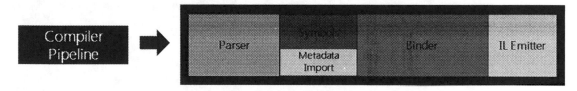

Figure 10-3. *Compiler pipeline (Source: Microsoft)*

Diagnostic API

The diagnostic API is what gives us the "squiggly lines" in our code. It's an API that analyzes syntax, assignments, and semantics based on Roslyn analyzers. It generates warnings or errors. This API can be used by linting tools to, for example, fail a build when certain team guidelines are not respected in a pull request.

Scripting API

This is part of the compiler layer and can be used to run code snippets as scripts. This is used by, for example, the C# Read, Evaluate, Print Loop, or REPL to run snippets of C# against a running assembly.

Workspace API

The workspace API provides the entry point for code analysis and refactorings over entire solutions. It powers IDE functions like Find All References and Formatting.

Syntax Tree

The syntax tree is a data structure exposed by the compiler API. It's a representation of the syntax structure of your code. The syntax tree enables tools to process and analyze the structure of your code. Using the syntax tree add-ins and IDE software can detect patterns in your code and change it when deemed necessary. A syntax tree has three characteristics:

- It contains the full information of the code that was typed by the developers, including comments, compiler pre-directives, and whitespaces.

- The exact original code can be reconstructed from a syntax tree. A syntax tree is an immutable construct that was parsed from the original source code. In order to provide the full power of analytics and code refactoring, the syntax tree needs to be able to reproduce the exact code it was parsed from.

- Syntax trees are thread-safe and immutable. A syntax tree is a state snapshot of the code. In-framework factory methods make sure that requested changes are pushed back to the code and a new syntax tree is generated based on the latest state of the source code. Syntax trees have a lot of optimizations in place so that new instances of a tree can be generated very fast with little memory use.

Roslyn SDK

As mentioned before, Roslyn is extendable. To be able to develop your own Roslyn analyzers, you need to install the Roslyn SDK. The SDK is part of the Visual Studio installer; it's available as an optional item as seen in Figure 10-4.

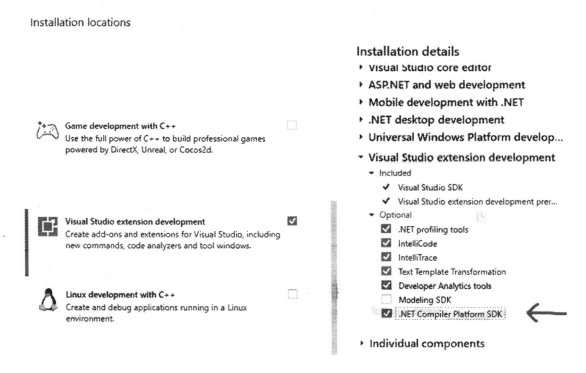

Figure 10-4. *Installing the .NET Compiler Platform SDK*

With the SDK comes the Syntax Visualizer. The Syntax Visualizer is an extra window in Visual Studio, under View ➤ Other Windows ➤ Syntax Visualizer, that lays out the syntax tree of the current open code file in Visual Studio. Its position synchronizes with your cursor in the source file. Figure 10-5 shows the visualizer docked to the side in Visual Studio 2022.

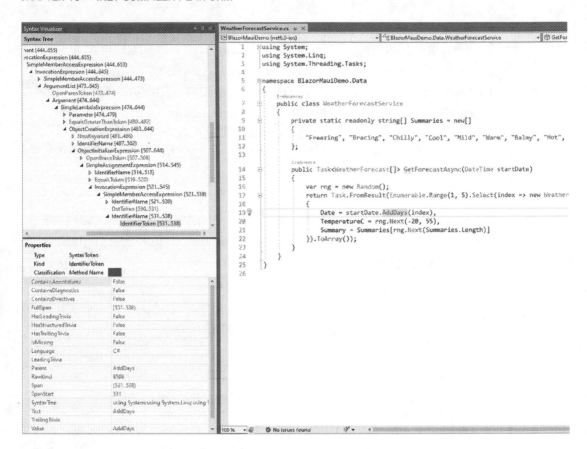

Figure 10-5. *Syntax Visualizer*

Figure 10-6. Roslyn project templates

The Syntax Visualizer is a great visual aid when working with the syntax tree. After installing the .NET Compiler Platform SDK, you will have access to new project templates in Visual Studio.

With these templates, you can build your own analyzers, code fixes, or code refactorings, both as a stand-alone console application and as a Visual Studio extension in the VSIX format. These templates are available for both C# and Visual Basic.

281

Creating an Analyzer

Let's create a stand-alone code analysis. Notice that the code analysis tools need to be written in .NET Framework; don't worry about that; they do support analyzing .NET 6 code. The default template queries the available version of MSBuild on your system and lists them to select which version you want to analyze code against. Figure 10-7 shows the default output when we run the unchanged template; this list might be different for you depending on what is installed on your system.

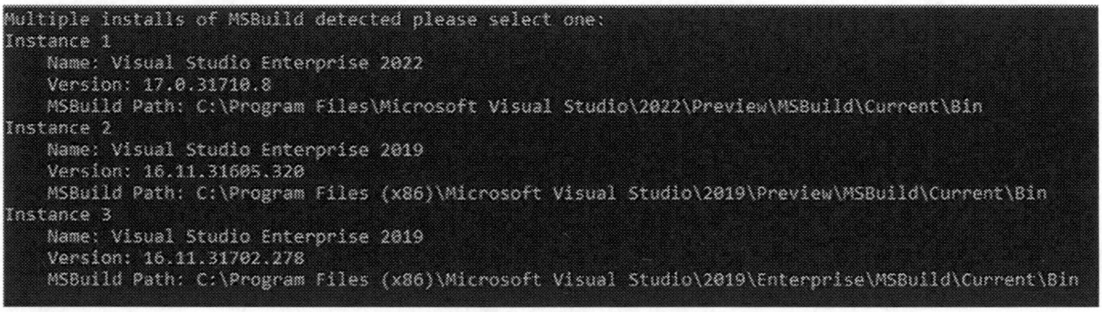

Figure 10-7. *Listing the available MSBuild instances*

The logic of detecting MSBuild instances is abstracted away by the Roslyn SDK; all we need to do is call `MSBuildLocator.QueryVisualStudioInstances().ToArray()` to get a list of versions installed. Let's empty the `Main` method and start implementing a code analyzer ourselves.

When analyzing code, we will need a `SyntaxTree` object. A `SyntaxTree` holds a parsed representation of a code document. In our example, we will inspect a piece of code and print the using statements in the console. Once we have our syntax tree parsed, we can extract a `CompilationUnitSyntax` object. This object represents our code document, divided into members, using directives and attributes.

Listing 10-1 shows how to get the syntax tree and compilation unit from a piece of code.

Listing 10-1. Generating the syntax tree and compilation unit

```
static Task Main(string[] args)
{
    const string code = @"using System; using System.Linq; Console.
    WriteLine(""Hello World"");";

    SyntaxTree tree = CSharpSyntaxTree.ParseText(code);
    CompilationUnitSyntax root = tree.GetCompilationUnitRoot();
```

We are using a very simple code example to get the point across. We parse the code into a SyntaTree and extract the CompilationUnitRoot from there.

Next we will need a CSharpSyntaxWalker object. A syntax walker is an implementation of the Visitor design pattern. The Visitor pattern describes a way to decouple an object structure from an algorithm; more information on the pattern is found at https://en.wikipedia.org/wiki/Visitor_pattern.

The CSharpSyntaxWalker class is an abstract class so we will need to create our own class that inherits from CSharpSyntaxWalker. For this example, we add a class called UsingDirectivesWalker. Listing 10-2 shows the code for this class.

Listing 10-2. Custom using directive syntax walker

```
class UsingDirectivesWalker : CSharpSyntaxWalker
{
    public override void VisitUsingDirective(UsingDirectiveSyntax node)
    {
        Console.WriteLine($"Found using {node.Name}.");
    }
}
```

In this example, we are overriding the VisitUsingDirective method from the CSharpSyntaxWalker base class. The base class comes with many override methods that each visits a specific type of syntax nodes. The VisitUsingDirective method visits all using directives in our syntax tree. The complete list of methods that can be overwritten is found at https://docs.microsoft.com/en-us/dotnet/api/microsoft.codeanalysis.csharp.csharpsyntaxwalker.

For each using node we visit, we print its name. All there is left now is to use this custom syntax walker. Listing 10-3 shows the complete Main method.

Listing 10-3. Using the UsingDirectivesWalker

```
static Task Main(string[] args)
{
    const string code = @"using System; using System.Linq; Console.
    WriteLine(""Hello World"");";

    SyntaxTree tree = CSharpSyntaxTree.ParseText(code);
    CompilationUnitSyntax root = tree.GetCompilationUnitRoot();

    var collector = new UsingDirectivesWalker();
    collector.Visit(root);

    Console.Read();
    return Task.CompletedTask;
}
```

We instantiate our new syntax walker class and call its Visit method, passing in the CompilationUnitSyntax. This triggers the methods in the CSharpSyntaxWalker base class, from which one is overwritten in our own syntax walker class. This results in the output visible in Figure 10-8.

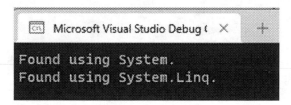

Figure 10-8. *Analyzer output*

This has been a very simple example of how to extract a specific piece of code from a code snippet. This should help you get started with Roslyn. If you want to read more and dive deeper into Roslyn, the complete Roslyn documentation is a great resource: https://docs.microsoft.com/en-us/dotnet/csharp/roslyn-sdk/.

Source Generators

A recent addition to the Compiler Platform is source generators. Source generators run during the compilation of your code. They can generate extra code files based on analysis of your code and include them in the compilation.

Source generators are written in C#; they can retrieve an object that is a representation of the code you have written. That object can be analyzed and used to generate extra source files based on the syntax and semantic models that are in the compilation object. Figure 10-9 shows where in the compilation pipeline the source generators live.

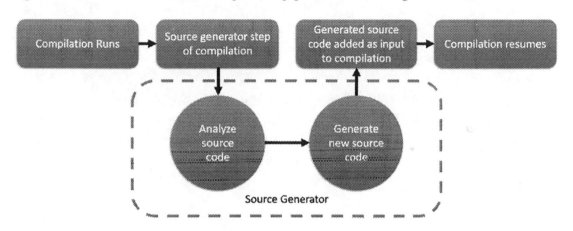

Figure 10-9. *Compiler pipeline (image by Microsoft)*

Source generators can be used to prevent the use of reflection. Instead of generating runtime classes, it might be possible to generate extra classes at compile time, of course depending on your use case. Being able to generate extra classes at compile time instead of runtime almost always means a performance increase. It is important to know, and remember, that source generators can only generate and inject extra code; they cannot change the code that was written by the developer.

Writing a Source Generator

Let us look at an example. For the example, we are going to write a source generator that takes any class that is decorated with a certain attribute and generate a record-type DTO from that class; DTOs are explained in more detail in the previous chapter. We will keep it quite simple for this demo generator, so do not worry about violating any DTO best practices in the generated code.

Source generators work with .NET 6 projects, but they need to be defined in a .NET Standard 2.0 library at the time of writing. After creating a .NET Standard 2.0 class library, we add a class that implements ISourceGenerator. To get the ISourceGenerator, we first need to install the Microsoft.CodeAnalysis NuGet package. Listing 10-4 shows the interface with its members.

Listing 10-4. ISourceGenerator interface

```
public interface ISourceGenerator
{
    void Initialize(GeneratorInitializationContext context);
    void Execute(GeneratorExecutionContext context);
}
```

ISourceGenerator consists of two methods. The Initialize method sets up the generator, while the Execute method does the actual generating of code.

For testing our generator, we will create a .NET 6 console application. After creating the project, we start by defining a very simple attribute. Listing 10-5 shows the attribute declaration.

Listing 10-5. Defining the attribute to filter on

```
internal class GenerateDtoAttribute : Attribute
{
}
```

We only need this attribute to do filtering at the time of generating, so no extra implementation is needed on the attribute class. Finally we add some classes and decorate them with the GenerateDto attribute, as shown in Listing 10-6.

Listing 10-6. Example of a decorated class

```
[GenerateDto]
public class Product
{
    public string Name {  get; set; }
    public string Description {  get; set; }
    public double Price{  get; set; }
}
```

Next we turn to the .NET Standard 2.0 project to implement our source generator. First thing we need to do is identify what classes are decorated with the GenerateDto attribute. To do this, we need to traverse the syntax tree and inspect the class nodes; this is done by an object called a *Syntax Receiver*. Syntax Receivers are objects that visit nodes and allow us to inspect them and save them to a collection that can be used for generating code. The Syntax Receivers are configured in GeneratorExecutonContext's SyntaxReceiver property. The GeneratorExecutonContext is an object that gets passed into the Initialization of a source generator, which we will get to in a moment. Every time the source generator runs, it creates exactly one instance of its Syntax Receiver, meaning that every inspected node is done by the same receiver instance. Listing 10-7 demonstrates a Syntax Receiver that filters out class nodes that are decorated with our GenerateDto attribute.

Listing 10-7. SyntaxReceiver

```
internal class SyntaxReceiver : ISyntaxReceiver
{
    public List<ClassDeclarationSyntax> DtoTypes { get; } =
    new List<ClassDeclarationSyntax>();

    public void OnVisitSyntaxNode(SyntaxNode syntaxNode)
    {
        if (!(syntaxNode is ClassDeclarationSyntax classDeclaration) ||
        !classDeclaration.AttributeLists.Any())
        {
            return;
        }

        bool requiresGeneration = classDeclaration.AttributeLists.
        Count > 0 &&
                classDeclaration.AttributeLists
                .SelectMany(_ => _.Attributes.Where(a => (a.Name as
                IdentifierNameSyntax).Identifier.Text == "GenerateDto"))
                .Any();
```

```
        if (requiresGeneration)
        {
            DtoTypes.Add(classDeclaration);
        }
    }
}
```

A Syntax Receiver is a class that implements the ISyntaxReceiver interface. The interface contains one member, an OnVisitSyntaxNode method. This method will be executed for every node in the syntax tree build by the Compiler Platform SDK. In this implementation, we inspect every node to see if it is of type ClassDeclarationSyntax. There are declaration syntax types for every type of node we can expect, including ClassDeclarationSyntax, InterfaceDeclarationSyntax, PropertyDeclarationSyntax, and so on. Once we have a ClassDeclarationSyntax that contains attributes, we use LINQ to check if the class contains our custom attribute. Once we have the IdentifierNameSyntax, we can verify if it has the name of the attribute we are filtering on, in this case *GenerateDto*. At this point, we have successfully detected a class that was decorated with the GenerateDto attribute, but we are not generating code yet; we are just traversing the syntax tree; that is why we save the found class nodes in an immutable property. The syntax receiver is single instance for every generator run anyway, so we can safely use properties to bring data from the receiver to the generator.

Let's have a look at implementing the actual generator. We'll start with the Initialize method that is part of the ISourceGenerator contract.

Listing 10-8. Initializing a source generator

```
[Generator]
public class MySourceGenerator : ISourceGenerator
{
    public void Initialize(GeneratorInitializationContext context)
    {
        context.RegisterForSyntaxNotifications(() => new SyntaxReceiver());
    }
```

In a source generator, a GeneratorInitializationContext object is passed into the Initialize method and a GeneratorExecutionContext is passed into the Execute method; this allows the Initialize method to, well, initialize the source generator. In this example, we use it to register our SyntaxReceiver into the generator pipeline. From this point on, whenever the generator runs, it will pass every syntax node through the receiver. The Execute method runs as part of the compilation pipeline whenever a source generator is installed into a project.

Listing 10-9. Checking for the receiver

```
public void Execute(GeneratorExecutionContext context)
{
    if (!(context.SyntaxReceiver is SyntaxReceiver receiver))
    {
        return;
    }
```

Our Execute method only works when the context contains the correct receiver. A quick typecheck makes sure everything is in order.

Listing 10-10. Grabbing properties and using statements

```
foreach (ClassDeclarationSyntax classDeclaration in receiver. DtoTypes)
{
    var properties = classDeclaration.DescendantNodes().OfType<Property
    DeclarationSyntax>();
    var usings = classDeclaration.DescendantNodes().OfType<UsingDirective
    Syntax>();
```

Next we loop over the list of class declarations we have captured in the receiver. By the time we get to this point in the code, the receiver will have done its work and the list will be filled with class declarations of classes that are decorated with the GenerateDto attribute. From every class declaration, we grab the properties, by looking for nodes of type PropertyDeclarationSyntax and the using directives by looking for UsingDirectiveSyntax. We need these because if we are going to generate records for every class, we need to know the properties so we can copy them and the using directives so that all the types can be resolved in their namespaces.

Listing 10-11. Generating the using directives

```
var sourceBuilder = new StringBuilder();

foreach (UsingDirectiveSyntax usingDirective in usings)
{
    sourceBuilder.AppendLine(usingDirective.FullSpan.ToString());
}
```

In Listing 10-11, we finally start generating code. We are using a `StringBuilder` to write out the entire code file before inserting it into the code base. First things to generate are the using directives. We already have a collection containing them, so we simply loop over the directives and call the `AppendLine` method to write it out. We use the `FullSpan` property on the `UsingDirectiveSyntax`; that property contains the entire instruction the node was parsed from, for example, `using System.Linq`.

Listing 10-12. Generating namespace and class declarations

```
var className = classDeclaration.Identifier.ValueText;
var namespaceName = (classDeclaration.Parent as
NamespaceDeclarationSyntax).Name.ToString();

sourceBuilder.AppendLine($"namespace {namespaceName}.Dto");
sourceBuilder.AppendLine("{");

sourceBuilder.Append($"public record {className} (");
```

The next things we need are namespace and record declarations. We can get those from the class declaration we are currently processing. The class name can be found in the Identifier property of the ClassDeclarationSyntax object. In this example, we are assuming that there are no nested classes, so the parent object of a class should always be a namespace object. By casting the parent object as a NamespaceDeclarationSyntax object, we can get to the Name property. Using the StringBuilder from Listing 10-11 and some string interpolation, we add the needed code. Be careful with the brackets, try to envision what the generated code will look like, and make sure that all necessary brackets are there and properly closed when needed. We are building code as a simple string, so no intellisense here.

Listing 10-13. Generating parameters and injecting the code

```
foreach (PropertyDeclarationSyntax property in properties)
{
    string propertyType = property.Type.ToString();
    string propertyName = property.Identifier.ValueText;

    sourceBuilder.Append($"{propertyType} {propertyName}, ");
}

//remove the final ', '
sourceBuilder.Remove(sourceBuilder.Length - 2, 2);

sourceBuilder.Append(");");
sourceBuilder.AppendLine("}");

context.AddSource(classDeclaration.Identifier.ValueText, SourceText.
From(sourceBuilder.ToString(), Encoding.UTF8));
```

Finally we use the list of properties we have from the class declaration to generate the record parameters. We can grab the datatype from the property's Type property and the name from the Identifier property. We use the StringBuilder's Append method to make sure that all parameters are appended on one line instead of adding a line break between each one. The parameters are separated with a comma, and the final comma is removed. Finally we close the brackets and our code is finished. We can use the AddSource method on the GeneratorExecutionContext object to inject the source into the codebase right before the code gets compiled. Our generated code is now part of the user code and will be treated as such by the compiler.

The final step in the process is linking the source generator to the project where we want to use it. Source generators are added as analyzers into the csproj file.

Listing 10-14. Adding a source generator to a project

```
<Project Sdk="Microsoft.NET.Sdk">

  <PropertyGroup>
    <OutputType>Exe</OutputType>
    <TargetFramework>net6.0</TargetFramework>
    <ImplicitUsings>enable</ImplicitUsings>
  </PropertyGroup>
```

```
<ItemGroup>
  <ProjectReference Include="..\SourceGeneratorLibrary\
  SourceGeneratorLibrary.csproj" OutputItemType="Analyzer"
  ReferenceOutputAssembly="false" />
</ItemGroup>

</Project>
```

The ItemGroup node in Listing 10-14 shows how to add a source generator. From this moment on, the source generator will run every time the project gets build. We can see if it works by loading the generated assembly in a decompiler like ILSpy. Upon inspection, we immediately see the Dto namespace appearing.

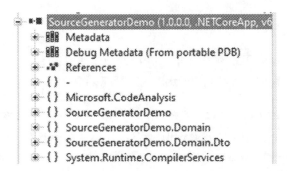

Figure 10-10.   *Dto namespace in ILSpy*

When we inspect the namespace, we'll see generated records for every class that was decorated with the GenerateDto attribute.

```
Person
// SourceGeneratorDemo.Domain.Dto.Person
using ...

public record Person(string Firstname, string Lastname, string Title, string Email, string Phone, string Address, string City, string Region, string PostalCode, string Country)
{
    public override string ToString()
    ...

    protected virtual bool PrintMembers(StringBuilder builder)
    ...
}
```

Figure 10-11.   *Generated record*

Since we have these objects available now, we can also instantiate them from code.

Listing 10-15.   Using the generated DTO objects

```
var product = new Product("Introducing .NET 6", "Book by Apress about .NET 6", 50.0);
```

Note that you might need to restart Visual Studio before Intellisense recognizes the generated objects.

Debugging Source Generators

As you might have guessed, debugging source generators is not as simple as setting a breakpoint and hitting the run button, but it is not much harder either. Instead of placing breakpoints, we can use the Debugger class from the System.Diagnostics namespace to programmatically pause the generator's execution. Listing 10-16 shows the statement right at the start of code generation.

Listing 10-16. Debugging a source generator

```
public void Execute(GeneratorExecutionContext context)
{
    Debugger.Launch();
```

If we trigger the source generator again, by rebuilding the program that uses the generator, the message in Figure 10-12 will pop up.

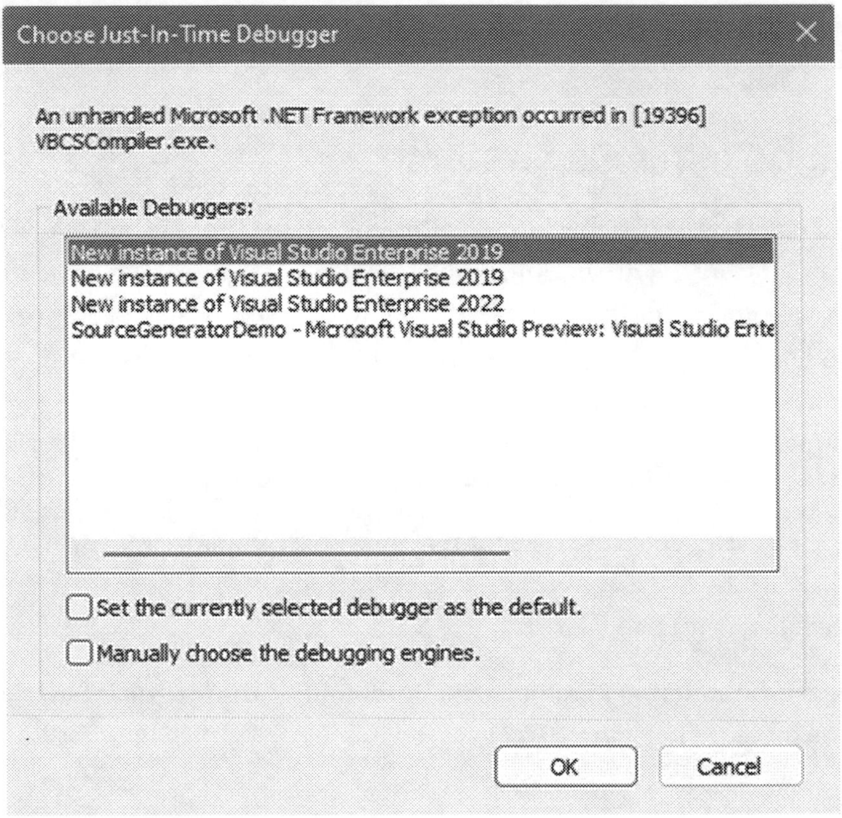

Figure 10-12. *Selecting a debugger*

Select *New instance of Visual Studio 2022*. VS2022 will start up, load in the source file for the generator, and pause right at the Debugger.Launch statement, just like if it was a breakpoint. From this point on, we are in debug mode; we can inspect variables, step over or into statements, and so on. The Debugger.Launch call can be placed anywhere in the generator, even in a syntax receiver.

Wrapping Up

.NET's compiler platform is a powerful platform that does so much more than just compiling code. It is a complete inspection and linting tool. The platform ships with an SDK that allows us to write our own inspections and fixes; this helps when working in teams to guard team agreements on code style but also for detecting bugs and anti-patterns.

Since .NET 5 the platform also has source generators. With source generators, we can generate code at compile time that gets injected into the compiler pipelines as if it was user-written code. Source generators can be a great help and can often replace places where previously we would have used reflection, for example, to generate DTO types like we have seen.

CHAPTER 11

Advanced .NET 6

A lot of the things in .NET that we use on a daily bases are often taken for granted. We reserve memory to store data, and we just assume that that memory gets released at some point. We ask the framework for a thread and we get one, but where does that thread come from? And how does async work again? Let's go into some more detail and explore how these concepts actually work.

Garbage Collector

One of the greater advantages of writing managed code is the access to a garbage collector, or GC. A garbage collector manages memory usage for you; it allocates memory when requested and releases memory automatically when no longer in use. This helps greatly in preventing out of memory issues; it does not eliminate the risk completely; we as developers need to be smart about memory allocation as well, but it is a great help.

Before we dive into the garbage collector, let's refresh our memory about memory. Memory consists of two pieces, a *stack* and a *heap*. A misconception that has been going around is that one is for value types and the other is for reference types; that is not entirely correct. Reference types do always go on the heap, but value types go where they are declared. Let me clarify.

Every time we call a method, a frame is created; that frame is placed on the stack. A stack is a tower of frames and we only have access to the top most one; once that frame is finished, it gets removed from the stack and we can continue with the next one. When an error occurs in one of the methods, we often get a StackTrace in Visual Studio; this is an overview of what was on the stack the moment the error occurred. Variables declared in a method usually go on the stack. Let's use Listing 11-1 as an example to illustrate what happens.

© Nico Vermeir 2022
N. Vermeir, *Introducing .NET 6*, https://doi.org/10.1007/978-1-4842-7319-7_11

Listing 11-1. A simple method with local variables

```
public int Sum(int number1, int number2)
{
    int result = number1 + number2;
    return result;
}
```

When calling the method, the Stack will look like Figure 11-1.

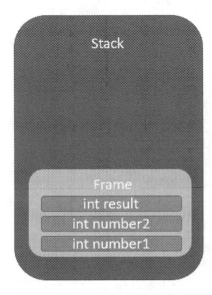

Figure 11-1. *Stack when calling Sum method*

Let's expand our example.

Listing 11-2. Calling a method on a class instance

```
Math math = new Math();
int result = math.Sum(5, 6);

public class Math
{
    public int Sum(int number1, int number2)
    {
```

```
    int result = number1 + number2;
    return result;
  }
}
```

This time we are instantiating a class and calling a method on that class. That results in the memory in Figure 11-2.

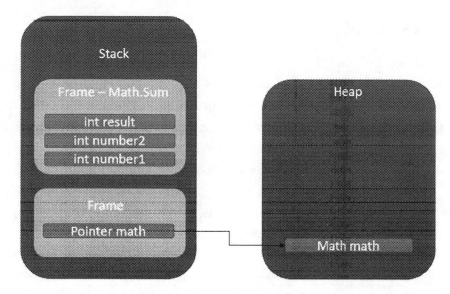

Figure 11-2. *Stack and heap*

The class instance lives on the heap with the stack containing a pointer to the instance. The call to the class member Sum() results in a second frame on the stack where the variables live as well.

The Heap

There are two object heaps in .NET. The large object heap and the small object heap. The small object heap contains objects that are smaller than 85K in size; all the others go on the large object heap. The reason for this split is performance. Smaller objects are faster to inspect so the garbage collector works faster on the small object heap. Objects on the heap contain an address that can be used to point to this object from the stack, hence the name Pointers. What determines the size of an object is beyond the scope of this book, so we won't go into detail here.

The Stack

The stack is used to track data from every method call. For every method a frame is created and placed on top of the stack. A frame can be visualized as a box or container, containing all objects, or pointers to those objects, the method creates or encapsulates. After a method returns, its frame is removed from the stack.

Garbage Collection

Back to the garbage collector. The garbage collector is a piece of software included in the .NET runtime that will inspect the heap for allocated objects that are no longer referenced by anyone. If it finds any, it will remove them from the heap to free up memory. This is just one place where the garbage collector works; other places are, for example, global references or CPU registers. These are called GC Roots.

The garbage collection consists of several passes. First the GC will list all GC Roots. It will then traverse all reference trees of the roots, marking the objects that still have references. A second pass will update the references to objects that will be compacted. The third pass reclaims memory from dead objects. During this phase, live objects are moved closer together to minimize fragmentation of the heap. This compacting usually only happens on the small object heap because the large object on the large object heap takes too much time to move. However, compacting can be triggered on the large object heap manually when needed.

The garbage collector runs automatically in a .NET application. There are three possible scenarios in which garbage collection is triggered:

- Low memory. Whenever the physical memory is low, the operating system can trigger an event. The .NET runtime hooks into this event to trigger garbage collection to help restore memory.

- Threshold on the heap is passed. Every managed heap, there is a managed heap per .NET process, has an acceptable threshold. This threshold is dynamic and can change while the process is running. Once the threshold is crossed, garbage collection is triggered.

- GC.Collect() is triggered. `System.GC` is a static wrapper around the garbage collector. Its Collect method triggers garbage collection. We can call this manually for testing purposes or in very specific scenarios, but usually we do not need to worry about this

A Look at the Threadpool

The threadpool in .NET is a pool of background threads that we can schedule work on. Depending on the system your application is running on, the runtime will create a set of background workers. Should we request more threadpool threads than the amount available, it will create extra background threads and keep those alive for future use. Since the threadpool threads are background threads, they cannot keep the process alive. Once all foreground threads have exited, the application will close and all background threads will terminate.

The threadpool has been favored over creating threads manually ever since .NET 4. The main reason is performance; threadpool threads already exist; they just need to be given a unit of work, while manual threads still need to be created and that creation is an expensive operation. An easy example of using the threadpool can be created by using the Task Parallel Library, or TPL.

Listing 11-3. Using the Task Parallel Library

```
var strings = new List<string>();

for (int i = 0; i < 1000; i++)
{
    strings.Add($"Item {i}");
}

Parallel.ForEach(strings, _ =>
{
    Console.WriteLine(_);
    Thread.Sleep(1000);
});
```

We have a list of 1000 strings. Using the TPL, we can loop over this in a parallel way with `Parallel.ForEach`. For each item in the list, work will be scheduled on a threadpool thread. The Thread pane in Visual Studio can visualize this.

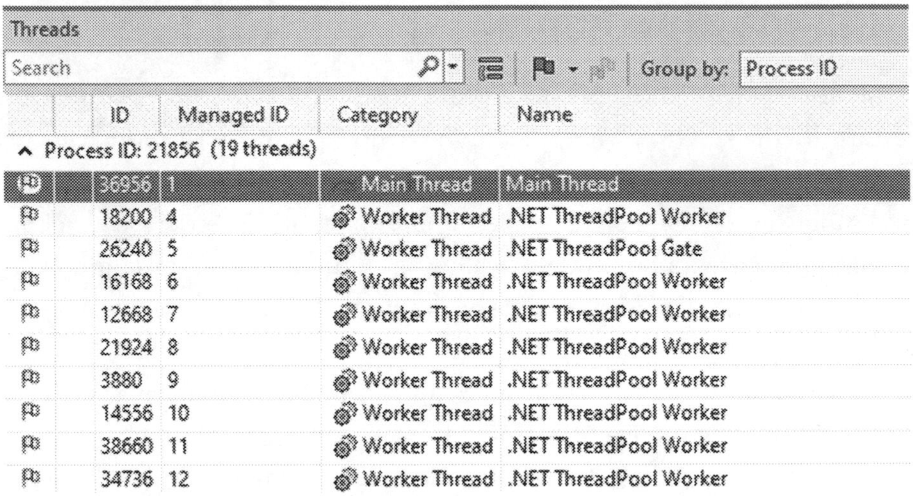

Figure 11-3. *Visualizing threadpool threads*

Running a foreach loop in parallel also means that the order of the outcome can be unpredictable.

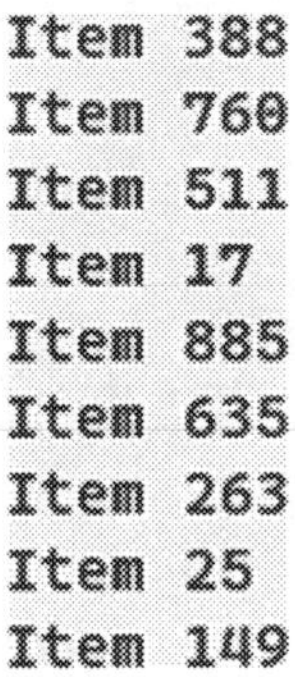

```
Item 388
Item 760
Item 511
Item 17
Item 885
Item 635
Item 263
Item 25
Item 149
```

Figure 11-4. *Parallel ForEach output*

A different way to loop over a collection in a parallel manner is using the AsParallel extension method. AsParallel is a method in the LINQ library. It returns a ParallelQuery object. By itself it does not do any parallelization; we need to execute a LINQ query on the ParallelQuery object it returns. Listing 11-4 shows how to use this method.

Listing 11-4. Using the AsParallel method

```
var strings = new List<string>();

for (int i = 0; i < 1000; i++)
{
    strings.Add($"Item {i}");
}
foreach (string item in strings.AsParallel().Select(_ => _))
{
    Console.WriteLine(item);
    Thread.Sleep(1000);
}
```

There is no major difference in using `Parallel.ForEach` versus `AsParallel`. The way to use it differs, but the results are similar.

The static `ThreadPool` class in .NET can tell us how many threadpool workers we can have simultaneously. Listing 11-5 shows how; Figure 11-5 shows the result on my Intel i7 device with 32GB of RAM.

Listing 11-5. Listing ThreadPool information

```
ThreadPool.GetMaxThreads(out int workerthreads, out int completionports);

Console.WriteLine($"Max number of threads in the threadpool:
{workerthreads}");

Console.WriteLine($"Max number of completion ports in the threadpool:
{completionports }");
```

```
Max number of threads in the threadpool: 32767
Max number of completion ports in the threadpool: 1000
```

Figure 11-5. *Max number of workers in the threadpool*

The threadpool consists of two types of threads: worker threads and completion ports. Completion ports are used for handling asynchronous I/O requests. Using completion ports for I/O requests can be much more performant than creating your own threads for I/O work. There are not that many cases where we want to use completion ports. The usage of these types of threads usually happens in the .NET libraries themselves; the parts that handle I/O interrupt and request.

Most of the time, it is better to use worker threads from the threadpool, but there are a few scenarios where it might be useful to create your own threads.

- Change priority of a thread.

- Create a foreground thread.

- Work that takes a long time.

Threadpool threads cannot be made into foreground threads, so if that is what you need, for example, to keep the process open when the main thread exits, then you need to create your own thread. Same with thread prioritization that also requires a new thread. Long running tasks can be scheduled on threadpool threads, but the number of threads there is limited before the system starts creating new ones, which is something we want to avoid if possible because of performance reasons. So if we schedule a lot of long running tasks, we might run out of threadpool threads; for that, we might switch to creating our own threads. As always this is very dependent on your situation, so handle with care.

Async in .NET 6

Async/Await has been around for a while now in .NET, and most .NET developers should be familiar with how to use it. .NET 6 comes with a few new additions to the await/async pattern, but let's explore the basics before we dive into the new stuff.

Await/Async

Listing 11-6. Async operation

```
public async Task<string> FetchData()
{
    var client = new HttpClient();
    HttpResponseMessage response = await client.GetAsync("https://www.
    apress.com").ConfigureAwait(false);
```

```
string html = await response.Content.ReadAsStringAsync().
ConfigureAwait(false);

return html;
}
```

As an example, Listing 11-6 shows a simple method that uses HttpClient to fetch a
web endpoint. We notice a couple of different things; first we have marked the method as
async; we can only use the await keyword in a method, lambda or anonymous method
that is modified with the async keyword. Await/async does not work in synchronous
functions, in unsafe contexts, or in lock statement blocks. The return type of the method
is Task<string>. Task is one of the go-to return types of asynchronous methods. Task
comes from the Task Parallel Library in .NET and symbolizes a unit of work and its
status; whenever we await a Task we wait for its status to become complete before
continuing executing the rest of the method. When we await GetAsync, for example, the
method execution stops there, scheduling the rest of the method as a continuation. Once
the HTTP call completes, the result is passed into the continuation and the rest of the
method executes. If we decompile this using a decompiler like ILSpy, we can clearly see
how the framework is introducing statemachines into our code to keep track of the state
of Tasks.

Listing 11-7. State machines

```
.class nested private auto ansi sealed beforefieldinit '<FetchData>d__0'
        extends [System.Runtime]System.Object
        implements [System.Runtime]System.Runtime.CompilerServices.
        IAsyncStateMachine
{
.override method instance void [System.Runtime]System.Runtime.
CompilerServices.IAsyncStateMachine::SetStateMachine(class [System.
Runtime]System.Runtime.CompilerServices.IAsyncStateMachine)
```

Listing 11-8 shows more intermediate language; this is the part where the HTTP calls
and the reading of the data happens.

Listing 11-8. Async calls in IL

```
// num = (<>1__state = 0);
IL_004d: ldarg.0
IL_004e: ldc.i4.0
IL_004f: dup
IL_0050: stloc.0
IL_0051: stfld int32 Foo/'<FetchData>d__0'::'<>1__state'
// <>u__1 = awaiter2;
IL_0056: ldarg.0
IL_0057: ldloc.2
IL_0058: stfld valuetype [System.Runtime]System.Runtime.CompilerServices.
ConfiguredTaskAwaitable`1/ConfiguredTaskAwaiter<class [System.Net.
Http]System.Net.Http.HttpResponseMessage> Foo/'<FetchData>d__0'::'<>u__1'
// <FetchData>d__0 stateMachine = this;
IL_005d: ldarg.0
IL_005e: stloc.s 4
// <>t__builder.AwaitUnsafeOnCompleted(ref awaiter2, ref stateMachine);
IL_0060: ldarg.0
IL_0061: ldflda valuetype [System.Runtime]System.Runtime.CompilerServices.
AsyncTaskMethodBuilder`1<string> Foo/'<FetchData>d__0'::'<>t__builder'
IL_0066: ldloca.s 2
IL_0068: ldloca.s 4
IL_006a: call instance void valuetype [System.Runtime]System.Runtime.
CompilerServices.AsyncTaskMethodBuilder`1<string>::AwaitUnsafeOnCo
mpleted<valuetype [System.Runtime]System.Runtime.CompilerServices.
ConfiguredTaskAwaitable`1/ConfiguredTaskAwaiter<class [System.
Net.Http]System.Net.Http.HttpResponseMessage>, class
Foo/'<FetchData>d__0'>(!!0&, !!1&)
// return;
IL_006f: nop
IL_0070: leave IL_01a3
```

As you can tell, a lot of code is generated when using await/async. That is why I want to advise you to use this carefully; async is not always better or faster than synchronous development.

The Task object generated when awaiting an action captures the context it was called from. When you await an async method, and don't specify `ConfigureAwait(false)`, the method will do its work on the thread pool and switch back to the caller's context when finished. This is exactly the behavior that you want when you request a webresult and immediately put the data into a property that is bound against, since binding happens on the UI thread. But this is not what we want when we're executing code in a library or in a service class, so that's where we'll use `ConfigureAwait(false)`.

AsyncState	null
CancellationPending	false
CreationOptions	None
▷ Exception	null
Id	18
▷ Result	null
Status	WaitingForActivation
▲ Raw View	
AsyncState	null
▷ Context	{System.Threading.ExecutionContext}

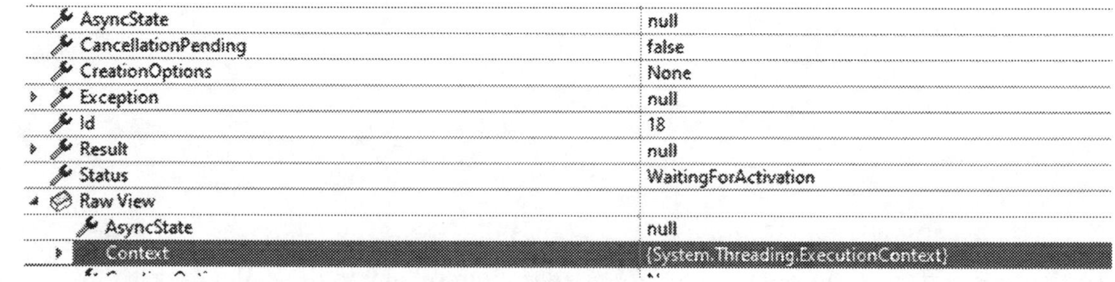

Figure 11-6. *Captured context in a Task*

In ASP.NET, ever since .NET Core 3.1, we do not need to call ConfigureAwait(false) because there is no SynchronizationContext to return to. Blazor on the other hand does have a SynchronizationContext.

Listing 11-9 shows an example of where to use ConfigureAwait(false) and where not to. The example is done in a WinForms application.

Listing 11-9. Usage of ConfigureAwait(false)

```
private async Task FetchData()
{
    var service = new ResourcesService();
    var result = await service.FetchAllResources();

    //textblock is bound against Json
    JsonTextbox.Text = result
}
```

```
public class ResourcesService
{
    public async Task<string> FetchAllResources()
    {
        var client = RestClient.GetClientInstance();
        var result = await client.GetAsync("/api/data").
        ConfigureAwait(false);
        string json = await result.Content.ReadAsStringAsync().
        ConfigureAwait(false);

        return json;
    }
}
```

The FetchAllResources method has two calls that are awaited and uses ConfigureAwait(false) because we do not need to switch back to the caller context. By not returning to caller context in that method, we prevent two context switches to occur.

The FetchData method doesn't use ConfigureAwait(false) because it needs to return to the caller context. The caller context here is the UI thread. The property that the returned value is being set to will trigger a change notification, so we need to be on the UI thread.

Cancellations

In Async operations, we often make use of CancellationTokens to cancel long running tasks. These tokens are used quite a lot across the base class library as well. However, cancelling tasks does not happen that often so it would be interesting to be able to reuse CancellationTokenSource, the object that generates CancellationTokens. Up until now, we couldn't do this safely because we couldn't be certain that some tasks were still referencing this token. In .NET 6, CancellationTokenSource was extended with a TryReset method. Listing 11-10 shows the use of the TryReset method.

Listing 11-10. Try to reset a cancellation token

```
CancellationTokenSource _cancellationTokenSource = new
CancellationTokenSource();

private void CancelButton_OnClick(object sender, EventArgs args)
{
    _cancellationTokenSource.Cancel();
}

public async Task DoWork()
{
    if (!_cancellationTokenSource.TryReset())
    {
        _cancellationTokenSource = new CancellationTokenSource();
    }

    Task<string> data = FetchData(_cancellationTokenSource.Token);
}

public async Task<string> FetchData(CancellationToken token)
{
    token.ThrowIfCancellationRequested();

    var client = new HttpClient();
    HttpResponseMessage response = await client.GetAsync("https://www.
    apress.com", token).ConfigureAwait(false);
    string html = await response.Content.ReadAsStringAsync(token).
    ConfigureAwait(false);

    return html;
}
```
Once a token was actually cancelled it cannot be recycled and the
TryReset method will return false.

The example shown here comes from a WinForms application where we can load
data and cancel it using a cancel button. When calling the DoWork method, we try to
reset the CancellationTokenSource; if we don't succeed, we instantiate a new one.

The CancellationTokenSource's CancellationToken is passed to the LoadData method. LoadData checks if the token is not cancelled and uses it for loading and deserializing the data. As long as the token was not cancelled, we can keep resetting the CancellationTokenSource for reuse.

WaitAsync

In .NET 6, Microsoft is giving us more control over when to cancel or timeout asynchronous operations by adding WaitAsync methods to Task. With WaitAsync, we can specify a cancellation token or a timeout to a task.

Listing 11-11. WaitAsync with a cancellation token

```
CancellationToken token = _cancellationTokenSource.Token;

var client = new HttpClient();

Task<HttpResponseMessage> response =
client.GetAsync("https://www.apress.com", token)
    .WaitAsync(token);

await response;
```

Listing 11-12 shows the three different options.

Listing 11-12. All WaitAsync overloads

```
Task<HttpResponseMessage> taskWithToken = client
    .GetAsync("https://www.apress.com", token)
    .WaitAsync(token);

Task<HttpResponseMessage> taskWithTimeout = client
    .GetAsync("https://www.apress.com", token)
    .WaitAsync(new TimeSpan(0, 0, 10));

Task<HttpResponseMessage> taskWithBoth = client
    .GetAsync("https://www.apress.com", token)
    .WaitAsync(new TimeSpan(0, 0, 10), token);
```

Do not mistake WaitAsync with Wait. Wait is an actual blocking operation; it will block the thread until the Tasks completes and should only be used in very specific cases. WaitAsync is a way to add cancellation or timeout configuration to an asynchronous task that will run non-blocking.

Conclusion

.NET is an easy-to-use framework. It abstracts a lot of difficult concepts away from us as developers. While it does abstract these concepts away, we still have the possibility to dive deeper and actually use the more advanced concepts. We can get full control of the garbage collector and even implement our own garbage collectors should we really want to.

.NET 6 comes with big improvements on performance, on I/O-based operations, but also in general. Await/async is extended to give more fine-grained control to us developers; `CancellationTokenSource` is extended to allow more reuse of tokens. The examples in this chapter are just a few examples. There are some very good resources out there that dive deep into .NET.

- Async/Await - Best Practices in Asynchronous Programming - `https://docs.microsoft.com/en-us/archive/msdn-magazine/2013/march/async-await-best-practices-in-asynchronous-programming`

- Pro .NET Memory Management - `https://link.springer.com/book/10.1007/978-1-4842-4027-4`

- Task Parallel Library (TPL) - `https://docs.microsoft.com/en-us/dotnet/standard/parallel-programming/task-parallel-library-tpl`

Index

A

Active Server Pages (ASP), 177
AppendLine method, 290
Application architecture
    microservices application, 264, 265
    monolith application, 263
    record types, 259–262
Application.EnableVisualStyles
        method, 80
Application Programming Interface
        (API), 200
AsParallel extension method, 302
AsParallel method, 303
ASP.NET Core
    source code, 177
    templates, 178, 179
Await/async pattern, 304–306, 311
Azure Container Registry (ACR), 240
Azure functions
    attributes, 249
    BookFunctions class, 250
    book service, 249
    code, 248, 249
    deployment
        API Management step, 255
        create function, 254, 255
        function type, 254
        Plan Type, 254
        portal, 255, 256
        Postman, 256, 257
        publishing, 253
        url, 256

FetchBooks, 251
    by ID, 252
    Swagger UI, 251
FunctionsStartup, 250
GET request, 253
IBookCatalogService, 250, 251
In-proc *vs.* out-proc projects, 247
languages, 245
modes, 246, 247
parameter, 252
POST request, 252, 253
startup object, 249, 250
Storage account, 254
Swagger UI, 247, 248
template, 247
triggers, 245, 246
Azure integrations, 221
Azure portal, 221
Azure SDK ships, 221
Azure trials, 221

B

Blazor, 15, 234
    definition, 125
    desktop, 148–152
    server
        definition, 144
        SignalR, 144–148
    WebAssembly
        client project, 129–132
        client/server architecture, 127
        component system, 134, 135

313

N. Vermeir, *Introducing .NET 6*, https://doi.org/10.1007/978-1-4842-7319-7

Blazor (*cont.*)
    creating Wasm project, 126, 127
    definition, 125
    .NET 6, 132, 133
    pages, 136–139
    progressive web
      application, 127–129
    Razor component lifecycle, 140
    running app, 140–143
Blazor Wasm, 126
Blazor WebAssembly, 4
BooksViewModel, 171

C

CancellationTokens, 308
Clean Architecture (CA), 265
Cloud providers, 221
Command line interface (CLI) tools, 8
    commands, 31, 32, 63, 64
    Dotnet build, 46–51
    dotnet new command, 33–35, 37, 38
    Dotnet publish, 52–56
    dotnet restore command, 38–43
    Dotnet run, 56, 57
    Dotnet test, 58, 59
    GitHub actions, 60–63
    .NET CLI commands, 33
    nuget.config file, 43–45
    toolset, 31
Compiler platform
    anti-patterns, 295
    creating analyzer, 282–284
    source generators
      compiler pipeline, 285
      debugging, 293, 294
      definition, 285
      writing, 285–292

Containerized applications, 238
Container orchestrator
    Dapr, 270
    definition, 265
    docker compose, 268, 270
    k8s, 265–268
Containers, 238
CoreCLR, 23
CoreFX, 23
CreateMauiApp method, 160

D

Dapr.Client NuGet package, 272
DataGridView's DataSource
    property, 89
Design patterns, 177
Desktop development
    mobile apps, 65
    WinAPI, 66–68
    WPF application, 65
Distributed Application Runtime (Dapr)
    definition, 270
    installation, 270, 271
    State management, 272, 273
Docker Compose, 268
Docker container
    ACR, 240, 241, 243
    authentication, 243
    building, 243
    CLI, 243
    debug target, 239
    definition, 238
    Docker build command, 242
    Docker Desktop, 238
    Dockerfile, 242
    Docker registry, 238
    Docker Support, 239

error, 241, 242
images, 239
images, ACR, 244
Linux, 239
pushing images, 243
repository, 240
requirements, 238
running containers, 240
Visual Studio, 239
wizard, 244
Domain-Driven-Design (DDD), 265
dotnet new command, 33
DotnetSixWinForms, 10
DoWork method, 309

E

Execute method, 286
eXtended Application Markup Language
(XAML), 91

F

FetchAllResources method, 308
foreach loop, 302
Frameworks, 234
FullSpan property, 290

G

Garbage collector (GC), 297, 300
GenerateDto attribute, 287, 289

H

Heap, 299
HTTP Strict Transport Security
(HSTS), 184

I, J

IncrementCount method, 131
Initialize method, 286
Inversion of Control (IoC), 182

K

Kubernetes (k8s), 265

L

Long Term Support release (LTS), 2

M

Microservice architecture, 264
Microsoft Azure, 221
Microsoft's cross-platform strategy, 21
Microsoft's Xamarin framework, 153
Model-View-Controller (MVC)
    AddControllersWithViews method, 182
    app.UseHttpsRedirection, 185
    ASP.NET
        templates, 178, 179
        Visual Studio, 179
    authentication type, 179
    building blocks, 178
    controllers
        adding view, 192
        attributes, 196
        BookCatalogService, 190
        Book class, 190
        BookController, 191
        create Book, 196
        create form, 198
        creation, 190
        data annotations, 199, 200
        datastore, 196

Model-View-Controller (MVC) (*cont.*)
    definition, 189
    elements, 198
    generated view, 194, 195
    Html.ActionLink, 195
    Html.DisplayFor tag, 195
    Index method, 191
    inspecting request, 196, 197
    methods, 196, 197
    model declaration/ASP tags, 193
    .NET-based logic, 189
    parsed data, 197
    Razor template, 192, 195
    Razor view, 194
    route defaults, 191
    routing system, 189
    scaffolding, 192
    singleton, 190
    table creation, 194, 195
    token, 197
    validation rules, 199, 200
    validations, 197–199
    View method, 192
    view type, 192
  core strength, 177
  design pattern, 177, 178
  development, 184
  Docker container, 180
  HSTS, 184
  HTML pages, 178
  HTTPS, 180
  IServiceCollection, 182
  launchsettings.json file, 184
  MapControllerRoute, 185
  middleware components, 184
  .NET 6, 179
  pipeline, 182, 183, 185
  pipeline configuration, 183
  profile configuration, 184
  Program.cs, 181
  project structure, 180, 181
  project wizard, 180
  routing
    default, 185
    mapping, 185
    parameter, 186
    parts, 186
    URL, 185
  UseAuthorization, 185
  UseRouting, 185
  UseStaticFiles, 185
  views, 186, 187
    CSS file, 187
    extensions, 187
    h2 elements, 188
    home component, 189
    HTML response, 189
    Index.cshtml file, 188
    _Layout.cshtml file, 187
    Razor, 187, 188
    @RenderBody method, 187, 188
    scaffolding, 193
    Shared folder, 187
    title, rendering, 189
    ViewData, 189
  WebApplication instance, 182
  WebApplicationBuilder, 181
Model-View-ViewModel (MVVM), 164
Mono, 23
Multi-Application User Interface (MAUI)
  application lifecycle, 161–163
  ASP.net, 156
  cross platform world, 159, 160
  definition, 153
  iOS application, 157–159
  MVVM, 164–170

MVVM toolkit, 170–176

project structure, 154, 156

Xamarin forms, 153, 157

N

nameof() method, 169

.NET 6

architecture, 21, 22

Blazor, 15–17, 20

CLI, 8, 9, 11

definition, 1

desktop development, 12, 14, 15

desktop packs, 25–29

framework, 1

libraries, 1

managed execution process, 24, 25

MAUI, 17–19

Migration, 119–121

operating systems, 6–8

platform, 4, 5

platform-native APIs, 29

roadmap, 5, 6

supported versions, 3

types, 2

upgrade assistant, 122

version support, 2, 3

Ngen, 25

NuGet packages, 12

NuGet references, 120

O, P, Q

OnParametersSet, 139

OpenAPI Initiative (OAI), 204

R

Roslyn

built-in analyzers, 276

compiler API, 277

compilers, 275

diagnostic API, 278

IDE features, 275

LINQ, 277

scripts, 278

SDK, 279–281

syntax tree, 278

workspace API, 278

Run method, 82

Runtime identifier (RID), 49

Runtimes

CoreCLR or Mono, 23

CoreFX, 23

languages, 22

WinRT, 24

S

Serverless computing, 245

ServerPrerendered, 147

SetCompatibleTextRenderingDefault method, 82

SignalR, 144

Single-threaded apartment (STA), 71

Stack, 298–300

StackPanel, 101

StackTrace, 297

StartupUri property, 95

Statemachines, 305

STAThread attribute, 71

Static apps
  application name, 237
  Blazor app, 237
  creation, 235
  deployment details, 236
  domain name, 237
  frameworks, 237
  GitHub Actions, 236
  hosting plan, 235
  hostname, 236
  zip file, 236
SynchronizationContext, 307
SyntaxReceiver property, 287
Syntax tree, 278

T, U

TargetFramework, 10
Threadpool, 301–304

V

Virtual machines, 238
Visual Studio, 221

W

WaitAsync methods, 310
WebAPI
  API controller, 202, 203
  checkbox, 202
  controller-based APIs
    adding book, 211, 212
    attribute, 203
    BookController, 205, 206
    book detail, 210
    client implementations, 209
    framework, 203

    FromBody attribute, 212
    HTTP form data, 214
    HTTP request, 214
    HTTP status codes, 206
    HTTP verbs, 213
    JSON, 204, 205, 207–209
    lines of code, 215
    methods, 206, 210, 212
    OAI, 204
    OAS, 204
    openAPI information, 207
    parameters, 211
    POST request, 212, 213
    Program.cs, 203, 204
    REST controller, 203
    specification, 204
    Swagger, 204
    testing, 209
  creation, 202
  definition, 200
  guidelines, 200
  minimal APIs
    book details, 217
    bootstrapping, 215
    vs. controller-based APIs, 216
    endpoints, 216, 218
    extension methods, 218
    framework, 217
    GET request, 216
    helper methods, 216
    lines of code, 215
    NodeJS, 215
    parameters, 217
    posting data, 217
    Program.cs, 216
  MVC principle, 200
  project type, 201

Web Apps
  applications, 222
  App Service
    Application Insights, 229
    application logs, 231
    App Service Plan, 227
    Azure portal, 230, 231
    Azure pricing calculator, 225, 226
    CI/CD, 228
    configuration, 225
    deployment, 225, 230–232
    GitHub Actions, 228, 230
    monitoring, 228, 229
    publish profile, 231–234
    publish wizard, 232
    region, 226
    Resource Group, 225
    runtime stack, 225
    selection screen
      groups, 227
    SKU, 227
    subscription, 224
    tagging, 229
    third-party services, 223
    Visual Studio, 232
    YAML file, 228
  ASP.NET Core 6, 222
  Azure portal, 223
  containers (*see* Docker container)
  creation, 224
  setting, 244
WinAPI, 66
Windows App SDK
  building, 110–113

definition, 109
features, 110
packaging, 115–118
Windows API, 113–115
Windows Forms (WinForms), 4
Windows Presentation Foundation
    (WPF), 4
  AssemblyInfo, 92
  data binding, 106–109
  definition, 91
  layout, 95–103
  startup, 93, 94
  visual tree, 103–106
  XAML, 91
Windows Runtime (WinRT), 24
WinForms
  API set, 69
  application, 309
  default Program class, 70
  definition, 69
  designer, 70
  form designer, 83–86, 88–91
  message loop, 82
  STA, 71, 72
  startup
    configuration, 72
    DPI mode, 72, 73, 75, 76
    scale events, 76–79
    text rendering, 81
    visual styles, 79–81

X, Y, Z

Xamarin, 5

Printed in the United States
by Baker & Taylor Publisher Services